Abbey Road to
Zapple Records
A Beatles
Encyclopedia

Abbey Road to Zapple Records
A Beatles Encyclopedia

by Judson Knight

Taylor Publishing Company
Dallas, Texas

Designed by Hespenheide Design

Published by Taylor Publishing Company
1550 West Mockingbird Lane
Dallas, Texas 75235
www.taylorpub.com

p. ii *The Beatles enjoy the waters on the Florida coast, February 15, 1964.* AP/Wide World Photos

p. vi *Paul, John, Ringo, and George take a fake punch from heavyweight contender Cassius Clay, later known as Muhammad Ali, in Miami Beach, Florida, on February 18, 1964.* AP/Wide World Photos

p. xii *The Beatles (with manager Brian Epstein in the background) return to Britain on September 22, 1964, following their tour of the United States.* Archive Photos/Express Newspapers

Library of Congress Cataloging-in-Publication Data:

Knight, Judson
    Abbey Road to Zapple Records : a Beatles encyclopedia / by Judson
  Knight
       p.   cm.
    ISBN 0-87833-240-5
    1. Beatles Miscellanea.   I. Title
  ML421.B4K65   1999
  782.42166'092'2—dc21   99-16883
                                            CIP

10 9 8 7 6 5 4 3 2 1
Printed in the United States of America

To Deidre, who made it all happen;
To Jon, who never got to see;
And to Tyler, whose smile lights up my world.

Table of Contents

I

J-K

L

Introduction

In response to the inevitable question, "What special qualifications do *you* have to write *yet another book* about the Beatles?" I would have to answer honestly, succinctly, and with economy of phrasing: "Not many."

That is, I never knew John Lennon; nor do I know Paul McCartney, George Harrison, or Ringo Starr. I was never acquainted with any of the other people around them, and to calculate my closest approach to them, I would have to go for the old "Six Degrees of Separation" rule. Together with my wife, Deidre (who's also my agent), I calculated that she has a relative who knows the manager of a well-known star who was once close to a member of the group. So where does that put me? Three degrees away? Or maybe four, if you add Deidre to the chain.

But insider knowledge—the claim, for instance, that "I was the guy who told John Lennon to put in that backward stuff on 'Rain'"—has never been a prerequisite for writing about the Beatles. The majority of volumes I researched in writing this one were written by people who had no interaction with the group; yet their account of events tends to be no less reliable than the recollections of those who knew the Beatles personally.

It might seem, in fact, that a certain degree of distance from the group would aid a writer in maintaining a sense of perspective about them, though in reality "outsiders" are at least as likely as insiders to portray the Beatles as demigods. You won't find such hagiography in this book, however. At the time the group broke up, none of the members were any older than thirty, and when John and Paul did some of their most fruitful work, they were in their mid-twenties. In other words, they were just youngsters, and even if they *were* creating some of the greatest rock music ever written, that doesn't mean that their emotional or intellectual growth was on a par with their creative development. (For instance, observe the rather petty incident which ultimately led to the writing of "Across the Universe," as noted in the entry on that song.) Therefore it's senseless to present the Beatles as all-seeing, all-knowing wizards; if nothing more, their solo work would deflate that notion.

On the other hand, the purpose of this work is not to shovel up dirt either. Plenty of other books do that, and frankly, I'm not—and this book is not—all that concerned with the Beatles' personal affairs. It's the music that matters most.

What It's All About

The focus of this little encyclopedia is, therefore, primarily on the songs themselves: their inspiration, their recording, the public's (often mistaken) interpretation . . . and *who wrote the song*. That's an element of this book with which some readers may take issue, but I'm going on the fairly well-established premise that, starting with *Rubber Soul*—at least—Lennon and McCartney seldom actually wrote their songs together. There were occasional collaborative efforts bringing together separate fragments by each, but the two artists were much more likely to compose on their own.

Hence in listing the songs, I list also the likely author of each putative Lennon-McCartney collaboration from 1965 on. After all, does anybody really think that John Lennon helped write "Yesterday"? Or that Paul McCartney had anything to do with writing "The Ballad of John and Yoko"? As for the determination of authorship, there are many clues, and when in doubt, the simplest thing is to observe who sings lead vocal on the song.

Just as the concentration is on songs rather than sex lives, likewise it is on the offbeat details rather than the basics, which one can find in any number of other works about the Beatles. This book is really a series of stories about the Beatles and their music, and my criterion for inclusion was rather simple, and certainly subjective: if there wasn't anything particularly fascinating to say about a subject, I didn't give it an entry. On the other hand, the book *does* treat matters than wouldn't normally come to mind when discussing the Beatles—see for instance the entry listed simply as **I.**

Regarding the focus on minutiae, I have found that after all these years and all the millions of words written about the Beatles, that's what most fans care about: Is it true that you can hear the squeak of the piano bench at the end of "A Day in the Life"? What was the shortest Beatles song ever recorded? On what songs did George *actually* play the sitar? What was the longest song title? What banned album cover featured the group holding slabs of raw meat and dismembered dolls? Who *was* the Walrus?

Another aspect of this book is the relation it establishes between events and concepts, drawing together disparate elements. A simple example of what I mean can be found in the many places where I have attempted to translate population or monetary figures—the size of the audience that watched the live satellite broadcast of "All You Need Is Love," or the amount of money the group earned per show at the Cavern Club—into numbers that would have meaning for contemporary readers.

There are other places in which I have sought to tie together facts in ways that no one, to my knowledge, yet has: for example, the events taking place around the time of the *Abbey Road* cover photograph shoot, or the strange intersecting lines of people and occurrences surrounding the Dakota Apartments. (Unfortunately, those two examples are both closely tied to the macabre, but then again, the Beatles' music—from "Baby's in Black" to "Maxwell's Silver Hammer"—often was as well.)

It has been said that *The Guinness Book of World Records* originated from the disputes over sports records which Irish bar patrons would often debate over pints of Guinness. Likewise the origins of this book lie in all the intriguing little stories I used to hear from my elders concerning the Beatles—some of them true; some . . . shall we say, *embellished*. In writing this book, I set out to test all the little rumors for myself. Is it true that "Strawberry Fields Forever" is about drugs? Did the Beatles once record as "the Beat Brothers"? Was *Abbey Road* really the Beatles' last album? (The answers, working backward in true Beatles style, are *yes*, *no*, and *most likely not*.) But back to those stories. . . .

A Soundtrack for Childhood

On the day I was born, September 29, 1964, the Beatles had returned from their first North American tour, and began taping songs—"Every Little Thing," "I Don't Want to Spoil the Party," and "What You're Doing"—for their next album. My mother has told me that when she was in the hospital giving birth to me, she heard from the woman sharing her room that the hotel bedsheets slept on by the Beatles in Kansas City and Detroit had been cut up and sold in one-inch pieces. (See **United States of America** in this book.)

Obviously, if I was just showing up then, I can't profess to remember seeing the group on Ed Sullivan almost eight months before. I do have the distinction of having been in two countries, on two continents, where the group toured. The second time was in the Philippines in 1966. My family was living in Manila, and I still sometimes think *Wouldn't it have been neat if Mom and Dad had known that the Beatles were in trouble and had helped them get out of the country? Then maybe we could have been The Family Who Saved the Fab Four.* (If you don't know what I'm talking about, see **Philippines**.)

One of my brothers brought home *Sgt. Pepper* one day, and I can still recall vividly the effect it had on my young imagination. My sister later told me that I would often stand outside of church after services, charging other kids money to recite the lyrics to "Mr. Kite"—lyrics which I had made up, because I didn't understand lines such as "late of Pablo Fanques Fair," and hadn't yet learned to read.

After that, there follow memories many of us share, in one form or another, from the late 1960s and early 1970s: the endless hours spent listening to my older brothers' albums, the vague rumors that Paul was dead, and then the awareness that the group had broken up. In 1973—when the breakup of the Beatles did not seem at all a well-established fact, at least to me—I remember another kid telling me that the group members were all living in a giant house down the street from us, perhaps recording a new album. So I wrote them a note and slipped it through the gate. Later I watched from a nearby tree as the groundskeeper swept up the piece of paper with the leaves and other debris that had accumulated on the driveway.

Seven years after that, in 1980, I recall how, with a girl at my high school in Atlanta, I tried to call John Lennon in New York. (And I can remember another girl asking us who John Lennon was—talk about the dumbing down of America!) Then, a few weeks later, my friend called me early in the morning with some very shocking news about John. At first I couldn't believe she was telling the truth, that it wasn't some sick joke.

Five months after the world lost John Lennon, I lost my *brother* Jon, the one who had first brought home *Sgt. Pepper* all those years before. As with John Lennon, the killing—in this case by a drunk driver—seemed purposeless, the gulf between the killer and the victim so vast as to be ludicrous.

From the Beatles' arrival in the U.S. to the death of John Lennon was sixteen years, and now much, much more time has elapsed since 1980. Around the Beatles, there have been more losses: Ringo's first wife Maureen in 1994, Apple press agent Derek Taylor in 1997, Linda McCartney in 1998. . . . And where there is death there is also life, with Sean Lennon—past the age his dad was when he appeared on *Ed Sullivan* the first time—recording music as well.

I think of all this as I search the "Paul Is Dead" Web sites while giving my baby daughter a bottle. I've already taught her "Octopus's Garden" and "I Should Have Known Better," both of which make her giggle and stick out her tongue.

Why am I telling you all this? Not because my experience with the Beatles was special, but precisely because it was so ordinary. We all have our little stories, which is why I think we were all so deeply affected by the killing of John Lennon. It wasn't just him we were crying for: it was our youth, our childhood, all the unfulfilled longings which found expression in the Beatles' music. And that, ultimately, is the reason that justifies the existence of not only this, but the next hundred books about the Beatles.

Judson Knight
Atlanta
March 1999

Some Notes

In discussing songs and albums, preference is given to the "canon," or the definitive body of the group's works. Specifically, these are pieces recorded with EMI/Parlophone after Ringo Starr joined the group, and items which were intentionally and lawfully released by the Beatles through May 1970.

This excludes not only bootlegs, but the Tony Sheridan recordings and other early works, as well as any number of other items unavailable legally prior to the release of the *Beatles Anthology* CDs. That being said, such items *are* discussed, as for instance in entries on Sheridan and the *Anthology* respectively. Also, a handful of solo releases—ones which are of particular interest, usually because they involved more than one ex-Beatle—receive special attention; but for the most part, the songs warranting entries are the ones defined as "canonical."

Likewise with albums: Though repackaged presentations such as *Meet The Beatles!* or *Love Songs* receive mention, the bias is in favor of albums that the Beatles recorded as such, from *Please Please Me* to *Abbey Road*. This volume, however, is not a discography, and as with all other topics presented here, discussion of albums is far from exhaustive.

Readers may find what they perceive to be "holes" in the list of entries. Why no entry, for instance, on Elvis Presley, or "This Boy," or the film of *Let It Be*? First, this book was not intended to be comprehensive; and second, all three of those items, for instance, are mentioned in several places even if they do not have entries. But third and most important is the fact that the purpose of this volume, as mentioned in the Introduction, is to present only the most quirky, interesting, and anecdotal information—not mere facts, which are available in other books. The emphasis here is on legend, myth, and minutiae; if a particular topic involved insufficient quantities of these, it did not warrant an entry.

Finally, most pound-to-dollar exchange rates found in this book are computed on the February 1968 *Monetary Fund Report*, in which £1 in British currency equals $2.40 in American money. Most population figures for the "modern" world—as opposed to the 1960s, that is—are for 1995.

Abbey Road

The last album ever recorded by the Beatles, *Abbey Road* saved future generations from having to accept *Let It Be* as the final word from the world's greatest band. And yet because of complications involving the other project, this album actually came out almost eight months earlier, in October 1969.

After the disastrous recording sessions of January 1969, which would ultimately yield *Let It Be*, the Beatles had begun to drift apart, each man developing his own career separate from the group. Then in the summer, the four went into the studio on Abbey Road where they had recorded many an album before, and did it one more time.

But "it" wasn't the same as the elaborate recording process they had gone through on *Sgt. Pepper* or even the White Album: they put together *Abbey Road* more quickly than they had any LP since *Help!* in 1965. After recording the album and thus fulfilling their contractual obligations, the four Beatles were out the studio doors and on the way to the rest of their lives.

Their diverging directions are evident in the striking differences between the album's two sides. Side One represents John Lennon's ideas of what a rock album should be: lean, mean, minimalist, unsentimental. There is no doubt that all six songs on the first side are separate compositions, and except for George Harrison's "Something," it's pretty clear that they are all rock songs too.

Paul McCartney, however, had different ideas. For one thing, "rock" didn't necessarily mean straight rock 'n' roll to him: it could pull in a little from show tunes, a little from classical music, a little from the music of the 1930s and '40s. Nor did a song have to have a definite ending. Side Two is his side, and he welds fragments of his compositions (along with three of Lennon's) into a nine-song "pop symphony." On earlier Beatles albums, of course, Paul had toyed with the idea of stringing together a long sequence of songs, but his use of the form reached its fullest maturity on *Abbey Road*.

Originally the group had considered calling the album *Everest,* though not for any lofty reasons—no pun intended—but because that was the brand name of the cigarettes smoked by engineer Geoff Emerick. In the end, however, they chose instead to name it after the street on which the EMI studios were located. It was there they had recorded all but one of their preceding albums (the exception being *Let It Be*, recorded at Apple Studios), and it was there that they would record their last.

Plagiarism and Popularity

Each of the Beatles indulged in a little plagiarism on *Abbey Road*. According to the owners of the rights to Chuck Berry's "You Can't Catch Me," Lennon's "Come Together" had taken its first two lines and much of its melody from Berry's tune. "Something in the Way She Moves" was already the title of a song by James Taylor before George Harrison resurrected it as the first line of his own "Something." Paul wasn't so vulgar as to steal from fellow pop musicians; instead, he reached all the way back to the seventeenth century to pinch some lines from the dramatist Thomas Dekker, which he used in "Golden Slumbers." But Ringo topped them all, in the subtlest musical heist of the four: his "Octopus's Garden" bears an uncanny resemblance, in theme at least, to Lennon and McCartney's 1966 classic, "Yellow Submarine."

Abbey Road was the only Beatles album to include synthesizers (George's contribution), and the only one with a drum solo by Ringo (a sixteen-second piece during "The End.") It was also the first Beatles album issued solely in stereo, since by that point the mono vs. stereo wars had finally ended. And "Something" / "Come Together," released a month after the LP, was the first Beatles single issued *after* the album of its origin.

Manager Allen Klein made the decision to release the single later, an unorthodox move at the time, though it has since become much more common. In 1970 Klein issued sales figures for various Beatles albums in an attempt to prove that the group's receipts had soared during his watch. This, too, was an unusual move, and as a result of Klein's self-promotion, the world got a rare glimpse at information usually guarded with care by record labels.

According to Klein, *Abbey Road* had already sold 5 million copies, putting it in first place ahead of *Meet the Beatles!* (4.3 million) and *Hey Jude* (3.3 million). One can only imagine how many additional copies this best-selling Beatles album has sold in the decades since. Its success, however, probably had as much to do with other factors—say, the Beatles' artistry, for instance—than it did with Klein's ability as a manager.

The Photograph: A Gruesome Synchronicity

Perhaps no single photograph of the group together is as famous as the one that appears on the front, showing the four men walking across Abbey Road, presumably to the studio. Each is dressed distinctively: George in blue jeans, Ringo in a somber black suit and tie, Paul like a hippie businessman with suit but no tie or shoes, and John serene in white. Though they are walking in the same direction, each appears as an individual headed ultimately on his own path, and in fact later during the day that the picture was taken, they went inside and recorded "The End"; twelve days after that marked the last time the four ever worked together.

But there was more to this picture than met the eye, or so some people claimed. By the time the album came out, the urban legend concerning the death of Paul McCartney had reached its apogee, and this would prove another element motivating the heightened sales of *Abbey Road*. Whereas the "Paul Is Dead" phenomenon had primarily been fueled up to that point by a misreading of song lyrics, with *Abbey Road* the best "clues" appeared on the cover: Paul is walking out of step, his eyes closed, smoking a cigarette, as the others—preacher John, undertaker Ringo, and grave-digger George—prepare to bury him. . . . It could only mean one thing, couldn't it? (See **The "Paul Is Dead" Phenomenon.**)

And yet there was another bizarre, grisly significance to the *Abbey Road* cover photo, a chilling synchronicity that eluded the "Paul Is Dead" clues-seekers because it did not come to light until much later. The photo shoot for the cover began at 11:35 a.m. on Friday, August 8, 1969, when the four Beatles met photographer Iain Macmillan outside the Abbey Road studios. Macmillan climbed a ladder to take the shot from a commanding view, and a policeman stopped the traffic as the Beatles crossed the road. Macmillan snapped six shots, of which McCartney selected the best, and by 2:30 p.m. the Beatles were in Studio Two, working on overdubs not only for "The End," but also for "I Want You"—the "She's So Heavy" part would only emerge the following Monday, when they returned to the studios—and "Oh! Darling."

At 11:35 a.m. in London, it was 3:35 a.m. in Los Angeles, where five people had begun the last day of their lives. In fact they had about twenty-one hours to live; that night, in a house at 10050 Cielo Drive in Benedict Canyon, they would die in one of the most gruesome murders in history.

The Beatles finished their recording session at 9:00 p.m., or 1:00 in California. Around that time, a thirty-four-year-old drifter and former convict, leader of an obscure cult headquartered in the desert outside L.A., informed his chief lieutenant that the five victims had to die. But he didn't call them by name: he merely said that it was time for a racial war to begin, and since he had once known someone who lived in the house on Cielo Drive, he had decided that it should begin there.

The killing of actress Sharon Tate and the four other victims (as well as Tate's unborn child) took place at 12:30 that night. The following night, Leno and Rosemary LaBianca, a couple likewise unknown to the killers, would die; and by the time the Beatles returned to Abbey Road Studios on Monday at 2:30 p.m., news of the two murders had reached the world press.

But as for the motivation behind these unspeakable acts, police would remain perplexed for months, their primary clues a series of slogans written in blood at the murder scenes: "HELTER SKELTER," "RISE," and "POLITICAL PIGGY." In the end, of course, it would turn out that the killers had acted on orders from their messianic leader, Charles Manson, and that Manson in turn believed he had received his "instructions" from the Beatles themselves. (See **Charles Manson.**)

* * * * *

Abbey Road Song List

Title	Composer	Time
Side One		
Come Together	Lennon	4:16
Something	Harrison	2:59
Maxwell's Silver Hammer	McCartney	3:24
Oh! Darling	McCartney	3:28
Octopus's Garden	Starkey	2:49
I Want You (She's So Heavy)	Lennon	7:49
Side Two		
Here Comes the Sun	Harrison	3:40
Because	Lennon	2:45
You Never Give Me Your Money	McCartney	3:57
Sun King	Lennon	2:31
Mean Mr. Mustard	Lennon	1:06
Polythene Pam	Lennon	1:13
She Came in Through the Bathroom Window	McCartney	1:58
Golden Slumbers	McCartney	1:31
Carry That Weight	McCartney	1:37
The End	McCartney	2:04
Her Majesty	McCartney	0:23

"Across the Universe"

"Across the Universe" started as an angry reply from John Lennon to his wife, Cynthia, with whom he had just had an argument. Sitting at the kitchen table of his London home, he had written the line "words are flowing out like endless rain into a paper cup," meaning to describe what he considered her nagging; instead, quite another song took shape.

John later said that the words came through him as though he were a transmitter rather than the originator of the thoughts. In an instant, what had started out as petty became something that verged on profound, and

John and Cynthia Lennon, followed by Beatles manager Brian Epstein. Archive Photos/Popperfoto

he wrote this song in a way unlike any other: as poetry, without a single note of music to go with it.

The recording of "Across the Universe" came out in two different versions, the first made in early 1968, just before the group departed for the Maharishi Mahesh Yogi's ashram in India. Paul McCartney had once said that he wanted no female voices on a Beatles record (an ironic statement, given the fact that later his wife Linda would play with Wings) but for this recording, he and John invited fans Lizzie Bravo and Gaylene Pease into the studio to sing backup. An overdub with the sound of birds taking flight at the beginning of the song accentuated the simple acoustic backing.

Originally this version had been in the running for inclusion on a single, but it ultimately lost out in favor of "Lady Madonna." So instead, John donated the song to the World Wildlife Fund, which used it on their 1969 benefit LP, *No One's Gonna Change Our World.* Six months later, Version 2 appeared on *Let It Be.*

The first time around, John had more or less total artistic control; but by the time Phil Spector was reworking the track in early 1970, John no longer wanted to be bothered with the Beatles—much less with a song he had written nearly two years before. Spector removed the birds and all the vocals except for John's, and added a heavenly chorus with a string overdub that most die-hard Lennon fans considered a bit . . . over the top. But even in this sugary incarnation, it was still a great song.

It wasn't until a decade later, when the *Rarities* albums came out in America and Britain, that most listeners got to hear what they had been missing in Version 1.

"Act Naturally"

By the time they recorded *Help!* in the winter and spring of 1965, the Beatles had adopted a pattern of including on each album at least one song with Ringo as vocalist. (*A Hard Day's Night* was an exception.) For *Help!*, they had recorded "If You've Got Trouble" on February 18, but it proved a lackluster effort, and didn't see commercial release until 1995, when it appeared on *The Beatles Anthology 2.* In place of the aborted recording, Ringo suggested "Act Naturally," written by Vonie Morrison and Johnny Russell, which had been a hit for country singer Buck Owens in 1963.

Owens would later become a familiar part of the American cultural fabric as cohost (with Roy Clark) of *Hee Haw* during its glory days—the years of Minnie Pearl et al., from 1969 to 1976. In 1989, Ringo joined Owens for a recording of "Act Naturally" on an album by the country singer, and the two hammed it up in a video. As for "Act Naturally," it was the last Beatles release of a song not written by a member of the group.

Albums

The term "album" is often mistakenly understood as referring only to long-playing vinyl records. The latter have mostly gone the way of dial telephones, but albums—that is, collections of songs, whether on compact disc, cassette, or in formats to be known to future generations—will continue to exist as long as there is music.

There have been hundreds of Beatles albums: aside from the canonical albums listed below, there were compilations, versions from different countries, all manner of pre-Ringo recordings, live recordings, specialty or non-musical albums (e.g. of interviews), and of course bootlegs. But most of these are not, strictly speaking, "Beatles albums"—that is, a collection of songs that the four Beatles recorded together for the purpose of releasing those songs as a unit. By this purest of definitions, there were only eleven canonical albums—that is, albums that constitute the canon, or definitive body of work:

> *Please Please Me* (March 1963)
> *With the Beatles* (November 1963)
> *A Hard Day's Night* (July 1964)
> *Beatles for Sale* (December 1964)
> *Help!* (August 1965)
> *Rubber Soul* (December 1965)
> *Revolver* (August 1966)
> *Sgt. Pepper's Lonely Hearts Club Band* (June 1967)
> *The Beatles* (November 1968)
> *Abbey Road* (September 1969)
> *Let It Be* (May 1970)

The first seven of these titles refer specifically to British releases on the Parlophone label. Of those seven, three—*Please Please Me, With the Beatles,* and *Beatles for Sale*—were never released in the United States. *A Hard Day's Night, Help!, Rubber Soul,* and *Revolver,* by contrast, all saw Stateside release on the Capitol label, but with a different and less complete song list than their British counterparts. In each case, the American albums were merely truncated versions that U.S. record executives had developed in an effort to stretch their profits. But from *Sgt. Pepper* onward, the Beatles held a much greater degree of artistic control, and an album came to be viewed as an inviolate unit, one that could not be cannibalized for parts like an automobile.

All the Songs in One Collection

In order to possess all 215 of the Beatles' canonical songs—again, the definitive body of their work, leaving out all the live or pre-Ringo recordings, as well as studio outtakes and bootlegs—one would have to own the eleven above-named *British* albums plus four others. None of these four are "albums" as such, but rather collections of songs recorded at different times. These, too, are all British releases, with one exception:

> *A Collection of Beatles Oldies* (December 1966)
> *Magical Mystery Tour* (U.S., November 1967)
> *Yellow Submarine* (January 1969)
> *Rarities* (October 1979)

Of these, the first is a collection of songs previously released only on singles in Britain; the second is the soundtrack to the *Magical Mystery Tour* film, along with assorted singles; the third, another soundtrack with just four "new" songs, all of them throwaways to one degree or another; and the last, a collection of material unavailable in LP form in Britain prior to its release. There is some overlap, to be sure—e.g., "Yellow Submarine" is on both *Revolver* and *Yellow Submarine*—but this is still the most economical way to assemble all the Beatles' recordings.

American Versions

What about those "cannibalized" American albums? Prior to the release of *Sgt. Pepper,* U.S. record company execs managed to turn eight British albums into eleven. All were released by Capitol, with one noted exception:

> *Meet the Beatles!* (January 1964)
> *The Beatles Second Album* (April 1964)
> *A Hard Day's Night* (United Artists, June 1964)
> *Something New* (July 1964)
> *Beatles '65* (December 1964)
> *The Early Beatles* (March 1965)
> *Beatles VI* (June 1965)
> *Help!* (August 1965)
> *Rubber Soul* (December 1965)
> *"Yesterday". . . and Today* (June 1966)
> *Revolver* (August 1966)

How did the record company achieve this feat of multiplication? In the era of the personal computer, one would say they "cut and pasted": half a dozen songs from this album, two or three from that one, a couple of B-sides and *voila!*—a new album. For more about the contrived U.S. non-albums, see the entry on *"Yesterday". . . and Today,* as well as **Appendix 3: A Cross-Reference of British and American Releases Prior to *Sgt. Pepper;*** suffice it to say, however, that when it came time to reissue all the Beatles albums on CD in 1987, only the British versions saw rerelease—both in Britain and the U.S.

Capitol did, however, rerelease its *Magical Mystery Tour* on CD, since it contained *more* songs than the old British version, which was an EP (extended-play) record. So superior was the American *MMT,* in fact, that Parlophone released the U.S. version on CD, thus making the Beatles catalogue uniform on both sides of the Atlantic. And to make it easier to complete one's collection with songs left off of albums, the two companies released *Past Masters, Vol. I* and *Past Masters, Vol. II* in 1988. These included material previously found on *A Collection of Beatle Oldies* and *Rarities,* with liner notes by Mark Lewisohn, perhaps the world's leading authority on Beatles recordings.

Anomalous Songs of the Pre-1967 Era

The following twenty-four pre-*Sgt. Pepper* songs are somewhat anomalous in that they failed to see album release either in Britain or America, or in both countries, until long after they appeared on a single—or, in the case of Britain, an EP. (All eventually wound up on *Past Masters.*) Listed is the song name, the country, and the record on which it made its latter-day appearance:

"All My Loving"—U.S., *The Beatles 1962–1966* (April 1973)

"Bad Boy"—Britain, *A Collection of Beatles Oldies* (December 1966)

"Day Tripper"—Britain, *A Collection of Beatles Oldies* (December 1966)

"From Me to You"—Britain, *A Collection of Beatles Oldies* (December 1966); U.S., *The Beatles 1962–1966* (April 1973)

"I Call Your Name"—Britain, *Rock 'n' Roll Music* (June 1976)

"I Feel Fine"—Britain, *A Collection of Beatles Oldies* (December 1966)

"I Want to Hold Your Hand"—Britain, *A Collection of Beatles Oldies* (December 1966)

"I'll Get You"—Britain, *Rarities* (October 1979)

"I'm Down"—Britain and U.S., *Rock 'n' Roll Music* (June 1976)

"Komm, Gib Mir Deine Hand"—Britain, *Rarities* (October 1979)

"Long Tall Sally"—Britain, *Rock 'n' Roll Music* (June 1976)

"Matchbox"—Britain, *Rock 'n' Roll Music* (June 1976)

"Misery"—U.S., *Rarities* (March 1980)

"Paperback Writer"—Britain, *A Collection of Beatles Oldies* (December 1966); U.S., *Hey Jude* (February 1970)

"Rain"—Britain, *Hey Jude* (May 1979); U.S., *Hey Jude* (February 1970)

"She Loves You"—*A Collection of Beatles Oldies* (December 1966)

"She's a Woman"—Britain, *Rarities* (October 1979)

"Sie Liebt Dich"—Britain, *Rarities* (October 1979); U.S., *Rarities* (March 1980)

"Slow Down"—Britain, *Rarities* (October 1979)

"Thank You Girl"—Britain, *Rarities* (October 1979)

"There's a Place"—U.S., *Rarities* (March 1980)

"This Boy"—Britain, *Love Songs* (November 1977)

"We Can Work It Out"—Britain, *A Collection of Beatles Oldies* (December 1966)

"Yes It Is"—Britain, *Rarities* (October 1979)

Post-*Sgt. Pepper* Anomalies

In the post-*Sgt. Pepper* era, there were a handful of songs which, though they eventually made it onto LPs, were never intended to be part of "albums" as such; instead, they were merely singles later collected on albums. Interestingly enough, most of these saw LP release in the U.S. long before they did in Britain. All eventually wound up on the *Past Masters* CDs:

"All You Need Is Love"—*Magical Mystery Tour* (U.S.), November 1967

"Baby You're a Rich Man"—*Magical Mystery Tour* (U.S.), November 1967

"The Ballad of John and Yoko"—*Hey Jude* (U.S.), February 1970

"Don't Let Me Down"—*Hey Jude* (U.S.), February 1970

"Hey Jude"—*Hey Jude* (U.S.), February 1970

"Lady Madonna"—*Hey Jude* (U.S.), February 1970

"The Inner Light"—*Rarities,* Britain, October 1979

"Old Brown Shoe"—*Hey Jude* (U.S.), February 1970

"Penny Lane"—*Magical Mystery Tour* (U.S.), November 1967

"Revolution"—*Hey Jude* (U.S.), February 1970

"Strawberry Fields Forever"—*Magical Mystery Tour* (U.S.), November 1967

"You Know My Name (Look Up the Number)"—*Rarities,* Britain, October 1979

"All My Loving"

When people think of America's introduction to the Beatles on the *Ed Sullivan Show,* they usually remember them opening with "I Want to Hold Your Hand." In fact the group closed with that number; the first of the five songs they played—the one by which they proclaimed that they had arrived on the American stage—was "All My Loving."

One of the most memorable aspects of that song, aside from George Harrison's country-and-western solo in the middle, is Paul McCartney's cleverly worded promise: "I'll pretend that I'm kissing the lips I am missing." It was the kind of double-talk that would have put a politician to shame: taken one way, it could mean "I'll be kissing somebody else, but I'll be pretending it's you."

Ed Sullivan stands with the Beatles during a rehearsal for the band's first American appearance, February 9, 1964. AP/Wide World Photos

"All Those Years Ago"

From George Harrison's 1981 *Somewhere In England* album, "All Those Years Ago" was written as a tribute to the late John Lennon and recorded by all three remaining former Beatles. The three would play together again—and this time with the recorded voice of Lennon as well—on their recordings of two Lennon songs, "Real Love" and "Free As a Bird," in the mid-1990s.

"All Together Now"

It is common knowledge that the Beatles recorded some of their greatest music during the spring of 1967, sessions that would yield *Sgt. Pepper*. Less well-known, however, is the fact that they also recorded some of their least remarkable songs during the same period—timeless classics such as "Only a Northern Song," "You Know My Name (Look Up the Number)," and "All Together Now." Such recordings suggest that after *Sgt. Pepper,* the group's artistic energies had been temporarily exhausted.

In all fairness, however, "All Together Now" is a cute children's song, and would do well on a compilation of Beatles songs for little ears, along with "Yellow Submarine" and "Good Night."

"All You Need Is Love"

The Beatles recorded "All You Need Is Love" on June 25, 1967, for the *Our World* television broadcast, part of the Canadian EXPO 67 celebration. This, the first worldwide satellite program in history, went out to twenty-four countries and an audience of somewhere between 25 million and 700 million people. (Obviously, estimates vary widely.) The best guess is about 200 million, a number approximating the entire U.S. population at that time, meaning that one person out of every seventeen on Earth saw and heard the broadcast.

In view of the global broadcast, John Lennon had deliberately written simple, easily translatable lyrics with a universal message. "All You Need Is Love" has few words with more than two syllables, and the concepts it contains could easily be understood by a child.

During the recording of the song, members of the group and others in the studio with them wore placards bearing the message "Love is all you need" and "All you need is love" in English, Spanish, French, and German. As of 1999, these were respectively the second-, fourth-, and tenth-most commonly spoken languages in the world. (French and German were tied.) First, third, and fifth through ninth places go to Mandarin, Hindi, Russian, Arabic, Bengali, Portuguese, and Malay-Indonesian.

Except for the overdub of the rhythm section, recorded earlier that day, the entire recording took place live. The Beatles performed as the centerpiece of a miniature orchestra that included their producer, George Martin, on piano, along with thirteen other musicians: four violins, two cellos, two trumpets, two trombones, two saxophones, and one accordion. Among the backup singers on the chorus were Mick Jagger and Keith Richards of the

Paul, George, Ringo, and John take a break in the EMI Studios in London during a June 24, 1967, rehearsal for the live broadcast of "All You Need Is Love." AP/Wide World Photos

Rolling Stones, along with singer and then-Jagger associate Marianne Faithfull; Keith Moon, drummer for the Who; Graham Nash, then with the Hollies; George Harrison's wife, Patti; Paul's girlfriend, Jane Asher; and Gary Booker of Procol Harum.

Immediately before the TV broadcast, communication broke down between the television producer and the cameraman inside the recording booth. George Martin had to relay instructions to and from the cameraman, as well as supervise the recording—with millions of people watching.

In the Mood for a Lawsuit

Nor was that the end of the bad luck this simple little song would bring George Martin. The group had asked him to score the introduction and fade-out of "All You Need Is Love" to give it an international flair. He used the French national anthem, the *Marseillaise*, at the beginning, and the old English folk song "Greensleeves," along with Glenn Miller's "In the Mood," at the end.

The first two were in the public domain, but it turned out that though the copyright had run out on "In the Mood" itself, its *arrangement* was still under protection. As soon as "All You Need Is Love" came out, the copyright owners sued. They expected Martin, who had only earned £15 ($36) for his arrangement, to pay royalties on every copy of the song sold anywhere in the world. Given the popularity of the single, that could ultimately mean many years' worth of income for Martin. But fortunately EMI, owners of the Beatles' recording labels, agreed to pay the copyright holders.

The televised version of the song lasted for six minutes, though for the single—which features a different recording of Lennon's vocal—George Martin trimmed it down to just under four minutes. The group recorded the track at least twice: once before the broadcast, then the main recording. The version on *Yellow Submarine* is the first recording, made in true stereo, unlike the single and the version on the *Magical Mystery Tour* album.

"And I Love Her"

"And I Love Her," from the *Hard Day's Night* album on both sides of the Atlantic, contains a bit of grammatical trickery which may have been unintentional on the part of Paul McCartney. Throughout the song, he speaks in second person—that is "you"—but the identity of that second person appears to change. In the introduction, he addresses the listener by saying "and if you saw my love, you'd love her too"; later, however, he speaks directly to the woman referred to earlier as "my love": "a love like ours will never die, as long as I have you near me."

"And I Love Her" came at a time when the Beatles were just starting to discover the lyrical intricacies of Bob Dylan. More than a decade later, Dylan would weave a much more elaborate series of shifts—in this case, from first to third person (or from "I-me" to "they-them") in his classic "Tangled Up in Blue."

Apple

Just as the word *beetles* had once designated nothing more than an insect, so *apple* gained new meaning in 1968, when the Beatles formed the largest counterculture corporation of the 1960s. "Counterculture corporation," of course, is an oxymoron, which might help to explain why the ambitious project nearly went bankrupt in its first year of business.

The group's first association with the name *Apple* came in the fine print on the back cover of *Sgt. Pepper's Lonely Hearts Club Band*, released in June 1967: "Cover by M.C. Productions and The Apple." What "The Apple" was and what it meant became more apparent on December 5, 1967, when the Apple Boutique at 95 Baker Street in London opened for business.

Invitations to the shop's opening, where guests were served apple juice, struck a whimsical tone: "Come at 7:46. Fashion show at 8:16. . . ." The building that housed the boutique had been painted in outlandish colors and psychedelic designs, which included mystical symbols and illustrations of nebulous planetary bodies. Neighboring businessmen attempted, to no avail, to have the building painted in a more conservative manner.

Paul McCartney said the group had conceived of the Apple Boutique so that people might have "a beautiful place where you could buy beautiful things." Some people might have questioned the *beautiful* part. The store chiefly featured designs by The Fool, a group of four Dutch artists who had also decorated George Harrison's bungalow and John Lennon's piano. The Fool's fashions had an appropriately esoteric and transcendent and impractical quality, with titles like "Water," "Fire," and "Space."

Throughout their collective career as Beatles, the members of the group would often exhibit a tendency to become excited about a project, work on it for a while, then tire of it and go on to other things. This had some good results, especially the rapid changes in musical styles from one album to another; but in the case of Apple, their short attention spans and lack of patience for details spelled doom. It was a bad sign, for instance, that even at the time of the boutique's opening, Paul's and Ringo's enthusiasm had ebbed so much that they didn't bother to show up.

Boredom soon turned to disgust, as The Fool siphoned considerable sums from the Beatles' pocketbooks. So on July 30, 1968, as Paul put it, "We decided . . . the retail business wasn't our particular scene, so we went along, chose all the stuff we wanted—I got a smashing overcoat—and then told our friends. Now everything that's left is for the public." They gave away $25,000 worth of clothing, and pulled down the curtain on the Apple Boutique—but not on the overall Apple project.

The Blossoming of Apple

Around the time of the boutique's opening in December 1967, the group had brought out a disastrous film called *Magical Mystery Tour*, produced by Apple Films. By then, their manager, Brian Epstein—the one person who might have saved them from the impending Apple folly—was dead, and they had come under the spell of another kind of mentor, the Maharishi Mahesh Yogi. Just before leaving for the Maharishi's ashram in India, the group released a single, "Lady Madonna" / "The Inner Light." This would be the last Beatles release not issued on the Apple label.

After each became more or less disenchanted with the Maharishi, the Beatles returned to England one by one in the summer of 1968 and began making arrangements to set up their own business. Apple was about to be born.

Lennon and McCartney flew to New York and held a press conference aboard a Chinese junk on the Hudson River. There they unveiled to the world Apple Corps, an enterprise to include not only records, but books, inventions, films, and whatever else excited their whims. This corporation, founded on the principles of what Paul called "Western Communism," would be—in John's words—"a system where someone doesn't have to go on his knees in someone's office—probably yours." That got a laugh out of the reporters.

Soon afterward, a strange advertisement appeared in British newspapers. It showed a photograph of a man (actually Alistair Taylor, Apple general manager), along with these words:

> THIS MAN HAS TALENT. . . . One day he sang his songs to a tape-recorder, and remembering to enclose a picture of himself, sent the tape . . . to Apple Music, 94 Baker Street, London W.1. If you were thinking of doing the same thing yourself—do it now! This man now owns a Bentley!

They might as well have put out an ad saying "Come take our money!" But this was 1968, when people did a lot of things that would seem laughable with the passage of time.

And of course, the predictable happened: the Beatles and their new enterprise were deluged with tapes and other submissions, and cranks and con artists came from miles around. But there was a lot of good in with the bad, and in its beginnings, Apple promised to be a huge financial success. After all, the first Beatles single released on the Apple label turned out to be their biggest-selling—and one of the best-selling singles of all time: "Hey Jude" / "Revolution."

The Beatles were far from the only talents on the Apple label. James Taylor, Billy Preston, and Mary Hopkin ("Those Were the Days") got their start on Apple, as did Badfinger, who took their name from the original title of "With a Little Help from My Friends"—"Badfinger Boogie."

There were other, more . . . *unusual* musicians on the label as well. Grapefruit, the first group signed by Apple, unfortunately left without recording any material. Other Apple artists included Jackie Lomax ("Sour Milk Sea"—written, produced, and assisted by George Harrison); the Black Dyke Mills Band ("Thingumybob," written by Paul McCartney); Ringo's friend John Tavener, who recorded *The Whale*, a classical work; and the London branch of the Radha Krishna Temple, who recorded chants. Asked by John Lennon if their single would reach Number One on the British charts, members of the temple answered, "Higher than that." As it turned out, it did not go any higher than Number Twelve.

Art, Absurdist Art, and the Merely Absurd

The Apple symbol appeared on the label of every Beatles record issued between August 1968 and April 1973, when *The Beatles 1962–1970* albums came out. The idea for this distinctive, tangy trademark came from a Magritte painting owned by McCartney.

According to one account, designers, typographers, and fruiterers spent six months in New York and London, searching for the perfect apple to use as a model. George Mahon did the final design, with a whole apple on Side One of every record, and a perfectly sliced apple on Side Two. Alan Aldridge, a sculptor reported at the time to be building a foot-high nude statue of John Lennon and Yoko Ono, did the italic "Copyright reserved" calligraphy on the original label.

The Apple offices themselves were something of an artwork as well—though "performance art" was more like it. Whoever and whatever happened to be in London at the time brought sleeping bags and little else to the three-story building on Saville Row, prepared to stay at Apple on the Beatles' tab.

A "family" arrived from San Francisco, announcing their intention of establishing a utopia with John and Yoko in the Fiji Islands. Another Apple camper was a person nicknamed "Stocky" who spent his days sitting on a filing cabinet, drawing pictures of sexual organs.

At Christmas of 1968, a group of Hell's Angels appeared at the Apple offices. An entourage of two men, 'Frisco Pete and Billy Tumbleweed, with a dozen-woman harem, they had come, they said, on the invitation of George Harrison. Harrison had met them while in San Francisco's Haight-Ashbury district eighteen months before, and—perhaps caught up in the spirit of the "Summer of Love"—had apparently made an offhanded invitation for the men to stop by if they were ever in London.

Well, they were . . . and they did. When they arrived, however, it was with the unfortunate news that they would have to cut their visit short because of urgent business on the other side of the continent. They were on their way, they said, to Czechoslovakia—where the Communist government had cracked down on a people's revolution earlier that year—"to straighten out the political situation."

From time to time, there were more or less traditional events at the Apple headquarters. More or less. During the same Christmas when the Hell's Angels came to call, John and Yoko dressed up in Santa Claus suits and handed out presents to children of the Apple staff and friends. Those on hand had a forty-two-pound turkey for dinner, guaranteed by the merchant who sold it to be the largest in Britain.

Despite the fact that drugs of all shapes, sizes, and side-effects appeared at Apple as regularly as tea or coffee at more orthodox British businesses, the Saville Row Police Station was only 200 yards away. On occasion, the alert of an approaching bobby would cause a rise in the company's water bill, as Apple toilets flushed away illegal substances.

Apple also had a resident inventor, a friend of John's called "Magic Alex," or Alex Mardas, as he was known to his parents back in Greece. His ideas included fruit-shaped radios, a "nothing box," and a transistor radio that would receive sounds from a turntable without the use of wires. He also claimed to be building a recording studio for the Beatles, but when George Martin inspected this alleged state-of-the-art facility, he discovered that it had an air conditioner loud enough to drown out any music in the vicinity. To the best knowledge of anyone in a position to know, Magic Alex never produced anything during his lengthy stay at Apple—except a lot of hefty invoices.

It's hard to imagine anyone trying to conduct business in the middle of all this, and it seems the idea was equally difficult for the people who actually did work there. One day Apple press agent Derek Taylor's receptionist came into his office and said, "Derek, Adolf Hitler is in Reception." Taylor replied, "Oh, Christ, not that asshole again. Okay, send him up."

The End of the Cocktail Party

If Brian Epstein had not died in August 1967, Apple probably would never have been born. Prior to his death he expressed regret that since the group had played their last concert a year before, his help as manager was no longer needed. Actually, though no one knew it at the time, they needed him more than ever.

In the end, freedom from supervision by Brian, or any other grown-ups, proved more of a curse than a blessing. In January 1969, John Lennon confessed to a reporter, "Apple is losing money. If it carries on like this, we'll be broke in six months." They had kept the offices stocked with food and drink and drugs, and had taken in every leech and vagabond that happened along: left unchecked, "Western Communism" and the "counterculture corporation" would have sent four of the world's wealthiest artists into bankruptcy.

But instead, in early 1969 the Beatles took on a new manager, Allen Klein, who set about turning Apple into a real business while the group turned its attention to the business of breaking up. Apple continued to function until early 1976, though the Beatles had ceased to function six years before. The label concerned itself with the reissue of old Beatles albums and with the issue of new albums by the former Beatles. In 1976, when its contract expired, the Apple catalogue reverted to Parlophone Records in Britain and Capitol Records in America, the group's labels prior to August 1968.

But at the end of each two-hour installment in *The Beatles Anthology*, which aired in the U.S. on ABC-TV in November 1995, there appeared the logo of Apple Corps, a holding company which continues to oversee Beatles-related projects under the supervision of former Beatles road manager Neil Aspinall. And furthermore, the *idea* of Apple—the original group-owned label, to be followed by Rolling Stone Records, Led Zeppelin's Swan Song, and a few others—would not die.

As for that *other* company called Apple, its existence did not escape the attention of Apple Corps' legal counsel. In 1991, Apple Corps and Apple Computer reportedly reached a settlement over the computer company's allegedly unauthorized use of the apple logo. God and Nature are, as of this writing, still authorized to produce apples.

Apple was one of the few record labels ever to be immortalized both in book and song. *Apple to the Core* by Peter McCabe and Richard D. Schonfeld discusses the financial problems that helped break up the group. *The Longest Cocktail Party* (Playboy Press) is an account of the wild and crazy days at 3 Saville Row, written by Richard DiLello, an office worker hired by the Beatles to keep the Apple offices stocked with the finest drugs available.

As for songs, Paul's "You Never Give Me Your Money" from *Abbey Road* is generally regarded as a not-so-veiled account of the group's breakup in general, the Apple fiasco in particular. "Apple Scruffs," from George Harrison's 1970 *All Things Must Pass* album, celebrates all the fans who waited in the cold outside the Apple offices, hoping for a glimpse of a Beatle.

In Yoko Ono's native language, Japanese, the word for "apple" is *ringo*.

Australia

Australia gave the Beatles the biggest crowds of their career. Two hundred fifty thousand people greeted them in Melbourne in June 1964, and 300,000 in Adelaide on the same tour—the largest gathering in the history of the Australian continent. That's a lot of people, especially considering that the population of Australia, even in 1995, was only about 18.3 million. In proportion to the national population, this would be equivalent to a group of more than 4 million people in America, all coming together to welcome just four men.

But not everybody Down Under loved the Beatles. In Brisbane, a group of students threw rotten eggs, pies, and slabs of wood at the group. Beatles fans, angry and intent on retribution, nearly killed the students before the police stepped in and stopped the altercation.

A number of books have celebrated the Beatles' sojourn in, and effect upon, the antipodean realms. These include *The Beatles Down Under* by Glenn A. Baker with Roger Dilernia (Wild & Woolley Press, 1982), *The Beatles in New Zealand: The Land of the Long White Crowd* by Bruce Renwick (1993), and *A Special Madness: Celebrating the 30th Anniversary of the Beatles in Australia* (Melbourne: Victoria Press, 1993).

"Baby You're a Rich Man"

"Baby You're a Rich Man" started as two entirely different songs. John Lennon intended "One of the Beautiful People" for a *Sgt. Pepper* follow-up album, but the group needed a new song to back "All You Need Is Love" on the single released in July 1967. So Lennon mated it with an unfinished piece by Paul McCartney called "Baby, You're a Rich Man," and they gave it Paul's title minus the comma.

The song features John on the clavioline, an ancient keyboard instrument on which only one note can be played at a time. A studio engineer added vibes, and George Harrison puts in a rare appearance playing the tambourine rather than his usual guitar.

Though not one of the Beatles' immortal works, "Baby You're a Rich Man" is interesting as a progress report rather than as a song. On a track released at the peak of the group's artistic and commercial success, the question seems fitting: "How does it feel to be one of the beautiful people?"

That phrase, incidentally, made it into *Bartlett's Familiar Quotations*.

"Baby's in Black"

"Baby's in Black," from *Beatles for Sale* in the U.K. and *Beatles '65* in the U.S., appears to be the first of many Beatles songs dealing with the macabre: the girl in the song mourns for a boy who is dead, and the protagonist feels unable to compete.

During the taping of "Baby's in Black" on August 11, 1964, a BBC film crew came into Abbey Road Studios and took some footage of the group for the *Top of the Pops* TV show. They later aired these clips, with "A Hard Day's Night" overdubbed onto them, as a sort of primitive rock video. Stylistically, it was a long way from "A Hard Day's Night" to "Baby's in Black": once again, the Beatles were miles ahead of anyone who tried to pinpoint their progress.

"Back in the U.S.S.R."

According to George Harrison, "Back in the U.S.S.R." was originally a patriotic song, "I'm Backing the U.K." Instead, what resulted was a wonderful tribute to Chuck Berry ("Back in the U.S.A.") and the Beach Boys ("California Girls"), with a sly reference to Ray Charles ("Georgia On My Mind") thrown in.

However, the joke escaped members of certain political factions, who automatically assumed that this was yet another endorsement of Communism by a group who had only three months before put out a song called "Revolution." The Reverend David Noebel, author of *The Beatles: A Study in Sex, Drugs, and Revolution*, wrote that "the lyrics have left even the Reds speechless." Assuming that anyone in the Kremlin even cared about the Beatles, they probably were speechless indeed, since the song lampooned all things Soviet.

On this first White Album track, Paul McCartney plays lead guitar while George plays bass for the first time ever on a Beatles record. John Lennon plays six-string bass guitar, another first (and only) for him on a Beatles record. It appears that in overdubs, all three took turns on the drums as well, because during the recording of the song, Ringo was absent, having briefly quit the group in disgust with the bickering of the others. He departed on August 22, 1968, the first of two days' recording, and had resolved his differences by September 3—just in time for the group's famous televised recording of "Hey Jude."

Also interesting, in light of the reference to his group, is the rumor that Mike Love of the Beach Boys allegedly helped write the song's chorus. Though this is improbable, it is true that Love was with the Beatles in India at the Maharishi's ashram when they were writing many of the songs that would appear on the White Album.

"Back in the U.S.S.R." actually made it to the top of the pop charts on Rozglasnia Harcerska, the official Polish radio station. The Poles have a well-established history of animosity towards Russia (and vice versa), which pre-dates Communism by a couple of centuries.

Badfinger

Formed in 1968, a group called the Iveys signed on to Apple Records in the same year. Soon they had a new name, Badfinger, taken from the working title of "With a Little Help from My Friends"—"Badfinger Boogie."

Their first hit was "Come and Get It," written by Paul McCartney, which appeared on *The Magic Christian*—the soundtrack to a movie starring Peter Sellers and Ringo Starr. (McCartney, whose demo version of "Come and Get It" appears on *The Beatles Anthology 3*, also produced the album.) Three years later, in 1971, they appeared with George Harrison at the Concert for Bangladesh.

Badfinger established itself with Beatlelike harmonies and instrumentation in songs such as "Day After Day," but they weren't simply imitators: their song "Without You" became a hit for singer (and later John Lennon associate) Harry Nilsson in 1972.

But Badfinger's glory days were short. In 1974 Joey Molland, the group's lead vocalist, quit, and in the following year fellow vocalist and guitarist Pete Ham committed suicide by hanging. Molland and bassist Tom Evans—who also sang vocals—resurrected the band in 1978, but then *Evans* hanged himself, in 1983. Molland and drummer Mike Gibbins still tour occasionally under the Badfinger name.

"The Ballad of John and Yoko"

Only two Beatles took part in the recording of "The Ballad of John and Yoko," released as a single in May 1969 and (in the U.S.) on *Hey Jude* in February 1970.

John Lennon had just returned from his honeymoon, as documented in the song, and wanted to go ahead and record his "Ballad" even though George Harrison and Ringo Starr were not available at the time. So he summoned Paul McCartney, and the two of them performed all the vocals and the instrumentation—Lennon on lead vocal, lead guitar, and acoustic guitar, and McCartney on bass, piano, maracas, drums, and harmony vocals.

And therefore this ballad is not exactly as it appears: supposedly it was by a group called "the Beatles," though only half the group recorded it; and the songwriting credit on the label reads "Lennon-McCartney," but it is unlikely Paul wrote a word of it. After all, it wasn't *his* honeymoon.

Virtually everything in the song actually happened, from the denial of a French visa at the docks in Southampton to the men from the press welcoming the newlyweds back a week later. In two years' time, Lennon had

John and Yoko talk to journalists in a suite in the Amsterdam Hilton during their honeymoon. Archive Photos/Express Newspapers

gone from the utterly fanciful (e.g., "Lucy in the Sky with Diamonds") to the utterly factual. It was hard to say which was more surreal.

Many radio stations in the U.S. refused to play the song "The Ballad of John and Yoko," either because of its references to Christ and crucifixion, or because of a somewhat indelicate pun in the line, "The newspapers said, 'hey, what you doin' in bed?' / I said we're only tryin' to get us some peace." In some cases, DJs spliced in the offending lyrics backwards.

The Beach Boys

The Beach Boys were possibly the closest thing to an "American Beatles." The exquisite vocal harmonies of this California quintet often matched, and sometimes surpassed, the harmonic qualities of Lennon, McCartney, and Harrison.

Like the Beatles, the Beach Boys built their early careers around light-hearted songs about teenage love, and like the Beatles they grew out of that and into psychedelia. Both groups made the shift in the mid-1960s: Whereas the Beatles brought forth the ultimate "Double A-Side" single, "Penny Lane" / "Strawberry Fields Forever," in February 1967, the Beach Boys emerged with "Good Vibrations" in October 1966. This masterpiece of harmony, instrumentation, and (most of all) production cost the group about half as much as the entire album of *Sgt. Pepper's Lonely Hearts Club Band* cost the Beatles.

Both groups planned albums that never came to fruition. The Beach Boys had to scrap their ambitious *Smile* project, perhaps the greatest unrealized creation of rock history, and release the much less remarkable *Smiley Smile* in the late 1960s. Not long afterward, the Beatles would have to give up *Get Back*, another great album that never was, and funnel what remained into the uninspired *Let It Be*. .

Only one member of the Beach Boys, the late Dennis Wilson, was actually a full-fledged surfer, and he helped define the group's image as tanned troubadours of the waves. But Wilson himself had clearly ceased to be a clean-cut California boy by the time he befriended Charles Manson. He gave Manson one of the Beach Boys' gold records—the actual, physical gold record—and Manson sold it. Manson, whose "family" would later commit a series of murders based on their leader's claim to have received orders from the Beatles (see **Charles Manson**), wrote a song called "Cease To Exist," which with additional lyrics by Wilson became "Never Learned Not to Love" on the Beach Boys' *20/20* album.

Rumored Collaborations

There are all sorts of urban legends concerning alleged collaborations between members of the Beach Boys and the Beatles. *Smiley Smile* features a song called "Vegetables," which supposedly features Paul McCartney on bass and as co-producer. McCartney has said that he may have been in the studio during the recording of the song, but that was the extent of his involvement. According to another unsubstantiated rumor, he played bass on the Beach Boys' rendition of "On Top of Old Smokey," which has never been released.

In 1968, the Beach Boys released a song entitled "Bluebirds Over the Mountain," which later appeared on their *Rarities* album in the 1980s. Allegedly the author, Ersel Hickey, published the composition with Northern Songs, which had only two artists on its roster: John Lennon and Paul McCartney. Therefore some people believed Hickey was Paul McCartney, who had written Peter and Gordon's 1966 hit, "Woman," under the pseudonym "Bernard Webb." In fact the song was published by Brother Publishing Company, and in any case Hickey is a real person—not an alter ego—who has written other songs.

Beach Boy Mike Love went to the Maharishi's ashram in India at the same time as the Beatles. According to a story that McCartney himself has denied, Love helped him write the Beach Boys-style chorus of "Back in the U.S.S.R." Another rumor has it that the Beatles recorded a song called "Happy Birthday Mike Love" and left it to sit in the Abbey Road archives. At least one fact is indisputable: The Beach Boys *did* record "With a Little Help from My Friends," and the evidence may be found on their *Rarities* album.

The Beat Brothers

The Beat Brothers is a name often associated with the early Beatles. Many people assume that this was a stage name used by Lennon, McCartney, and Harrison before Ringo joined the group in 1962. However, the Beat Brothers were a completely different group whose only relation to the Beatles was that both bands played in Hamburg in 1961 and both backed singer Tony Sheridan on several recordings for Polydor.

The confusion is understandable. When Polydor issued a single of Sheridan and the Beatles playing "My Bonnie," it incorrectly identified the recording artists as "Tony Sheridan and the Beat Brothers." The single, a rocking version of the familiar old song, actually turned out to be a hit in

Germany—*before* the Beatles were famous. And later on, when the group hit it big, record companies eager to squeeze every possible dime from the Beatles phenomenon "padded" their releases of early Beatles recordings with material by Sheridan and the Beat Brothers.

An example of this is *The Beatles with Tony Sheridan and Their Guests*, issued in the U.S. by MGM Records in February 1964. (An ironic title in the first place: when they made the recordings, Sheridan was the big star, not the Beatles.) It features the Beatles themselves on "Cry for a Shadow" and "Ain't She Sweet"; Sheridan and the Beatles on "My Bonnie," "Take Out Some Insurance on Me Baby," "Sweet Georgia Brown," "The Saints," "Why," and "Nobody's Child"; and Sheridan and the Beat Brothers on four other songs. (See also **Tony Sheridan.**)

Beatlemania

The origins of Beatlemania, that strange malady that affected young people all over the world in the mid-1960s, could actually be traced to a specific date: October 13, 1963. That was the day when thousands of fans jammed the streets outside the London Palladium, where the Beatles had just played a show.

The group members themselves cited October 31 as the origination date of this mass cult phenomenon. On that day, five celebrities were due to arrive at Heathrow Airport in London: the newly elected Miss World and the four Beatles, fresh from a tour in Sweden. Fans caused immense traffic jams, and the prime minister himself got caught in the traffic and had to wait. As for Miss World, she went virtually unnoticed.

Beatlemania spread to the United States in January 1964, and probably reached its peak about the time *A Hard Day's Night* came out that summer. A year later, the Beatles had moved on to *Rubber Soul* and other things.

In the 1970s, a stage show called *Beatlemania*, featuring four "band members" who looked just like the Beatles and sang Beatles songs, had a hit run. By that time, some took a rather jaded view of Beatlemania-the-phenomenon, an example being a line from "London Calling" by the Clash in 1979, to the effect that "phony Beatlemania has bitten the dust."

The Beatles (a.k.a. the White Album)

The Beatles is the true title of the double album released by the group in November 1968. But like *Led Zeppelin IV* (often called *The Runes Album* or *Zofo*), this one is better known by its nickname than by its actual title.

Originally they wanted to call their album *A Doll's House*. This would have been an interesting choice, since the famous play by that title, a drama by Norwegian playwright Henrik Ibsen, is about a woman who chooses to leave her husband as an act of affirming her individuality. Exactly the same thing was happening with the Beatles, and the roots of their future breakup are evident on the White Album.

In fact, the title *The Beatles* is positively ironic, since in fact the album showcases not so much the work of a group called the Beatles as it does the individual talents of its members. The two principal Beatles songwriters—and, to an extent, George Harrison—could have released solo albums, using the material they had written for the White Album, and the songs would have sounded much the same.

In several instances, one member of the group recorded his song without any help from the others. John did it on "Julia," and Paul recorded a number of his songs solo: "Wild Honey Pie," "Blackbird," "Why Don't We Do It in the Road," "Mother Nature's Son," and more. As if to further shake the foundations of the group, the album marked the first appearance of a major rock performer from outside the group—Eric Clapton, who played lead guitar on Harrison's "While My Guitar Gently Weeps."

Since 1965's *Rubber Soul*, when John and Paul began to emerge as separate songwriters and the credit "Lennon-McCartney" became little more than a legal formality, Paul had begun to dominate the albums. He'd had more songs than John on *Revolver*, *Sgt. Pepper*, and *Magical Mystery Tour*. However, on *The Beatles*, John reasserted himself, offering this time around a quantity of songs equal to those of Paul. Of his thirteen White Album titles, Lennon's two favorites were "I'm So Tired" and "Happiness Is a Warm Gun." His least favorite of any song on *The Beatles* was McCartney's "Ob-La-Di, Ob-La-Da," which George seems to have despised as well. Paul, for his part, hated "Revolution 9" and attempted to have it removed from the album—an opinion shared by many fans.

Thirty Songs, Two Records

The group recorded between thirty-four and forty songs in the sessions that resulted in the White Album. Two of these came out on a single, "Hey Jude" / "Revolution," in August 1968. Two more, George's "Not Guilty" and John's "What's the New Mary Jane," only saw legitimate release on *The Beatles Anthology 3* nearly thirty years later. As for the remaining tracks alleged to have been recorded, including "Indian Rope Trick" and "Happy Birthday Mike Love," accounts of these are probably apocryphal.

Of the thirty that remained, George Martin had wanted to select the fourteen best tracks and release a really strong single-record album. It is interesting to speculate about what would have made the cut, and what wouldn't: certainly "Back in the U.S.S.R.," "Julia," and "While My Guitar Gently Weeps" would have passed the test; and certainly "Revolution 9" and "Wild Honey Pie" would have gotten canned. Many people could have lived with that, especially the part about "Revolution 9." But some of the album's best tracks—"Why Don't We Do It in the Road," for instance, or "Blackbird"— might have gotten left on the cutting-room floor as well, and that would have been a shame.

In any case, the group wanted a double album because it would put them an extra record toward fulfilling their contract with EMI. Once again, as often happens, the motivation for a supposed artistic choice was economic, or at least largely so. But as a result, Beatles fans discovered new realms afforded by the wide room of the expanded format, and the group got to explore various styles of music.

Many people mistakenly think that *The Beatles* was the first double album of entirely new material by a major artist. They're almost right, but as in many other instances, there was one performer just a step ahead of the Beatles: Bob Dylan, who in 1966 released the double *Blonde on Blonde*. At 93 minutes, 33 seconds, however, the White Album was certainly the longest release of new material by a major rock artist at that time. (And by definition, because it resulted from several talents rather than just one, it was more varied than *Blonde on Blonde*.) Most likely the album that shattered the White Album's record for length was George Harrison's triple-disc, twenty-three-song magnum opus, *All Things Must Pass*, which came out two years later. It clocked in at 103 minutes, 33 seconds—exactly 10 minutes longer than the White Album.

The Artwork

At the initial release of the album in November 1968, each copy came stamped with an individual number in the lower right-hand corner of the front cover. Thus no two copies of *The Beatles* were exactly the same. In later years, stamped copies of the White Album would make the rounds at various Beatles conventions, drawing high prices based on the condition and the number—the lower the better.

With the album came photos of the band, plus a lyrics sheet and poster. This idea—the inclusion of "goodies" with an album, which fans looked forward to getting the way kids looked for the prize in a cereal box—was not a first, though it had hardly become a standard practice. Dylan's *Greatest Hits* album, for instance, which came out a year before, had included a poster with a stylized portrait of the artist by Milton Glaser; before that, of course, there had been the Beatles' own *Sgt. Pepper,* which in its original form included mustache cut-outs and other novelties. As for the White Album poster, Linda Eastman, future wife of Paul McCartney, took some of the photographs and helped arrange the pictures for the collage.

The stark beauty of the album's white cover continued a long tradition of surprising and innovative Beatles cover art, beginning with *Rubber Soul*'s distorted faces and carried through *Sgt. Pepper*'s kaleidoscopic "group picture." Instead of trying to top the earlier artwork, the design went back to square one: solid white. It was around this time that John came under the influence of Yoko Ono, who had a penchant for solid white objects in her artwork; but if there was a connection between this and the album cover, it has not been clearly established.

There is a misconception that the original cover of the White Album had shown John and Yoko in the nude, and that the Beatles—forced by the record company to withdraw this cover—had opted for a solid white one as a protest. In November 1968, two different albums came out: the White Album, and John and Yoko's *Two Virgins*, with its infamous cover that showed them naked against a white backdrop. Because both albums involved John Lennon, and both came out the same month, the mistake is understandable.

Since the White Album, groups have had their own "color" record names, an intentional and sometimes ironic reference to *The Beatles*. There was Sonic Youth's *Whitey Album* in 1988, and in 1997 *The Brown Album* by Primus. In 1991, there was *Metallica*, like *The Beatles* an eponymous record that came to be known by its color—"The Black Album." And then there was the "Black Album" that never really existed—Spinal Tap's sanitized cover of *Smell the Glove*, as depicted in the 1984 film *This Is Spinal Tap*. (The original release of the film's soundtrack came in a plain black sleeve, just like *Smell the Glove*.) Finally, there are the "Red Album" and the "Blue Album," names sometimes used for *The Beatles 1962–1966* and *1967–1970* albums respectively.

Macabre Footnotes

The White Album came out in Britain on November 22, 1968, exactly five years—five *long* years—after the assassination of John F. Kennedy. The group's 1963 album, *With the Beatles*, had been released on the very day of the shooting in Dallas.

Without a doubt, *The Beatles* was probably the first rock album used as evidence in a murder trial: *The People of the State of California vs. Manson, Atkins, Krenwinkel, and Van Houten*. (See **Charles Manson**.)

* * * * *

The Beatles Song List

Title	Composer	Time
Side One		
Back in the U.S.S.R.	McCartney	2:45
Dear Prudence	Lennon	4:00
Glass Onion	Lennon	2:10
Ob-La-Di, Ob-La-Da	McCartney	3:10
Wild Honey Pie	McCartney	1:02
The Continuing Story of Bungalow Bill	Lennon	3:05
While My Guitar Gently Weeps	Harrison	4:46
Happiness Is a Warm Gun	Lennon	2:47
Side Two		
Martha My Dear	McCartney	2:28
I'm So Tired	Lennon	2:01
Blackbird	McCartney	2:20
Piggies	Harrison	2:04
Rocky Raccoon	McCartney	1:42
Don't Pass Me By	Starkey	3:52
Why Don't We Do It in the Road	McCartney	1:42
I Will	McCartney	1:46
Julia	Lennon	2:57
Side Three		
Birthday	McCartney	2:40
Yer Blues	Lennon	2:46
Mother Nature's Son	McCartney	2:46
Everybody's Got Something to Hide Except Me and My Monkey	Lennon	2:25
Sexy Sadie	Lennon	3:15
Helter Skelter	McCartney	4:30
Long Long Long	Harrison	3:08

Side Four

Revolution 1	Lennon	4:13
Honey Pie	McCartney	2:42
Savoy Truffle	Harrison	2:55
Cry Baby Cry	Lennon	2:34
[Can You Take Me Back]*	McCartney	0:27
Revolution 9	Lennon	8:15
Good Night	Lennon	3:14

*Not listed on the inside cover, lyrics sheet, or label.

The Beatles 1962–1970 Albums

In April 1973, two "new" Beatles double albums came out. The first featured selections of the group's music during the early phase of their career, from their first single, "Love Me Do," in 1962, to *Revolver* in 1966. The second covered their later phase, from the "Penny Lane" / "Strawberry Fields Forever" single in 1967 to *Let It Be* in 1970. Together, *The Beatles 1962–1966* and *The Beatles 1966–1970* introduced a whole new generation of kids—too young to remember the group's heyday—to the Beatles' music.

The four discs that constitute *The Beatles 1962–1970* albums feature fifty-four songs in all. Of these, forty-nine are Lennon-McCartney tunes; four are by George Harrison ("While My Guitar Gently Weeps," "Old Brown Shoe," "Here Comes the Sun," and "Something," all on *1967–1970*); and one is by Ringo, "Octopus's Garden," also on *1967–1970*.

The four ex-Beatles themselves picked the tracks for these two albums, and the song list generally received critical praise for its breadth and inclusiveness. Supposedly the former group members also picked the colors that frame the cover pictures of each: red on *1962–1966*, and blue on *1967–1970*. They chose these, allegedly, to pay homage to Liverpool's two football teams, Liverpool (whose color is red) and Everton, whose players wear blue.

The covers themselves were exceedingly clever. The first, clearly taken during the 1962 to 1966 era, shows the four moptops in identical uniforms looking down at the camera from a balcony. In the second photo, each man is standing in the same position and on the same balcony, but it's obvious that a lot of time has passed. All except Paul have some type of facial hair—John's is a beard as big as Karl Marx's—and each is dressed very differently from the others, in clothing that clearly identifies the period as the late sixties.

There was no trick photography at work here. The first picture was taken in 1963, for the cover of the group's first British album, *Please Please Me*. Six years later, when they were recording music for what they planned as a back-to-the-basics album called *Get Back*, the band members thought it would be a hoot to take a picture in exactly the same pose—exactly the same, only totally different. *Get Back*, of course, never materialized, and the group broke up; so the *1967–1970* album cover was most people's first exposure to the latter picture.

The British and American releases of *1962–1966* differ slightly. The British version features three seconds of strange whispering just before "I Feel Fine," while the American one precedes "Help!" with sixteen seconds of Monty Norman's "James Bond Theme."

The Beatles Anthology (CD)

The Beatles Anthology CDs are much more than a soundtrack for the film of the same title; they contain dozens upon dozens of Beatles tracks which had never been heard before by a wide audience. Many of these had been available on bootlegs, but many more had *never* been released, and certainly never with the quality afforded a legal EMI release.

The three CDs, released in succession between late 1995 and mid-1996, chronicled the Beatles' career from the first Quarry Men recordings in 1958 to the last *Let It Be* overdubs in 1970—and something more. These were the two "new" Beatles songs, "Free As a Bird" and "Real Love." Both had begun as demo tapes made by John Lennon in 1977 and 1979, respectively, and Yoko Ono offered both—along with a third song, "Grow Old with Me"—to the three remaining Beatles.

Paul McCartney, George Harrison, and Ringo Starr recorded "Real Love" and "Free As a Bird" without the participation of George Martin, who elected not to involve himself due to problems with his hearing; instead, Jeff Lynne (formerly of ELO, and more recently George's bandmate in the Traveling Wilburys) served as producer. The resulting productions became something much more than the original Lennon pieces, and thus "Free As a Bird" is credited to all four Beatles.

As interesting as the concept of two "new" Beatles songs were, however, these were far from the only items which recommended *The Beatles Anthology* CDs to fans everywhere. In the case of all but a very few of the tracks contained on the six discs, it is easy to agree with the Beatles' decision not to release them; but that being said, the songs make for endlessly fascinating listening.

Below is a very cursory overview of the material contained in the *Anthology* CDs. Much more information is available from the sleevenotes by Mark Lewisohn, probably the world's leading authority on the Beatles: These are three excellent little booklets with copious photos—many of these outtakes as well—and notes on each song, along with intros to each book by Apple Corps press agent Derek Taylor, who died in 1997. As with the *Anthology* film (see **The Beatles Anthology (Film)**), another great source is at the Mining Co. on the World Wide Web (http://beatles.miningco.com/mbody.htm).

Beatles Anthology 1

This first set of two discs covers the years from 1958 to 1964. This means that there are quite a few recordings of John, Paul, and George with persons other than Ringo—including Pete Best. (Note the cover, on which Ringo's face—from the *Please Please Me* photo shoot—covers Best's on the old leather-clad "Savage Young Beatles" poster.) This is the only *Beatles Anthology* CD to include spoken-word commentary from the Beatles and Brian Epstein, though all contain plenty of studio chatter.

Incidentally, before Capitol Records shipped this CD to stores, it kept its warehouses under armed guard in order to prevent anyone from getting a preview of "Free As a Bird." Through a special shipment arrangement with United Parcel Service, copies of the CD arrived at record stores with great fanfare on the day of release.

Disc 1

Free As a Bird: The March 1994 recording with all four Beatles together again—sort of—for the very first time since January 1970.

[John Lennon]: A snippet from an interview with Jann Wenner of *Rolling Stone* on December 8—note the date—1970.

That'll Be the Day • In Spite of All the Danger: The first recording by the Quarry Men, made in 1958. There was a rumor that the *Anthology* would include a recording made on the first day Lennon and McCartney met—July 6, 1957—but that did not happen. The second song, the B-side, is a rare McCartney-Harrison composition. (For the first recording of John, Paul, George, *and* Ringo, see **First Recording.**)

[Paul McCartney]: From a 1994 interview with Lewisohn.

Hallelujah, I Love Her So • You'll Be Mine • Cayenne: Two covers and a McCartney song, all from 1960. These are the only known Beatles recordings featuring Stuart Sutcliffe.

[Paul McCartney]: Talking to Malcolm Threadgill in 1962.

My Bonnie • Ain't She Sweet • Cry for a Shadow: Two covers and the only known Harrison-Lennon song, an instrumental. All were recorded in Hamburg on June 22, 1961, and on the first, the Beatles perform backup for Tony Sheridan.

[John Lennon]: Talking about Brian Epstein to David Wigg in 1971.

[Brian Epstein]: Reading from his book *A Cellarful of Noise* in 1964.

Searchin' • Three Cool Cats • The Sheikh of Araby • Like Dreamers Do • Hello Little Girl: Five of the fifteen songs recorded during the group's ill-fated Decca Records audition on New Year's Day 1962. The songs were all selected by Epstein: the first two are Lieber-Stoller numbers previously recorded by the Coasters; the third is from a 1940 movie; and the last two are Lennon-McCartney originals.

[Brian Epstein]: From *A Cellarful of Noise*—Epstein talks about the failure of the Decca audition.

Besame Mucho • Love Me Do: The earlier audition recordings were rather lame compared to these—made on the first session with George Martin and EMI on June 6, 1962—and it's not impossible to understand why Decca turned down the future greatest band of all time. This slower version of "Love Me Do," with Pete Best (as opposed to later ones with Andy White and finally Ringo), was not rediscovered until 1994.

How Do You Do It: From the second George Martin session, on September 4, 1962—this time with Ringo. The song is a Mitch Murray number that Martin liked a lot more than the Beatles did.

Please Please Me: This is from the session of September 11, 1962, during which the group recorded the "Love Me Do" single, with Andy White instead of Ringo. (See **"Love Me Do."**) Like the Pete Best "Love Me Do," this first recording of "Please Please Me," also with White, did not resurface until 1994.

One After 909 (sequence) • One After 909 (complete): The early Beatles song, never officially released until *Let It Be* more than seven years later. This is from a session of March 5, 1963, and the first version is a splice of several recordings, including one that broke down.

Lend Me Your Comb: A live recording on BBC's *Pop Go the Beatles* on July 2, 1963. The song is a cover, and the lyrics seem rather suggestive for the time.

I'll Get You: From the British TV show *Val Parnell's Sunday Night at the London Palladium,* recorded October 13, 1963—the day on which Beatlemania "officially" began. (See **Beatlemania.**)

[John Lennon]: From the Wenner/*Rolling Stone* interview.

I Saw Her Standing There • From Me to You • Money (That's What I Want) • You Really Got a Hold on Me • Roll Over Beethoven: An exuberant performance in Stockholm on October 24, 1963. Sweden—not Germany—was the first foreign country the Beatles toured as a group: their time in Hamburg was not a *tour* but a series of jobs, and it occurred long before fame or Ringo found them.

Disc 2

She Loves You • Till There Was You • Twist and Shout: From the November 4, 1963, Royal Command Performance—complete with Lennon's famous cheeky comment that introduces the last number: ". . . I'd like to ask your help. Would the people in the cheaper seats clap your hands? And the rest of you, if you'll just rattle your jewelry."

This Boy • I Want to Hold Your Hand • [comedy skit] • Moonlight Bay: From a December 2, 1963, appearance on *The Morecambe and Wise Show.* After playing two songs, the boys spar with Eric Morecambe and Ernie Wise, one of Britain's leading comedy acts. (The humor is almost incomprehensible to anyone who is not British.) They follow this with a comic rendition of a 1940s hit.

Can't Buy Me Love: An early rendition of the song, taped in Paris on January 29, 1964.

All My Loving: The first song of the group's first performance on *The Ed Sullivan Show,* February 9, 1964.

You Can't Do That • And I Love Her: Two interesting outtakes of songs recorded during the *Hard Day's Night* sessions in February 1964. Particularly noteworthy is the more rhythmic version of the latter track.

A Hard Day's Night: The first take, complete with laughter.

I Wanna Be Your Man • Long Tall Sally • Boys • Shout: From the British TV special *Around the Beatles,* recorded on April 19, 1964.

I'll Be Back (Take 2) • I'll Be Back (Take 3): The development of the song from a waltzlike number to the more well-known version.

You Know What to Do • No Reply (demo): The June 3, 1964, demo of "No Reply" sounds quite different from the released version; as for Harrison's "You Know What to Do," this was to have been his second Beatles song after "Don't Bother Me," but it never saw release until the *Anthology*.

Mr. Moonlight • Leave My Kitten Alone: Two covers from the *Beatles for Sale* sessions in August 1964: the first was released in 1965, the second not till 1995.

No Reply: An important attempt along the way to the finished song.

Eight Days a Week (sequence) • Eight Days a Week (complete): Various takes at Abbey Road on October 6, 1964.

Kansas City/Hey-Hey-Hey-Hey!: Take 1 of this song was the one released; this is Take 2.

Beatles Anthology 2

Of the three *Anthology* albums this one, covering the period from 1965 to early 1968, is perhaps the least satisfying. Expectations are understandably high, considering that Volume 2 includes the period of greatest experimentation and creativity, from *Rubber Soul* to *Sgt. Pepper*. Hence it is frustrating to find a number of live recordings of old Beatlemania-era material, along with some of the less interesting songs of the later period, such as "Your Mother Should Know" and "Only a Northern Song." But for treasures such as John Lennon's first demo of "Strawberry Fields," much can be forgiven.

Disc 1

Real Love: A second "Beatles" recording, made in 1995.

Yes It Is: Parts of two different takes, recorded on February 16, 1965.

I'm Down: A first, live-in-the-studio take—complete with Paul saying "Plastic soul, man, plastic soul."

You've Got to Hide Your Love Away • If You've Got Trouble: Outtakes from the *Help!* sessions. The latter was a song intended for Ringo, but was canned in favor of "Act Naturally."

That Means a Lot: Another song left on the cutting-room floor of the *Help!* album, this one became a hit for British pop singer P. J. Proby.

Yesterday: Take 1, made June 14, 1965, with just Paul on the acoustic guitar. A slightly different ordering of the lyrics.

It's Only Love: Parts of two takes.

I Feel Fine • Ticket to Ride • Yesterday • Help: A British TV performance most notable for the fact that this was the first time McCartney ever played "Yesterday" before an audience.

Everybody's Trying to Be My Baby: From the Shea Stadium concert on August 15, 1965.

Norwegian Wood (This Bird Has Flown): Though this is Take 1, and the released version came later, this recording of the song then titled "This Bird Has Flown" was already a clear indication of the painstaking process beginning to develop in the Beatles' studio work.

I'm Looking Through You: Another *Rubber Soul* outtake, this version lacks the "Why, tell me why" chorus that would later serve as an anchor to the song.

12-Bar Original: Had they released this recording made on November 4, 1965, it would have been the Beatles' first instrumental since the Hamburg days. Instead, "Flying" took that honor in 1967, and this track was not released until the *Anthology*.

Tomorrow Never Knows: Though it would wind up at the end of the *Revolver* album, this version of "Tomorrow Never Knows" was recorded on April 6, 1966, at the beginning of the *Revolver* sessions. At that time, the song was still called "Mark I," and this is Take 1—quite different from the released version, Take 3. This one is slower, with a less complex, but almost equally hypnotic, rhythm.

Got to Get You into My Life: Very different from the released version, this one features a prominent droning organ sound and additional lyrics.

And Your Bird Can Sing: Not strikingly different from the master recording, but notable nonetheless for the laughter.

Taxman: Take 11 (as opposed to Take 12, the released version). A few differences in the lyrics and the ending.

Eleanor Rigby (strings only): Because it features none of the Beatles—only hired classical musicians—this is not really a "Beatles" recording; nonetheless, it's moving to hear just the strings, specially remixed in 1995.

I'm Only Sleeping (rehearsal) • I'm Only Sleeping (Take 1): The rehearsal version features a vibraphone, and Take 1 includes both Lennon *and* McCartney on vocals.

Rock and Roll Music • She's a Woman: Two concert numbers from Japan on June 30, 1966—evidence of what was by then a wide gap between the songs the Beatles were playing on stage and the music they were creating in the studio.

Disc 2

Strawberry Fields Forever (demo sequence): At his home some time in mid-November 1966, John Lennon committed to tape the first version of a new song he had been writing during the filming of *How I Won the War.* The recording is very rough, and much would change as the song evolved; it's hard for a true Beatles fan to hear this for the first time and not get cold chills.

Strawberry Fields Forever (Take 1): A recording made on November 24, 1966, which shows that the lyrics and music were still continuing to develop.

Strawberry Fields Forever (Take 7 and edit piece): The entirety of Take 7, part of which went into the final recording or "master," along with a finale that includes a forceful performance by Ringo on drums.

Penny Lane: Parts of various takes, along with an extended version of the trumpet ending known to those who heard it on the *Rarities* album.

A Day in the Life: Also a composite of several versions, this presentation of "A Day in the Life" is itself a triumph of production. Again, hearing it is a cold-chills moment. For a full explanation of how it was made, one should read Lewisohn's liner notes.

Good Morning Good Morning: Almost alone among the *Anthology* tracks, this version of "Good Morning Good Morning," though noticeably different from the master, could have succeeded quite well if released in its place. It is funkier, bouncier, than the one on *Sgt. Pepper,* and does not include any animal noises at the end.

Only a Northern Song: Parts of several takes for this extraordinarily unmemorable song.

Being for the Benefit of Mr. Kite! (Takes 1 and 2) • Being for the Benefit of Mr. Kite! (Take 7): Parts of several takes, along with studio banter.

Lucy in the Sky with Diamonds: Once again, parts of various takes, mixed together to illustrate the most interesting aspects of the experimentation that went into this track.

Within You Without You (instrumental): All the instrumental parts to Harrison's exceedingly complex song—George on sitar, with guest musicians on violins, cellos, and Indian instruments.

Sgt. Pepper's Lonely Hearts Club Band (Reprise): The music is as strong as in the master, but in this take, McCartney's "guide vocal" sounds intentionally campy.

You Know My Name (Look Up the Number): For those who want to hear it, a stereo version of this over-the-top song, which runs two minutes longer than the version released as the B-side of "Let It Be."

I Am the Walrus: Take 16, the backbone onto which all the other effects were added to create the much-acclaimed master recording.

The Fool on the Hill: McCartney on piano, three weeks before the recording of the final version.

Your Mother Should Know: A September 16, 1967, recording, Take 27, with McCartney in a playful mood.

The Fool on the Hill (Take 4): Recorded on September 25, 1967, the day before the group scrapped all previous recordings of "Fool on the Hill" and developed what would become the master.

Hello, Goodbye: Parts of two different takes.

Lady Madonna: A remix involving several takes.

Across the Universe: Take 2 of the recording made on February 3, 1968, with Lennon and McCartney joined by two female fans. Take 1 would wind up on the World Wildlife Fund's benefit LP, and in extremely altered form, on Phil Spector's production of *Let It Be.*

Beatles Anthology 3

On this last set of CDs, covering the period from early 1968 to January 1970, the *Anthology* yields its finest moments. The creative highs may not be as great as during the *Revolver–Sgt. Pepper* phase, but there is still plenty to showcase—particularly because the vast majority of the Beatles' unreleased studio material came from this phase.

Disc 1

A Beginning: The intended orchestral introduction to "Don't Pass Me By," recorded by the same musicians who performed the backing for "Good Night" on the White Album.

Happiness Is a Warm Gun: One of several recordings from May 1968, made at George Harrison's house, this "routine" of Lennon's still-forming song includes an apparently impromptu section revolving around Yoko Ono's name.

Helter Skelter: A slow, bluesy version, edited down to five minutes from its original twelve. Included are a number of lyrical variations.

Mean Mr. Mustard • Polythene Pam • Glass Onion • Junk • Piggies • Honey Pie: All from the May 1968 routines at Harrison's bungalow in Esher, this is a treasure trove of material that would eventually be dispersed to the White Album, *Abbey Road,* and (in the case of "Junk") Paul's solo album *McCartney.* One notable fact is that in the acoustic version here, one can actually understand the lyrics to "Polythene Pam," which in its later rendition would become the Beatles' "Louie, Louie" (as it were). The lyrics of the other songs would all change to a lesser or greater extent before they saw final production.

Don't Pass Me By: An even more percussive and bouncy recording than the one which appears on the White Album.

Ob-La-Di, Ob-La-Da: Congas and three saxophones distinguish this take.

Good Night: A rehearsal, along with the orchestral backing to Ringo's vocal.

Cry Baby Cry: The first take, much like the master that emerged five hours later on the night of July 16, 1968.

Blackbird: Take 4, which once again is close to the master, Take 32—except for some background noise.

Sexy Sadie: An early take with a fade-out instead of the later coda.

While My Guitar Gently Weeps: A delicate acoustic rendering of a Harrison masterpiece, with a verse that did not make the final cut.

Hey Jude: A less lavish take, which begins with joking between Lennon and McCartney.

Not Guilty: Take *102* of a song that, after all that effort, never saw release on the White Album. Harrison would later include an acoustic version on his solo album *George Harrison* in 1979.

Mother Nature's Son: Take 2, as opposed to Take 26, the master.

Glass Onion: A recording made before George Martin's addition of strings, this one includes a "Revolution 9"–style conclusion, with a soccer announcer's repeated cry: "It's a goal . . . it's a goal . . . it's a goal. . . ."

Rocky Raccoon: A longer introduction for Rocky's story, along with some different lyrics.

What's the New Mary Jane: John's extraordinarily creepy song, which fortunately did not make the final song list for *The Beatles*. One can only wonder how it would have fit into Charles Manson's White Album schema.

Step Inside Love • Los Paranoias: An impromptu recording of a song McCartney had written for Cilla Black, another performer who had been managed by Brian Epstein, along with an equally off-the-cuff group composition.

I'm So Tired: A composite of three takes.

I Will: Take 1. (The master was Take 67.)

Why Don't We Do It in the Road: A kinder, gentler—and more bluesy— version.

Julia: A largely instrumental version of what turned out to be the last song recorded for the White Album, on October 13, 1968.

Disc 2

I've Got a Feeling: A January 23, 1969, recording with Billy Preston in the basement studios at Apple headquarters on Saville Row in London.

She Came in Through the Bathroom Window • Dig a Pony: A slower version of the first song than the one that appeared on *Abbey Road*, and a stronger recording of the second than on *Let It Be*.

Two of Us: Because the Beatles were now attempting to once again record live in the studio, each song required endless rehearsals. In this recording, McCartney can be heard saying "Take it, Phil" to Lennon—a reference to their Everly Brothers-style harmony.

For You Blue: Recorded the same day as the *Let It Be* version, January 25, 1969.

Teddy Boy: Two recordings of a song that ended up appearing on the solo *McCartney* album in 1970.

Rip It Up • Shake, Rattle and Roll • Blue Suede Shoes • The Long and Winding Road: Three oldies and an original—the latter the same recording as appeared on *Let It Be*, but without the strings and choir later added by Phil Spector.

Oh! Darling: Lennon takes part in this recording of a McCartney composition, and mentions the fact that Yoko Ono's divorce from her first husband has just become final.

All Things Must Pass: Recorded on February 25, 1969, Harrison's twenty-sixth birthday, this is a demo of the song that later became the title track of his first solo album.

Mailman, Bring Me No More Blues: A cover of an obscure Buddy Holly song, with touches of "Revolution 1."

Get Back: The third rendition of this song from the January 30, 1969, "rooftop concert" at Apple, this was the final song of the Beatles' final live performance.

Old Brown Shoe: Another demo recorded by Harrison on his birthday.

Octopus's Garden: Take 2 of 32, without the underwater sound effects.

Maxwell's Silver Hammer: Take 5, with a very nice piano intro from McCartney which sounds (to speak anachronistically) like the opening notes of Elton John's "Goodbye Yellow Brick Road," recorded four years later.

Something: The third and last of Harrison's "birthday demos." This one includes a rich countermelody later abandoned.

Come Together: Take 1 of 8, without echo or any guitar from Lennon.

Come and Get It • Ain't She Sweet: Paul's demo, which Badfinger recorded in an almost identical arrangement, along with a song the Beatles had covered many years before, during their time of apprenticeship in Hamburg.

Because: The extraordinary three-part harmony (which was duplicated twice to create nine voices), remixed, with all the instrumentation stripped away.

Let It Be: Paul plays his unfinished song for the rest of the band.

I Me Mine: The final recording of new material by the Beatles, on January 3, 1970.

The End: A new mix of the next-to-last song on the Beatles' next-to-last (and last recorded) album.

The Beatles Anthology (Film)

In 1995, on November 19, 22, and 23—just before Thanksgiving—ABC-TV broadcast *The Beatles Anthology,* a six-hour series which chronicled the story of the Beatles from the 1940s to their breakup. It was a huge media event, for which the network reportedly paid Apple Corps $20 million. In addition, ABC shelled out an additional $30 million for promotion of the event.

But the network in turn charged advertisers $300,000 for a thirty-second spot, and based on the vast enthusiasm generated among Beatles fans, it's a safe bet that they did pretty well on the entire proposition. The three-night show, after all, featured the world premiere of not one but two "new" Beatles songs, "Free As a Bird" and "Real Love"; extensive photographs and footage; and the full participation of all three surviving Beatles. It was, in a word, a Beatles fan's dream, especially when combined with the release, over the following year and a half, of three *Beatles Anthology* CDs—all part of what a Capitol Records executive called a "massive reintroduction of the Beatles."

The Long Road to the *Anthology*

The idea for the *Beatles Anthology* goes back almost to the time of the group's breakup. Derek Taylor, Apple Corps press officer, made a film called *The Long and Winding Road*, which never saw release due to legal problems—but which may have influenced the later *Rutles* parody. It certainly seems to have inspired *The Compleat Beatles*, a 1981 film which remained the most comprehensive of Beatles film histories until 1995. (The term *Compleat*, incidentally, is not a changed spelling to conform with the Beatles' variation on *beetles*; in fact it is an archaic spelling of *complete* most often associated with a 1653 book called *The Compleat Angler* by Izaak—who also had a funny way of spelling his first name—Walton.)

As for the project that would become *The Beatles Anthology*, it had to remain on hold until at least 1989, at which time all the bandmembers' twenty-year-old legal quarrels were settled. By then, most *personal* disagreements had long been put to rest as well, and Paul McCartney, George Harrison, and Ringo Starr were ready to work together.

It would still be years before the producers of the *Anthology*, with the help of the former Beatles, sifted through literally thousands of hours of footage and pictures that ranged from scenes of the group performing in their *Sgt. Pepper* uniforms to sequences from *Let It Be*, and from grainy Liverpool stills to Astrid Kirchherr's lush black-and-white portraits of the group with Stu Sutcliffe and Pete Best.

Eventually they narrowed it down to just five hours of material (six with commercials), which aired in Britain on ITV beginning the same night as the first ABC broadcast. As part of the continued "reintroduction of the Beatles," Apple Corps later issued *The Beatles Anthology Video*, eight tapes containing twice as many hours of material as the TV special.

For more information on the *Anthology*—as well as just about anything else on the Beatles—one of the best places to go is the Mining Co. on the World Wide Web (http://beatles.miningco.com/mbody.htm).

Beatles Merchandise

In 1964, when Beatlemania erupted in America, many in the business community saw a chance for instant riches. They could make some quick money before the fad died and American kids went back to life as it was before the Beatles—or so they thought. They may have been wrong about the group's staying power, but they weren't off the mark in their idea that people could make money from virtually any product with the name "Beatles" on it.

So it was that scores, perhaps even hundreds of Beatles products went into production in 1964. There were the usual items: Beatles buttons, Beatles trading cards, Beatles T-shirts, Beatles musical instruments, Beatles wigs. . . . But as a result of the group's phenomenal popularity, other products—often things that bore no relation to music at all—sold millions. There were Beatles pillowcases, Beatles coloring books, Beatles popsicles (and a flavor of ice cream called "Beatle Nut"), Beatles clothing (everything from bow ties to shoelaces to jewelry), Beatles balloons, Beatles talcum powder, licorice "long-eating" Beatles records, Beatles board games . . . and the list goes on.

The Beatles eventually developed legal authority over the use of their name, something a group nowadays would have done in the first place. Together with Brian Epstein, their manager, they set up Seltaeb ("Beatles" spelled backwards) as a licensing agency for all Beatles products sold Stateside. Seltaeb took a percentage from the profits of the fifty-million-dollar Beatles products industry, and reserved the right to reject any proposals not considered suitable for the use of the Beatles' names.

Not too many ideas failed the tastelessness test, but a few did. Such proposals included live jeweled beetles and Beatles sanitary napkins. Of all the products that did make it past Seltaeb, perhaps the most whimsical of all was canned Beatles breath, sold in New York.

Lest it be thought that Americans were the only people capable of such perversion, Lambretta, the Italian motorcycle corporation, considered a model with a Beatles wig on the seat.

A set of pin-back buttons featuring the Fab Four. Archive Photos/Blank Archives

"Because"

Both Paul McCartney and George Harrison referred to "Because," a John Lennon composition, as their favorite song on *Abbey Road*.

Lennon got the idea for the song's melody when he heard Yoko Ono playing Beethoven's "Moonlight" Sonata. (A fragment of "Because" appears on the couple's *Wedding Album*.) In writing his song, Lennon simply played Beethoven's piece backwards, with some rearrangements.

The *Abbey Road* recording features George Harrison on synthesizer, and one of only three notable cases of three-part harmony in a Beatles recording. The others, "This Boy" and "Yes It Is," were much earlier. For "Because," George Martin triple-tracked the vocals, to create the effect of *nine* voices singing in harmony.

"Being for the Benefit of Mr. Kite!"

"Being for the Benefit of Mr. Kite!," which closes out Side One of *Sgt. Pepper's Lonely Hearts Club Band*, is one of the most innovative songs from John Lennon's highly creative psychedelic period of 1966 and 1967.

Lennon's inspiration for the song came from an 1843 circus poster he had purchased at an antiques shop. "Being for the benefit of Mr. Kite!" announced the poster, intended to promote a circus at Rochdale, Lancashire. Essentially all the characters Lennon mentions in the lyrics—Mr. Kite, Henry the Horse, and the Hendersons of Pablo Fanques Fair—were to be found on the poster; John, as he explained later, did little more than to put them all together. (An ostentatious understatement.)

Though both Lennon and McCartney tended to downplay the idea that *Sgt. Pepper* was a "concept album" with a theme running through it, fans *perceived* a theme, and that was really what mattered most anyway. And inasmuch as there is a "concept" to *Sgt. Pepper*, it is in its bizarre mixture of Victorian and psychedelic motifs, a combination nowhere more evident than in "Being for the Benefit of Mr. Kite!"

Throughout the recording, George Harrison, Ringo Starr, and the Beatles' closest associates, Mal Evans and Neil Aspinall, play harmonicas. Paul performs on both bass and lead guitar, and John plays the Hammond organ and sings. As on other compositions from Lennon's psychedelic period, in this one his voice sounds not just otherworldly, but as though he were chanting from somewhere high above the listener. Lennon's Hammond organ can be heard in the middle ("Henry the Horse's Waltz"), while George Martin, on a Wurlitzer organ, supplies the "swirly noises"—chromatic runs based on the original tune.

In the middle of all this intriguing activity, it's easy to miss the most innovative element of the song. This is the backdrop to the waltzing horses and the godlike ringmaster's voice, a piece of sound like a Jackson Pollock painting put to music.

In fact, the effect of "Mr. Kite" comes largely from the artistry of the recording itself, the joint achievement of John Lennon and George Martin. Lennon had wanted recordings of Victorian steam organs in the background of "Mr. Kite," but both he and Martin knew that they might wind up with a lawsuit if they used the recordings just as they were. As it turned out, fear of possible copyright infringement caused the development of a fascinating technique.

George Martin took small portions of tape from different steam organ pieces and gave them to recording engineer Geoff Emerick with instructions to cut the tapes into "little parcels about a foot long, and don't be too careful about the cuts." This done, he told the engineer to throw the pieces of tape into the air, letting them fall where they might, then pick them up and piece them together in as random an order as possible.

Martin listened to the snippings Emerick had rearranged for him, then took the extra precaution of splicing in portions of the tape backwards if they sounded at all like the original. The result was a nonsensical jumble of squeaks and honks that meant nothing in terms of music. However, when used as a backdrop for the big-top antics of Messrs. K. and H., these sounds created an expressionist painting of a circus unlike anything the Ringling Brothers ever imagined.

Pete Best

In 1960, after four years of playing with a variety of drummers—and sometimes none at all—the Beatles finally acquired a serious percussionist named Pete Best. It looked as though the lineup of the group was set.

The boys had met Pete when they played at Liverpool's Casbah Club, owned by Pete's mother. The handsome and athletic Best impressed them with his drumming, and they asked him to join the group. He would continue to play with them for the next two years, through some of the hardest days of the group's history—including all three trips to Hamburg—until Brian Epstein asked him to leave, a request that came just when the Beatles were on the cusp of their long-anticipated success.

In old Astrid Kirchherr photos of the early Beatles—before Ringo, but with Best and Stu Sutcliffe—Best appears not to fit in. The others may not always be smiling, but they are open to the camera in a way that the saturnine Best is not. And he seems to belong to another time, with his James Dean-style ducktail in contrast to the others' "mod" look, which would revolutionize American fashion in just a few more years.

At performances in Hamburg and Liverpool, while the others clowned on stage, Best sat quietly and drummed, as if unaware of his companions' antics. He seemingly willed himself to be an outsider, and even after two years on the road in some rough venues—situations that should have created a bond—he had developed little rapport with the other group members. So it was easy to let him go.

On their return from Hamburg after their third trip in 1962, the Beatles were preparing to make their first recordings for Parlophone. Even though the group members were untrained, George Martin could see the raw talent in Lennon's, McCartney's, and Harrison's vocal and guitar performances, but he was not so pleased with Pete Best's drumming. When he told the other group members how he felt, they more or less agreed; at least, they didn't seem to feel any strong compulsion to step in on Pete's behalf.

So it fell to Brian Epstein to call Pete Best into his office and explain that the producer—and the other members of the group—wanted him out. Naturally, Best wasn't too happy about this, and had he known all that he was going to miss, he would have been truly upset. He had his own fans, distinct from the group's, which was another sign of the fact that he marched to his own beat; and when they found out about it, they were *really* steamed.

August 18, 1962: the Beatles appeared onstage at Liverpool's Cavern Club for the first time with their new drummer, Ringo Starr, formerly of Rory Storme and the Hurricanes. Dismayed at the loss of Pete Best, fans carried signs that read "Pete is Best" and "Pete Forever, Ringo Never." They even physically attacked members of the group, giving George Harrison a black eye.

Best's Luck Ultimately Changes

But Ringo and the other three clicked instantly, and Best was out. So he would go down in history as one of those people who got a seriously lousy deal—partly out of his own doing, partly out of sheer bad fortune. While his former bandmates went on to dizzying fame and fortune, Best went to work in a government office in Liverpool. Later, in the 1980s, he scored a minor splash with his own band, but his fame was like the light of the moon: it originated from another source, and had no power of its own.

In 1985, Best finally came out with a book, written with Patrick Doncaster, called *Beatle! The Pete Best Story,* published by Dell, and in 1998 British publisher Northdown released *Drummed Out!: The Sacking of Pete Best* by Spencer Leigh. Best himself in 1996 published *The Best Years of the Beatles.*

By then, *The Beatles Anthology* had given him a measure of the fame and fortune that had eluded him thirty-five years before. Because Best appeared on ten tracks, he received royalties in the millions: Though some of the early tracks had been legally released before, as for instance "Ain't She Sweet" on a 1970s K-Tel-style compilation called *History of British Rock,* there had never been a release with the full imprimatur of the Beatles, so Best had never seen real money from his work. Now he did, though it's actually a bit more complicated than that, and in fact involved the efforts of an attorney who secured a reported settlement of £2 million ($3.2 million) from Apple.

Best himself had begun touring with his Pete Best Band, whose other five members had not even been born at the time of the Beatles' breakup. In May 1996, Reuters caught up with him in Singapore, where he was joined by another figure from the Beatles' past: Allan Williams, their first manager.

Williams pointed out that in terms of onstage man-hours, Best actually drummed with the Beatles for much longer than Ringo.

In 1999, one of the principal stops on the Liverpool "Magical Mystery Tour," a tour of Beatles-related sites, was a visit to the old Casbah Club—reopened, with Pete Best on stage.

"Birthday"

"Birthday," which opens up Side Three of *The Beatles*, seems to have actually been cowritten by Lennon and McCartney. If so, it would be the only song on that album for which that is the case. As with most compositions from the White Album, they wrote this one while at the Maharishi's ashram in Rishikesh, India. Patti Harrison, whose birthday they were celebrating, sang the chorus along with Yoko Ono.

That's one version. In another, Paul alone wrote the song in the Apple studios, where the group recorded it on the spot. (It certainly sounds rather impromptu.) Either way, Patti and Yoko did both perform on the song.

Birth of the Beatles

Before the first meeting of John Lennon and Paul McCartney on July 6, 1957, Lennon's group was called the Quarry Men, and they—Lennon, McCartney, later George Harrison, and a number of others—continued to go by that name through 1959. (See **The Quarry Men.**)

Late in 1959, they played under the name Johnny and the Moondogs for the duration of one engagement: a trip to Manchester to compete on the Carroll Lewis Show, their first true talent contest. Each performer sang his number, and when the audience had heard them all, the performers were supposed to return to the stage for an encore to register audience applause and thus determine a winner. However, the Moondogs couldn't afford overnight lodging, and since the last train for Liverpool left before the final encore, they never got to find out whether they passed the audition.

In the months that followed, John and Paul would perform in a short-lived duo called the Nurk Twins, and the group would bill themselves as "The Rainbows" one night when all of them wore different-colored shirts to the club where they were playing.

Experimenting with Names

Stuart Sutcliffe joined the Quarry Men in January 1960, and despite John's later claim that "a man on a flaming pie" had given them the name Beatles, he and Stuart were the ones who came up with it.

Influenced by Buddy Holly's Crickets, they experimented with different spellings throughout the year 1960: first Beatals, then Silver Beats, then Silver Beetles. A fellow Liverpool musician told him they should call themselves Long John and the Silver Beetles, because the idea of a group without an individual's name at the front end (like Buddy Holly and the Crickets) seemed downright preposterous.

But they liked Silver Beetles, and under that name added a drummer, Tommy Moore—who was thirty-six years old, almost twice as old as the oldest band member, Lennon. In May 1960, they set out on their first "tour" as backup band for singer Johnny Gentle in Scotland. During the nine-day engagement, three of them adopted pseudonyms: Paul Ramon, Stu de Stael, and Carl Harrison (after one of George's heroes, Carl Perkins of "Blue Suede Shoes" fame.) Despite these cheery flourishes, it was a pretty unhappy trip: Johnny Gentle, who in 1998 published his recollections of the tour, wrecked the van, and Tommy Moore lost a few teeth. By the summer he was out of the group.

Meanwhile, Lennon and Sutcliffe had continued working on the group name. John changed the "e" to an "a" to show that the group played beat music, a style popular in Liverpool at the time. On August 6, 1960, they acquired a drummer, Pete Best, whose mother Mona owned the Casbah Club in Liverpool—a venue where the other Silver Beatles had hung out from time to time. They also found a manager, Allan Williams, who booked them for an inauspicious week-long gig backing a stripper named Janice with songs such as "Begin the Beguine."

But Williams found them better work when the steel band that played at his Jacaranda Club was lured away by the prospect of work in Hamburg. The manager saw a new opportunity booking British acts in Germany, and on August 16, 1960, an entourage including his five young musicians embarked for Hamburg.

Somewhere between August 6 and 16, they had dropped the "Silver" to become simply "The Beatles."

Minus 2, Plus 1, the Equation Is Complete

For the next year, the five—Lennon, McCartney, Harrison, Sutcliffe, and Best—would play together, both in Liverpool and Hamburg. Then in the summer of 1961 Stuart, never much of a musician, fell in love and quit the group. A year after that, Best was out.

The Beatles as the world came to know them—John Lennon, Paul McCartney, George Harrison, and Ringo Starr—first played together on August 18, 1962, before an angry crowd of Pete's fans at the Cavern Club.

(For more about the early Beatles, see **Pete Best; The Cavern Club and Other Clubs; First Recording; Hamburg; Lennon-McCartney Partnership; The Quarry Men; Tony Sheridan; Stuart Sutcliffe.**)

"Blackbird"

"Blackbird," an almost universally loved White Album track, illustrates Paul McCartney's ability to turn what was little more than a fragment into a fully realized song—without ever actually finishing the fragment. Thus the composition consists of just two verses and a break; but it works.

McCartney recorded the song by himself, and the only instrumentation is his acoustic guitar. On June 11, 1968, while he was busy going through the various takes until he reached the one he liked—Take 32, as it turned out—John Lennon was in another of the Abbey Road studios working on "Revolution 9." (Opinions of Lennon's "song," too, are almost universal—universally negative, that is—yet Charles Manson at least seems to have admired the two compositions equally.) This was the first time Lennon and McCartney had actually recorded separately and simultaneously, a portent of things to come.

Also on June 11, Paul worked on a short promotional film with Apple recording artist Mary Hopkin. In it he could be seen playing "Blackbird," then slipping into "Helter Skelter."

"Blue Jay Way"

"Blue Jay Way," George Harrison's contribution to *Magical Mystery Tour*, was the tenth of his songs to be recorded and released by the Beatles.

Harrison wrote "Blue Jay Way" in August 1967, while he and his wife Patti were visiting California. This was during the "Summer of Love," when Harrison walked the streets of San Francisco's Haight-Ashbury district, strumming his guitar and singing "Baby You're a Rich Man" for the thousands of flower children who swelled the district's population during that summer. Thirty years later, in *The Beatles Anthology*, George would speak of his visit to California in a way quite different from the usual media portrayal of the

"Summer of Love." It was far from Paradise, Harrison said; with all the unwashed hippies and whacked-out acidheads, it was more like being in the Bowery.

On the night described in the song, the Harrisons were staying in Los Angeles at a house called Blue Jay Way. Patti had gone to bed, but George sat up waiting for Beatles press agent Derek Taylor and his wife, whose plane was late due to heavy fog over L.A. While waiting for them, George began composing a song about people who become lost in the fog banks that sometimes shroud their own lives, and then "los[e] themselves instead."

The recording makes use of an electronic effect called phasing, produced by playing the same recording over two different tape machines slightly out of synchronization. Phasing helps give this song its foggy texture, as do the background vocals of George and Paul, which were recorded both backward and forward.

As the song fades out, Harrison repeats the phrase "don't be long" twenty-nine times.

Books About the Beatles

Almost since the beginning of the Beatles' career, people have been writing and publishing books about the group, ranging from the very good to the very bizarre; from chronology to critique to condemnation.

There have been group biographies by journalists such as Hunter Davies, Philip Norman, and Anthony Scaduto; then there are the more personal books, usually by people who worked with the group. Producer George Martin has published two, *All You Need Is Ears* (1982) and *With a Little Help From My Friends: The Making of Sergeant Pepper* (1994), and manager Brian Epstein had a book as well, *A Cellarful of Noise* (1964). So did press agent Derek Taylor—three, in fact, the last being *It Was Twenty Years Ago Today* in 1987. (Actually it was four, since in fact he ghostwrote Epstein's *Cellarful*.) Peter Brown, another Beatles business associate (who Lennon mentioned in "The Ballad of John and Yoko"), published *The Love You Make* with Steven Gaines—author of the 1998 bestseller *Philistines at the Hedgerow*—in 1983.

Quarry Man Pete Shotton, a lifelong friend of John Lennon, published two books with Beatles authority Nicholas Schaffner: *The Beatles, Lennon, and Me* (1983) and *John Lennon: In My Life* (1994). Fellow Quarry Man Len Garry wrote *John, Paul & Me: Before the Beatles: The True Story of the Very Early Days* (1997). A member of Stuart Sutcliffe's family published a book about him in 1996, and Pete Best had a book in 1995. In 1998, one of the singers the

The Beatles and friends enjoy a meal at a Swedish seaside resort in October 1967. Beatles publicist Derek Taylor appears on the far left. Archive Photos/Svenskt Pressefoto

Beatles had backed up in the very early days published *Johnny Gentle and the Beatles: First Ever Tour: Scotland 1960.*

Of course there were books by the Beatles' friends from Hamburg, Astrid Kirchherr and Jurgen Vollmer. By the 1970s, it began to seem as though everyone who had ever so much as waved at the Beatles had written a book about it. John's first wife, Cynthia, wrote about him in *Twist of Lennon* in 1978; so too did May Pang, who dated him during a period of separation from Yoko in the 1970s.

The one group of people who weren't writing books much were the former Beatles themselves. The closest thing to a Beatles autobiography was George Harrison's *I Me Mine* (Simon and Schuster, 1980), which originally came out in a leatherbound, signed limited edition that retailed for $200. Paul had a book of drawings, notes, and photos (by his wife Linda) called *Composer/Artist*, which came out in 1981.

As for John, in 1986 Harper published a book called *Skywriting By Word of Mouth*, including some autobiographical sketches he wrote shortly before his murder. Lennon also had two books of poems and short stories published in the mid-1960s (*In His Own Write* and *A Spaniard in the Works*, both by Simon & Schuster). There were several books of interviews, most notably *Lennon Remembers* by *Rolling Stone* publisher Jann Wenner (1971), and *The Playboy Interviews With John Lennon and Yoko Ono* a decade later. The *Rolling Stone* and *Playboy* interviews, in fact, provide an interesting counterpoint to one another, as they both have been published in book form and they represent Lennon at his worst in 1971 and his best in 1980, shortly before his death.

A biography of John published in 1988 excited perhaps more controversy than any other Beatles-related book ever did. In fact, the furor that greeted *The Lives of John Lennon* by Albert Goldman (William Morrow, 1988) recalled that which Lennon himself had caused when he said in 1965 that the Beatles were more popular than Jesus. It was indeed pretty sordid stuff, including (for instance) assertions that John abused Yoko, something most fans would find as hard to believe as the idea that she had numerous other lovers during the time of their marriage. Another Lennon postmortem is *Who Killed John Lennon?* by Fenton Bresler (New York: St. Martin's, 1989), which focuses on Mark David Chapman and the assassination.

Sublime Ridiculousness

Surprisingly few fictional works have involved the Beatles, though that could change in future years. Joe Orton, a British playwright murdered by his lover in 1967, wrote *Up Against It: A Screenplay for the Beatles,* which was not published until 1979. Robert Hemenway published *The Girl Who Sang with the Beatles, and Other Stories* in 1970; and then of course there's the screenplay, by Iain Softley and Stephen Ward, for the 1994 film *Backbeat.* The latter portrays the group's early Hamburg days, and presents Stuart Sutcliffe as a talent equal to John Lennon, whereas Paul McCartney is a mere wannabe—so yes, it's fiction.

The Beatles have inspired numerous literary studies such as *Beowulf to Beatles: Approaches to Poetry* (1972) by David Pichaske, or the essay "Learning from the Beatles" in *The Performing Self: Compositions and Decompositions in the Languages of Contemporary Life* by Richard Poirier (1971). Other "scholarly" writings on the group, most of which appear to be doctoral dissertations, include *The Music of Sound, or, the Beatles and the Beatless* by Joan Peyser (1967); *The Change of Leadership Within the Beatles* by Matthew M. Daiker (1997); *A Comparative Study of Three Cover Versions of the Beatles' Song "Eleanor Rigby"* by Peter A. De Vries (1988); *The Kaleidoscopic Rhetoric of the Psychedelic Counterculture: A Feminist Analysis of the Beatles' Sgt. Pepper's Lonely Hearts Club Band* by James M. Nesbit (1997); and *The Beatles: Twentieth Century Literary Figures and Cultural Icons* by Barri Ann Smith Piner (1997).

Certain titles seem to mystify rather than identify—e.g., *Epoch Moments and Secrets: John Lennon and the Beatles at the Mirror of Man's Destiny* by Richard Warren Lipack (1996), or *She Loves You: A Curious Tale Concerning a*

Miraculous Intervention by Elaine Segal (1997). Surely a much more digestible book would be *The Complete Idiot's Guide to the Beatles* by Richard Buskin (1998), presumably made for the world of *Windows for Dummies,* etc.

There have been numerous other Beatles-related books and writings that defy classification. One of these would certainly be *The Beatles* by Aram Saroyan, son of the novelist William Saroyan. This book of minimalist poetry, published in New York by Barn Dream Press in 1971, must be both the shortest (eight pages) and least expensive (five cents a copy) book about the Beatles ever written.

And its writing probably involved the least mental effort. The book consists of four two-word "poems," which were simply the names of the group members, starting with "Paul McCartney." Had Saroyan waited a couple of decades to pen his lyric masterpiece, it might have been praised as a triumph of postmodernism. How often, after all, are a title, text, and subject all the same thing?

"Boys" / "Kansas City"

The single "Boys" / "Kansas City" came out in the U.S. in October 1965, but a month later, Beatles manager Brian Epstein requested that it be removed from the U.S. market.

According to Epstein, "Boys" / "Kansas City" was "unrepresentative of current trends in Beatles music." His reasoning became clear a month later, when *Rubber Soul* appeared. The group was obviously moving on, and "Boys" and "Kansas City"—usually referred to as "Kansas City/Hey-Hey-Hey-Hey!" because it is actually two songs—were very much a thing of the past.

Even the authorship of the two songs harkens to the past, when the Beatles were more imitators than innovators. "Boys," by Luther Dixon and Wes Farrell, bears an uncanny resemblance to "What'd I Say" by Ray Charles. And "Kansas City" was a Lieber and Stoller song, with Little Richard's "Hey-Hey-Hey-Hey!" tagged on. (See also **"Kansas City/Hey-Hey-Hey-Hey!"**)

Canada

When the Beatles arrived in Toronto during their Summer 1964 North American Tour, cars of fans coming to the airport to greet them were backed up for seventeen miles. That's a lot of cars, considering that the entire population of Canada—spread over an area much larger than the United States—was not much greater than California's. Added to that is the fact that this event occurred at three o'clock in the morning. *Our Hearts Went Boom: The Beatles' Invasion of Canada* by Brian Kendall (Toronto: Penguin, 1997) is a record of the group's visit to the Great White North.

Five years after the Beatles' Toronto concert, John and Yoko Lennon held a ten-day "bed-in" at Montreal's Queen Elizabeth Hotel, during which time the Lennons and the Plastic Ono Band—which consisted of those people who happened to be present in the hotel room at the time—recorded "Give Peace a Chance." Later that year, Lennon testified before the Canadian Government Commission on Drug Use, asking that marijuana be legalized. During that visit he also met with Prime Minister Pierre Trudeau, who spent an hour talking with the former Beatle—more time than he had given to various heads of state who had recently visited his country.

Incidentally, the Beatles made a second trip to Toronto, in 1965. At their August 17 show, someone gave Paul McCartney an Ottawa Police Precinct badge which he would later wear on his *Sgt. Pepper* uniform. (The initials were O.P.P., not O.P.D. as "Paul Is Dead" enthusiasts believed.) According to George Martin, one of the policemen in the detachment guarding the group at the 1965 show was a Sgt. Pepper.

"Can You Take Me Back"

It is odd that Paul McCartney should have penned one of the Beatles' most obscure tracks, a twenty-seven-second snippet near the end of the White Album. Unlisted on the accompanying lyrics sheet, presumably the name of the song is "Can You Take Me Back," since the lyrics consist of that question and just five other words. Though the title should properly be rendered with a question mark, it probably would not have been, given the fact that other "question" titles—"Do You Want to Know a Secret" from the early days, "What Goes On" from *Rubber Soul,* and "Why Don't We Do It in the Road" on the White Album—are unpunctuated.

The "song" is simply a verse (or is it a chorus?). Paul recorded it on September 16, 1968, in the middle of the numerous takes on "I Will" (see **"I Will"**) necessary to get the rhythm track down pat. Originally "Can You Take Me Back" lasted two minutes, twenty-one seconds, but it was trimmed down and wedged between John Lennon's "Cry Baby Cry" and "Revolution 9." Its proximity to those two songs only enhances the aura of eeriness around this, the only Indian-inspired song in the Beatles catalogue. (*American* Indian, that is.)

"Can't Buy Me Love"

"Can't Buy Me Love," from the *Hard Day's Night* soundtrack, came out as a single in both Britain and America several months before the movie appeared. The song, backed with "You Can't Do That," gained a listing in *The Guinness Book of World Records* for the greatest advance sales on a single—three million copies.

Three of the Beatles recorded an alternate version of the song in a theater dressing room. John and Paul, who started out with one of the verses (instead of the chorus, as in the released version), played guitars while Ringo provided percussion on a suitcase. George, who had been in the bathroom during the recording, added only one touch: the sound of a flushing toilet. The Beatles wanted to release this recording, but George Martin thought it in bad taste.

"Can't Buy Me Love" is considered the last song of the Beatles' "rock 'n' roll stage." Three months after the release of this single came *A Hard Day's Night*, which featured the first classic Beatles ballads: John's "If I Fell" and Paul's "And I Love Her."

Capitol Records

Capitol Records in the United States, like Parlophone in the United Kingdom, was a subsidiary of EMI (Electric & Musical Industries), a vast British recording conglomerate established in 1931.

From the time the Beatles signed their contract with EMI/Parlophone in 1962 until the formation of Apple in 1968, and again after the dissolution of Apple in the mid-1970s, all Beatles releases in America came out under the Capitol imprint. American fans still get a little nostalgic when they see the old rainbow-rimmed label used by the record company in the sixties. (Likewise the Apple logo brings out a longing for days gone by, which may—along with the fact that Apple Corps shared copyright with EMI—have influenced Capitol's use of the Apple label on the *Anthology* CDs.)

Though Capitol would one day make millions of dollars from the Beatles catalogue, they were a bit slow to react at first. In late 1963 Brian Epstein wrote to them, requesting the U.S. release of the single "Please Please Me," which had hit Number One in Britain on February 16 of that year. A senior Capitol executive replied, "We don't think the Beatles will do anything in this market."

"Carry That Weight"

Paul McCartney's "Carry That Weight" belongs to the lengthy and much-acclaimed song cycle that fills the majority of *Abbey Road*'s second side. Though it is listed as a distinct composition, the Beatles recorded it along with "Golden Slumbers" as though they were one song.

At that point—in July 1969—the *Abbey Road* medley, which the group called "The Long One/Huge Medley," still had a considerable way to go before it took its final form. The song order as of July 30, less than six weeks before the album's completion, had "Her Majesty," which eventually came at the end of the nine songs, in the fourth position after "Mean Mr. Mustard" and before "Polythene Pam."

As for "Carry That Weight," it helps tie the medley together by reprising the "You Never Give Me Your Money" theme that opened it. Three Beatles sing on the recording (Lennon was absent), though as often happened when they sang together—e.g., on "Flying"—Ringo's voice dominates.

The Cavern Club and Other Clubs

The Cavern Club, the Liverpool bar where Brian Epstein "discovered" the Beatles in November 1961, became a significant part of the group's myth. The club paid the group only £5 ($12) for their first performance there, on March 21, 1961. By the time they left a year later, they were earning £300 ($720) per show. (Actually, the 1961 show was not really their first: the Quarry Men—without Paul and before George joined—had played there on August 7, 1957.)

According to Maureen Cox, one of the Cavern's many female patrons, girls would queue up for hours in front of the doors, dressed in their everyday jeans with rollers in their hair. When the doors opened, they would file into the club and wait while the opening bands did their sets. Then, when the hour drew near for the Beatles to appear on stage, a few girls at a time would steal off to the bathroom, make themselves up, and change into the nicer clothing they had smuggled in their handbags. That way, the girls always looked their best for the Beatles. Ringo Starr must have liked what he saw of Maureen, because he married her.

One night only three Beatles showed up at the Cavern, so Gerry Marsden of Gerry and the Pacemakers filled in, standing on an orange crate to reach the microphone.

The Casbah Club

During 1959 Johnny and the Moondogs, as the Quarry Men were currently calling themselves, often played at the Casbah Club in the basement of 8 Hayman's Green, Liverpool. Their engagement there, in fact, probably saved the group from a breakup ten years too early: all the members were becoming restless for a change, and without the common project of playing at the Casbah, they might have gone their separate ways.

The Casbah was owned by Mona Best, whose son Pete would join the group as drummer in the following year. Mrs. Best remembered John as being so nearsighted that he would often cause problems when he was only trying to help. (Lennon did not wear his glasses in public until his *Sgt. Pepper* phase many years later.) One day the Moondogs offered to help her paint the club; glad to have some extra assistance, she handed John, Paul, and George a paintbrush apiece and put them to work. When she came back to see how they were doing, Lennon had painted the pipes on the ceiling with the wrong paint—gloss instead of primer. And it was doubly wrong, because the pipes were not supposed to be painted in the first place.

Seven Clubs in Two Cities

In all, seven clubs in two cities played a vital role in the Beatles' development. Besides the Cavern and the Casbah, there was one other important Liverpool club, the Jacaranda, owned by Allan Williams, who became the group's first manager.

Most of these clubs, by the way, seem to have been ahead of their time by about thirty years: the Jacaranda and the Casbah, at least, were coffee bars, where kids such as Lennon, McCartney, and Harrison would nurse cups of espresso for hours.

Then there were the four clubs where the Beatles played in Hamburg, and these definitely were *not* coffee bars: the Indra, the Kaiserkeller, the Top Ten Club, and the Star Club. (See also **Hamburg.**)

Christmas Records

Every holiday season between 1963 and 1970, Beatles Fan Club members received a special Christmas gift from the group, the Beatles Christmas Record. It usually lasted about six minutes, and consisted of zany comedy sketches, as well as *thank you*s from the group to the fans for all the support they had received in the previous year.

Anyone who has ever watched *Monty Python's Flying Circus* has some idea of what these records were like. Also, the once-rare song "You Know My Name (Look Up the Number)" is similar in style to the Beatles' annual holiday greetings. Probably the most well-known of these seven recordings—the eighth is simply a compilation of the previous seven—is 1967's *Christmastime Is Here Again!,* the last Christmas record the members of the group recorded together. In 1968 and finally in 1969, the band members did their own bits, and an engineer put them on one record. The 1968 record contains Lennon's poem "Jock & Yoko," in which he airs his feelings regarding perceived mistreatment of his new love by his bandmates, and includes Tiny Tim singing "Nowhere Man."

The seven Christmas records were:

The Beatles Christmas Record (1963)
Another Beatles Christmas Record (1964)
The Beatles' Third Christmas Record (1965)
The Beatles' Fourth Christmas Record—Pantomime: Everywhere It's Christmas (1966)
Christmastime Is Here Again! (1967)
The Beatles' 1968 Christmas Record (1968)
The Beatles' Seventh Christmas Record (1969)
From Them To You (1970)

For more about the Christmas records, visit www.thadonline.com/cbd/xmasrecords.html on the World Wide Web.

Eric Clapton

In the 1960s there was an expression, "Clapton is God." It was a way of paying homage to the guitarist's legendary talent, which he brought to bear for John Mayall's Blues Breakers, the Yardbirds, Cream—and the Beatles.

A long-standing friend of George's, sometimes referred to by George as his "guitarist-in-law," Eric Clapton played lead on "While My Guitar Gently Weeps." His penchant for sweets led to the writing of another White Album track, "Savoy Truffle"; and later, George would write one of his biggest hits, "Here Comes the Sun," at Eric Clapton's house on a particularly beautiful spring day in 1969.

Clapton reportedly played on Harrison's first solo album, *Wonderwall Music,* under the pseudonym of Eddie Clayton, and George helped him write the Cream song "Badge." How did it get its title, which has nothing to do with the song itself? George and Eric were sitting across from each other, George writing the words down on a sheet of paper while he and Clapton composed them. When he came to the part for the song's bridge (a passage that usually connects the first verses to the last), George wrote the word "bridge" on the paper. Looking at the word upside-down, Clapton asked Harrison what he meant by "Badge." The two had a right laugh over the misunderstanding, and then decided to keep the word as the title.

George also played guitar on "Tell the Truth," from Clapton's 1972 masterwork, *Layla*. Clapton wrote the title track for the same woman who had inspired Harrison's "Something" three years before: Patti Boyd, formerly Mrs. George Harrison. By the time of "Layla," she and George had split up, and she and Clapton became involved soon afterward.

George and Patti didn't divorce until 1977, at which time she married Clapton. The two later divorced as well. As for Clapton and Harrison, despite the fact that they had loved the same woman—a circumstance that seldom improves a friendship—they seem to have remained friends.

Patti and the two men in her life later made a recording considerably less monumental than either "Something" or "Layla": a rendition of the Everly Brothers' "Bye Bye Love" on Harrison's 1974 *Dark Horse* LP. Patti sang backing vocals, while Clapton (of course) played guitar.

"Cold Turkey"

"Cold Turkey," John Lennon's second post-Beatles single, was the first song he ever released under his name alone, without the familiar Lennon-McCartney byline. Five months before, Lennon had released "Give Peace a Chance" as his first single, with the Plastic Ono Band. The song bore the "Lennon-McCartney" credit, even though Paul had nothing to do with its writing. But by the time of "Cold Turkey" in December 1969, Lennon was ready to go it alone.

The Plastic Ono Band that recorded "Give Peace a Chance" bore no relation to the one that performed "Cold Turkey," except that John Lennon belonged to both. In fact, the "band" was more of a concept than an actual group, and it could consist—as Lennon described it—of "whoever happens to be in the room at the time." For "Cold Turkey," Eric Clapton, Hamburg friend and bassist Klaus Voorman, and Ringo Starr happened to be in the room.

When he later returned his MBE award (see that entry) to the Queen, Lennon mentioned poor sales for "Cold Turkey" as one of his reasons for returning the medal. Later, however, he expressed regret for this flippant comment.

"Come Together"

John Lennon originally wrote "Come Together" for LSD guru Timothy Leary's campaign against Ronald Reagan for governor of California. However, as he was writing it, John Lennon realized that the song had nothing to do with Leary, Reagan, or California, so he abandoned the idea entirely, and the song became the first track on *Abbey Road*. (No doubt it was due to Lennon's apathy that Reagan beat Leary in the closely contested race. . . . But seriously, Lennon did later meet Reagan at a football game in the mid-1970s, and Reagan explained the rules of football to him.)

Maurice Levy, owner of the company that held the rights to Chuck Berry's "You Can't Catch Me," brought a lawsuit against Lennon, charging that he had lifted the first two lines of "Come Together," as well as much of its melody, from Berry's tune. Lennon settled the argument by agreeing to record "You Can't Catch Me" and "Sweet Little Sixteen" (another Berry song controlled by Levy) for his *Rock 'n' Roll* album, released in 1975. It was ironic—perhaps intentional—that Lennon should have chosen "Sweet Little Sixteen," since it already had its own courtroom history. Several years before, the Beach Boys had released "Surfin' U.S.A.," which had a tune virtually identical to Berry's, and they ended up having to pay royalties to the copyright holders for every record sold.

Although the Beatles had revolutionized hairstyles many years before, "Come Together" was the first Beatles song to actually mention long hair. Another reference in the song earned "Come Together" a place, along with "A Day in the Life" and "I Am the Walrus," on the list of Beatles songs banned by the BBC. The cause was the line "he shoot Coca-Cola," with which the authorities at the British Broadcasting Company took issue—not because of the drug references, but because it sounded like an advertisement for Coke.

Apparently the powers at the BBC failed completely to consider the possibility that "shooting Coca-Cola" could be a reference to something more serious than a soft drink. However, the line probably had nothing to do with either kind of coke; and in any case, Lennon seemed to enjoy putting false "clues" into his songs, as for example in "Glass Onion."

One particularly noteworthy reference in "Come Together" can be found in its opening passage: though it would be possible to hear the song a thousand times and not notice it, Lennon is clearly saying "Shoot me." This would of course assume a ghoulish significance eleven years later, when Mark David Chapman killed Lennon with a pistol. Just four months later, John David Hinckley tried unsuccessfully to do the same to Reagan, who unlike Lennon had the advantage of Secret Service bodyguards. Both

Chapman and Hinckley, it is said, had copies of J. D. Salinger's *The Catcher in the Rye* on their persons.

Concerts and Tours

The Beatles' concerts and tours broke records and almost broke a few of the group members' bones. There were many times when it seemed that over-enthusiastic fans might trample the group members to death or pull their hair out, hoping to get a "piece" of the Beatles.

To protect themselves, members of the group and their assistants, Mal Evans and Neil Aspinall, often devised ingenious means of escape. On one tour, for instance, all four tried to get away from a concert hall by wearing supposedly undetectable disguises of coats and beards. But one by one they were recognized—or at least, three of them were—and the admirers who swarmed around them completely failed to notice a 5'11" male passing by. This was Paul, who John later said was dressed as a "weird photographer, coming out with a lot of psychological gibberish." Paul's disguise must have been convincing, because not even Brian Epstein knew who he was.

Escape usually proved a better protection than disguise. In 1963, the Beatles got away from fans at a theater in Sunderland, England, by disappearing into a fire station next door. Once inside the station, they slid down the pole to where a police car was waiting for them. Meanwhile, a crew drove the fire engine out into the street to create a diversion while the boys rode off with the bobbies. Good thing there weren't any fires in Sunderland that night.

The Teddy Boy Days

Of course, the Beatles spent years building up enough of a reputation that fans would *want* to tear them limb from limb or crush them to death. In the early days, nobody cared; and even as their popularity grew, the group didn't yet have the money to hire bodyguards. So sometimes they got into difficult situations like the one at Liverpool's Grosvenor Ballroom in early 1960.

The group was in between drummers, since Tommy Moore had quit and Pete Best had not yet joined. So at the beginning of a show, John Lennon would often announce to the audience that if anyone could come up and play drums for them, they were more than welcome to do so.

In those days and for decades afterward, Liverpool was heavily populated by a species known as the teddy boy, or "ted." The teddy boy phenomenon belonged to a British tradition of lifestyles defined by musical affiliation which would include the later mod, rocker, punk, and skinhead movements. Many teds came from the lower classes, and in any case all of them affected a rough working-class style that revolved around drinking, fighting, music, and fashion. The Beatles at that time often imitated the teddy boy style of dress, wearing tight-fitting pants, or "drainpipes"; but they were no teddy boys.

When Lennon made his announcement at the Grosvenor, a burly ted named Ronnie bounded onto the stage and deposited his considerable frame into the drummer's seat. The stalwart teddy boy, whose talents no one felt at liberty to critique, proceeded to beat the skins with fury. When it became apparent that Ronnie considered this his audition, the group had to summon their manager, Allan Williams, to persuade the ted to remove his stout person from the drum set.

Incidentally, one promoter who hired the group devised a particularly ingenious method of battling the teds. He installed as his "bouncer" a tiny, bespectacled old woman. Whenever a ted proved particularly bothersome, the little old lady would shout, "You stop that or I'll call your mum!" Apparently the method worked beautifully.

A Mock Brawl After a Concert

It wasn't always the fans causing trouble. Though they left actual violence behind them in Hamburg, the Beatles were not above having a little good clean fun, as the movie *A Hard Day's Night* illustrated. One night after a concert in Bournemouth, England, Paul and George got into a mock brawl at a café. The "fight" woke up nearby residents, who called the police.

When the bobbies arrived, they discovered that the supposed brawl was only a gag by the Beatles, who were above reproach in those British touring days of 1963. (They would not lose favor with British law enforcement until 1969, when the authorities arrested John and George for possession of marijuana.) The policemen stayed for tea, asked the group for autographs, and then returned to the station.

Touring Gets Ugly

Undoubtedly the most bizarre and ultimately disturbing aspect of the Beatles' concerts and tours was the gathering of disabled people, hoping for the touch of a savior's hand, which greeted them in every city. No matter where in the world they went, upon returning to their dressing room after a concert, the group would usually find several men, women, or children in wheelchairs waiting to see them. Apparently people believed that because of their fame and glamour, the Beatles possessed some sort of Christlike powers of healing. Ringo discussed this phenomenon—which bore out John's observation about the Beatles being more popular than Jesus—in the 1995 *Beatles Anthology* film.

By 1966, most of the fun had gone out of touring, especially after a misunderstanding in the Philippines nearly got the group members killed (see **Philippines**). Then in San Francisco at the end of their tour, fans crushed a limousine supposedly containing the Beatles. Fortunately, the group was far away, hiding in an ambulance as it sped them through the city. It's little wonder that their August 29, 1966, show in San Francisco's Candlestick Park marked the end of the Beatles' touring.

Ambitious Tour Proposals

In the three years that followed for the Beatles as a group, they considered and rejected several concert proposals. According to *Rolling Stone*, Beatles representatives briefly attempted to negotiate a concert combining the Beatles, Leonard Bernstein, and the New York Philharmonic. During the "Get Back" period, in which they recorded the music that would later become *Let It Be*, Paul and director Michael Lindsay-Hogg had the idea of holding a concert either in an ancient Tunisian coliseum or on an ocean liner in the middle of the open sea.

After almost three years away from touring, the group members were starting to feel the lure of the stage again, but they couldn't agree on the place, size, or nature of the concert. George felt that Paul's ideas were absurd and impractical. As for John, when he observed all the bickering going on, he remarked, "I'm warming to the idea of an asylum."

The last live performance by the Beatles was the impromptu "Rooftop Concert" held on January 30, 1969, and preserved in the film *Let It Be*. Standing on top of the Saville Row offices of Apple Records, the group plugged in their amps and played five songs: "Dig a Pony," "I've Got a Feeling," "One After 909," "Don't Let Me Down," and "Get Back." Below them, traffic on Saville Row stopped completely and people flocked to see the Beatles perform.

After half an hour or so, the police arrived and put a stop to this disturbance of the peace, but unfortunately (from the group members' perspective) they didn't arrest anyone. If only they could have gotten some film footage of bobbies hauling the Beatles off to jail, Ringo later remembered, that would have been the crowning touch to the event. Instead, the police approached them politely and with deference, and simply *asked* them to stop playing.

"The Continuing Story of Bungalow Bill"

John Lennon wrote "The Continuing Story of Bungalow Bill," from the White Album, about an American staying at the Maharishi's ashram in India at the same time the Beatles were there. While the others were meditating and supposedly raising their spiritual consciousness, this American was off in the jungle shooting at tigers. Apparently he didn't get the idea of the whole karmic thing; or maybe he just didn't care.

"The Continuing Story of Bungalow Bill" features Yoko Ono on harmony vocal (such as it is). Yoko also sings on the chorus, along with several others, including Maureen Starkey, Ringo's wife. George Martin's assistant Chris Thomas plays the mellotron, the instrument that sounds a little like a horn that's heard during the handclapping at the end of "Bungalow Bill," just before Lennon shouts "Eh up!" and "While My Guitar Gently Weeps" begins.

Cover Versions

In their earliest days, the Beatles relied heavily on cover versions—that is, their own renditions of songs written by others. Later, during their recording career with Parlophone, they committed twenty-four covers to posterity, or twenty-five if one considers "Hey-Hey-Hey-Hey!" as a track separate from "Kansas City." (For a complete listing of the cover versions released by the Beatles, see **Songs.**)

With the exception of "Maggie Mae," an adaptation of a traditional tune for *Let It Be,* no Beatles album after *Help!* included any songs not written by Lennon, McCartney, Harrison, or Starkey. Meanwhile, other singers had been covering Beatles songs. Two notable instances were Del Shannon's "From Me to You," as well as "I Saw Her Standing There" by Tony Newley, both from 1963—the only American covers done *before* the Beatles suddenly came to Americans' attention in early 1964.

Obviously, the Beatles recorded those songs themselves as well; so, too, with "I Wanna Be Your Man," an early hit for the Rolling Stones in 1964. But there were twenty *Songs Lennon and McCartney Gave Away,* to use the title of a 1979 EMI album. These were pieces that the two wrote, but never released commercially. Perhaps the best-known example was "A World Without Love," recorded by Peter & Gordon in 1964. (Peter, incidentally, was Peter Asher, brother of Paul's girlfriend at the time, Jane Asher.)

But by far the greatest interest has been generated by songs the Beatles made famous in the first place. Artists ranging from Arthur Fiedler to Harry Nilsson to Count Basie to the Chipmunks have all interpreted the Beatles' music on albums of their own. There have been some memorable moments, as for instance when Joe Cocker sang "With a Little Help from My Friends" at Woodstock; or when Elton John covered "I Saw Her Standing There" live with John Lennon (though perhaps Lennon's presence keeps it from being a true cover); or when Frank Sinatra sang "Something." And there have been some pretty bizarre moments as well, not just Ted Nugent's fine rendition of "I Want to Tell You" in 1979, but Steve Martin singing "Mean Mr. Mustard," or Siouxsie and the Banshees' dark version of "Dear Prudence."

And there have been several tribute albums as well, starting with a bizarre compilation in the early 1970s called *All This and World War II*, which included Leo Sayer singing "I Am the Walrus." By the mid-1990s, there would be numerous tribute albums for artists ranging from Jimi Hendrix to Kiss; but as so often happened, the Beatles came first.

"Crippled Inside"

"Crippled Inside," from John Lennon's 1971 *Imagine* album, features George Harrison on the dobro, a country slide instrument. George also assisted John with guitar on "How Do You Sleep?" (widely regarded as an attack on Paul McCartney) and "Gimme Some Truth."

"Cry Baby Cry"

"Cry Baby Cry" is the not-so-traditional lullaby that begins Lennon's three-song fade-out on Side Four of *The Beatles*; interrupted only by McCartney's fragmentary "Can You Take Me Back," the series of compositions continues with "Revolution 9" and concludes with "Good Night."

This was the last song of Lennon's dreamy "Lewis Carroll phase." Two years before, he had fallen under the influence of the nineteenth-century author of *Alice in Wonderland*, and this interest had reached its peak in 1967 with "Lucy in the Sky with Diamonds." The title of "I Am the Walrus" refers to a character in Carroll's *Through the Looking Glass*.

A second inspiration for "Cry Baby Cry"—at least its title—came, as in the case of "Good Morning Good Morning," from a television commercial. The commercial used the slogan, "Make your mother buy."

Kircaldy, the duke and duchess of which are mentioned in the song, is a place in Scotland. The Beatles held a concert there five years before "Cry Baby Cry"—on October 6, 1963.

"A Day in the Life"

"A Day in the Life" is the last and—by general consent—best song on the album many consider the greatest of all time, *Sgt. Pepper's Lonely Hearts Club Band*.

In a 1976 poll by the fan magazine *Survey*, "A Day in the Life" won the title of Favorite Beatles Song. Critics have compared it with T. S. Eliot's *The Waste Land*, both for its dreamy yet apocalyptic quality, and for the way it captured the spirit of the twentieth century just as Eliot's 1922 poem had. Many have called "A Day in the Life" not merely the Beatles' finest song, but the greatest composition of the rock era.

The Fusion of Two Parts

Unlike most Lennon-McCartney compositions from 1965 on, this one was actually written by both Lennon and McCartney. It began as two very different song fragments which had nothing in common except their unremarkable quality; but when the two songwriters combined them, a process like nuclear fusion took over.

Lennon, who often kept newspapers propped up on his piano while he was writing songs, noticed an article about the death of Tara Browne, heir to the Guinness Beer fortune and friend of the Beatles and Rolling Stones. Browne, the article said, had died in a car crash.

Another clipping, from the London *Daily Mail*, referred to disastrous road conditions in Blackburn, Lancashire, in the northwestern section of England. According to the report, a town counselor had stated, "It's about time they did something. Do you know, I've been around Blackburn and I've counted four thousand holes."

John wrote a verse each about the newspaper articles, and another verse in which he remarked on the lackluster reception a recent film had received. The film was *How I Won the War*, directed by Richard Lester (who did *A Hard Day's Night*) and starring John Lennon.

He took what he had written to Paul, explaining that he had written a song, and could McCartney supply a bridge? Paul, too, had an unfinished work on his hands, a characteristically more lucid and down-to-earth piece about getting up for school, combing his hair, drinking a quick cup of tea, and running to the bus. But once he got to the upper floor of the double-decker bus, though. . . .

It was debatable whether the "smoke" he had in the song was a joint or a cigarette. Apparently it started out, in line with the song's schoolboy-ish setting, as just a plain old cigarette. But this was 1967, and Paul later admitted that he had used the part about "I went into a dream" as a direct reference to marijuana.

In Paul's words, "This was the only one in the album written as a delib-erate provocation. A stick-that-in-your-pipe . . . but what we want is to turn you on to the truth rather than pot." (On the other hand, plenty of other supposed "drug songs" on the album, such as "Lucy in the Sky with Diamonds," really had nothing to do with drugs—at least, according to the songwriter.)

The Alarm Clock

With Lennon's three verses and McCartney's bridge, they now had a song, of sorts. Still, a song that switches from newspaper headlines to sneaking smokes back to newspaper headlines sounds a bit silly without anything to connect the pieces. So between John's second verse and Paul's portion, they left open a space of twenty-four bars, which they planned to fill with . . . something.

McCartney played the measures on a piano while Mal Evans, road manager and assistant, counted the bars. Just for a little joke, Mal (or some-one) set an alarm clock to go off right when Paul reached twenty-four. It was supposed to startle Paul, and then they would take it off the recording; the problem was, as George Martin later recalled, "We couldn't get it off!"

But there was often a certain serendipity that followed the Beatles at that high point of their careers, fortunate mistakes that would later seem like the volitional works of genius—to paraphrase James Joyce. What could be better, to precede a line like "Woke up, fell out of bed," than an alarm clock going off? By the time it was all said and done, it seemed intentional.

Scoring the End of the World

They still had a lot of space to fill in, to go along with Paul's piano and Mal's counting. In his typically informal and unschooled way, John Lennon told George Martin he wanted a sound that went "from nothing to the end of the world." And just as typically, Martin helped his boys get the sound they wanted.

To create Lennon's "end of the world," Martin assembled a forty-one piece ensemble, half of a full symphony orchestra and by far the largest group of guest musicians ever to play on a Beatles record up to that time. (The only other song that would come close was "Hey Jude," recorded a year later with forty guest musicians.)

Since they could already see that this recording session would be a memorable event, Paul and the others decided that they would make a celebration of it. He asked that the musicians come to the recording session in full evening dress, which they did. The musicians, many of them old enough to be the Beatles' grandparents, were fascinated both by the opportunity to perform with the world's most talked-about composers, and by what they saw when they arrived at Abbey Road Studios.

The Beatles were there, along with Mick Jagger and other celebrities who had been invited for the final taping. The young people seemed to be holding some sort of psychedelic Mardi Gras, and they welcomed their elders with carnival disguises and joints. (The amused musicians donned the disguises, but as for the other—no one ever said. In any case, it was probably fairly easy to get a contact high in the studios that night.) One violinist wore a clown's nose, another a gorilla's paw. The conductor himself had on a bright red false nose and paper glasses. Smoke tinted in rich colors wafted through Studio One of Abbey Road.

On this historic evening, George Martin told the musicians that for the next few hours, they must unlearn everything that they had ever learned about music. To begin with, they had none of the essential equipment for orchestral performers—sheet music. Instead, Martin had drawn squiggly and ill-defined lines gradually drifting up the bar scale, indicating approximately what point the musicians should have reached at the end of each measure.

Then Martin told these musicians, who had spent their entire professional lives listening to their neighbors and playing in such a way as to produce smooth, unbroken harmony, to forget all about that too. To create the desired sound, Martin explained, each must completely ignore the person playing on either side of him. Not only that, each should try to drown the others out, and play as loudly, insanely, and chaotically as they had ever played in their lives. For the initial buildup of the orchestral portion, Martin used cellos and violas, requesting that the musicians slide their fingers up and down the frets instead of fingering the notes. The Beatles themselves played trumpets.

So they began, and forty-one woodwind, string, brass, and percussion instruments started to fight with each other, getting louder and louder and louder—loud enough, it seemed, to bring down the roof of the studio. They went through this musical agony not once but four times. Then Martin took the four tracks and placed them on the tape slightly out of synchronization so as to produce a fuller sound.

That Long, Long Note

The final chord of "A Day in the Life," possibly the most famous single note in rock history, lasts a staggering forty-two seconds—longer than a few entire *songs* by the Beatles.

Once again, John and Paul knew what kind of sound they wanted to create, but they didn't know how to get it. Initially they tried humming together—the four group members, Mal Evans, and a few others. But their attempts to do that just made them laugh, and they got no more than five seconds of this mantra-like humming.

So instead, Martin sat all four Beatles, along with Evans, down before three pianos—two uprights and a grand. Martin himself took a seat in front of a harmonium, a reed organ. On cue, all six men struck the same chord together.

Recording Engineer Geoff Emerick had his faders, which control volume input, turned as low as possible. As the note began to fade, Emerick slowly began turning his faders up until they reached full volume input. A squeaky chair, accidentally bumped by Ringo, can be heard in the fade-out, along with the hum of the air conditioners in the recording studio.

The chord itself, E Major, was associated in the 1700s with Heaven.

Whimsical Last Touches

Not completely satisfied with the many trappings and minute details of "A Day in the Life," Paul decided to add something on to the end. (Another version of the story has it that *John* suggested the addition.) Available only on British releases of *Sgt. Pepper*, this is a 20,000-Hertz (Hz) tone audible only to dogs. For comparison, the absolute highest pitch that the most sensitive human ear can detect is 16,000 Hz.

The 20,000-Hz tone lasts for eight seconds, and was supposedly a special message from Paul to his English sheepdog, Martha—for whom he later wrote "Martha My Dear"—and to all the dogs in Britain.

"Dear Prudence"

John Lennon wrote "Dear Prudence," his first song on the White Album, about actress Mia Farrow's sister.

Farrow and the others studying at the Maharishi's meditation school in India were often wont to relax after a day of study, but "Prudence" was not among them. Apparently she felt that her own quest for consciousness was too important a thing to leave long enough to go outside and play. John

Lennon, as shown in the song, attempted to coax her to relax a bit, but it was to no avail.

The recording of "Dear Prudence" features Paul McCartney playing the flugelhorn, an instrument not unlike a cornet or trumpet.

Decca Records

In January 1962, when the Beatles went through auditions with various recording companies, they took their demo to the Decca Record Company first. And Decca, of course, turned them down—in favor of the ever-popular Brian Poole and the Tremeloes.

A Decca executive explained to Brian Epstein that "groups with guitars are on their way out." The company later learned that Epstein had been willing to buy 3,000 copies of any Beatles single they released, which would have made the signing of a contract possible. However, they learned this much too late—by that time, the Beatles had signed with a down-and-out EMI subsidiary, Parlophone.

Decca is often singled out as *the* company that rejected the Beatles, but this is an unfair criticism: Columbia, HMV, Phillips, and Pye all made the same mistake. Unlike the other four labels, Decca's people at least considered signing on the group before rejecting what has been called (by Capitol Records Vice President Dan Davis) "the most valuable catalogue in the history of the recording industry." And furthermore, if one listens to the Decca audition tracks on *The Beatles Anthology 1,* they don't sound particularly remarkable—certainly nowhere near as good as "Love Me Do," recorded just a few months later.

In any case, Decca received an impressive consolation prize: the Rolling Stones.

"Dig a Pony"

Not one of John Lennon's more memorable compositions, "Dig a Pony" from *Let It Be* was one of five songs recorded live on the Apple Records rooftop. For the original *Get Back* album, however, the Beatles had intended to include a studio version of the song.

The lyrics of "Dig a Pony" are little more than linguistic found objects, items Lennon can profess to "dig" (along with other verbs). He also obliquely offers a tribute to the Rolling Stones in one line—"I roll a stoney."

The American version of *Let It Be* lists the song as "I Dig a Pony."

"Dig It"

The Beatles had two "dig" songs, both on *Let It Be.* "Dig It" distinguishes itself in part by being even less listenable than "Dig a Pony," but also by its catalogue of proper names such as the CIA and Richard Nixon. It is the second of only two EMI releases attributed to "Harrison-Lennon-McCartney-Starkey," the other being "Flying." (Then there's the *arrangement* of "Maggie Mae," also on *Let It Be,* which is also attributed to all four.)

"Do You Want to Know a Secret"

"Do You Want to Know a Secret" first appeared on *Please Please Me* in Britain in March 1963 and, in America, on *The Early Beatles* in March 1965. The recording features one of George Harrison's very first vocals. John Lennon, who wrote "Do You Want to Know a Secret," later said he took his inspiration from a song in a Walt Disney film that his mother had sung to him when he was two years old.

"Doctor Robert"

With "Doctor Robert," from the British *Revolver* and U.S. *"Yesterday". . . and Today,* John Lennon hinted at his new experiments with mind-altering substances. Whereas fans would later try to read drug references into "Strawberry Fields Forever" or other tracks from 1967 on, they were much too late: by then, drugs were no longer a new discovery, and hence they warranted less mention. By contrast, Lennon's songs from the *Revolver* era are littered with suggestions of altered reality, as for instance in "Doctor Robert."

The latter was ostensibly written about a doctor in New York City who wrote his friends prescriptions for hallucinogens. (One can assume that Lennon was one of those friends, if not a friend of a friend.) The lyrics might also refer to the dentist who first turned Lennon and George Harrison on to LSD in 1965—who might in turn be the same "bloody dentist" referred to by a spoken voice in "Revolution 9."

Donovan

Along with the Beatles, Bob Dylan, and the Byrds, Donovan (born Donovan Leitch) helped bridge what at the time seemed a vast gulf separating folk and rock music in the 1960s.

He became a good friend of the Beatles, and reportedly helped write "Yellow Submarine." By his own account, in fact, he added the words "sky of blue and sea of green." His "Sunshine Superman" showcases the guitar work of George Harrison, and Paul McCartney plays tambourine and sings background vocal on "Atlantis." Donovan attended the Maharishi's meditation school in India in early 1968 along with the Beatles.

"Don't Bother Me"

"Don't Bother Me," from *With the Beatles* (U.K.) and *Meet the Beatles!* (U.S.) became the first Beatles song written solely by George Harrison.

It is also the first track by the group to feature an array of instruments outside the range of those normally associated with rock music. Paul McCartney plays the claves, a set of cylindrical hardwood sticks struck against one another to produce percussion; Ringo, in addition to his regular drums, plays ordinary bongos and a loose-skinned Arabian bongo. It was a small start, and all in the area of percussion, but it set a pattern of unusual instrumentation for a group whose later recordings would include cellos, sitars, and white noise machines.

George wrote "Don't Bother Me" in a hotel room during a 1963 tour of Britain. Forced to stay inside because of the flu, he decided that it was about time that he wrote a song. Over the course of the next six years, he would emerge as a songwriter whose talents challenged those of Lennon and McCartney.

"Don't Let Me Down"

"Don't Let Me Down," the studio version of which was released as the B-side to "Get Back" in April 1969 and available on the *Hey Jude* LP in the U.S., was the only song from the Apple "Rooftop Concert" not released on *Let It Be*. For many years, however, the live "Don't Let Me Down" filled out the song list on a number of bootlegs.

John Lennon wrote "Don't Let Me Down" for the same person who had inspired many of his songs, starting with "I'm So Tired" and other White Album tracks: Yoko Ono.

In 1980, Lennon suggested that Rod Stewart had appropriated the tune of "Don't Let Me Down" for his own use in "The Killing of Georgie." He couldn't come up with the correct name for Stewart's composition, however, referring to it as "Maggie Don't Go."

"Don't Pass Me By"

"Don't Pass Me By," from the White Album, was the first Beatles song written solely by Ringo Starr, who had cowritten 1965's "What Goes On" with Lennon and McCartney—the only Lennon-McCartney-Starkey title in the entire Beatles catalogue.

"Don't Pass Me By" is one of only three and a half Beatles recordings that feature Ringo playing a nonpercussive instrument. The first of these was "I'm Looking Through You," in which he plays Hammond organ. On *Sgt. Pepper*, he plays harmonica on "Being for the Benefit of Mr. Kite!", and he plays piano on "A Day in the Life" for the duration of only one note—the famous *long* note. (Hence the "half.") And in "Don't Pass Me By" he plays the piano.

The recording also features some very down-home violin, which according to one rumor was played by George Harrison. In fact the performer was Jack Fallon, who in his dual career as a music booking agent had signed the Beatles for their first concert in the south of England more than six years before.

"Don't Pass Me By," which proved that Ringo was not a bad songwriter in his own right, came out as a single in Scandinavia, where it reached Number One. Ringo must have been a little shy about the song: he had actually written it back in 1963, five years before he recorded it with the group. As he later recalled, he would often write what he thought were original compositions, only to learn from other group members that he had simply appropriated another performer's tune.

The song was originally intended to include an incongruous orchestral introduction, the recording of which did not surface until the *Anthology* CDs (see ***The Beatles Anthology* [CD]**.)

"Drive My Car"

"Drive My Car" served as the opening track of *Rubber Soul* in Britain, but only appeared in the U.S. half a year later as part of the hodgepodge that was *"Yesterday"*. . . *and Today.*

The recording, made on the night of October 13, 1965, was significant because it was the first time a Beatles session at Abbey Road Studios went past midnight. From then on, this would become the pattern: not only are rock musicians nocturnal creatures almost as a vocational qualification, but it was easiest to get in and out of the studios at a time when most screaming fans would be at home asleep. By the time of *Sgt. Pepper* and later *The Beatles,* sessions that began in the late afternoon and ended in the wee hours of the morning had become the norm.

This was part of the reason why the January 1969 sessions that became part of "Let It Be" proved to be such a disaster: The film world is on an entirely different schedule than the music world, and in order to accommodate the crews recording their activity in the studio, the Beatles had to show up every day bright and early. No wonder everyone got testy.

Bob Dylan

Bob Dylan had more influence than anyone else on the Beatles' transition from the loveable moptops of 1964 to the experimenting folkies—and druggies—of 1965. During the 1960s, if there was anyone who shared center stage with the Beatles, it was Dylan. They may have sold more albums, but he had at least as much effect on what was happening in the culture around him.

Perhaps nothing illustrates this more than a story told by Paul McCartney of what he called an "homage visit" to Dylan in London a few weeks after the release of *Sgt. Pepper.* Dylan's stature was such that he kept McCartney, along with the Stones' Keith Richards and Brian Jones, waiting for an hour while he received other well-wishers in his suite at the Mayfair Hotel. When Paul finally got in to see the Great One and played him some songs from the group's new album, Dylan listened and said, "Oh, I get it.

You don't want to be cute anymore." This, Paul recalled later, was an extremely incisive observation.

Growing Up with the Beatles

Dylan (born Robert Zimmerman in 1941) became friends with the Beatles early, at a time when their two styles—bohemian folk on the one hand, middle-class pop on the other—seemed miles apart. One night during their Summer 1964 U.S. Tour, he showed up in their dressing room and introduced them to a mysterious herb. Actually, due to a misunderstanding, he thought the Beatles already smoked pot, which they never had. John Lennon recalled several years later, "He thought 'I Want to Hold Your Hand,' when it goes, 'can't hide'—he thought we were singing, 'I get high'—so he turns up—and turns us on, and we had the biggest laugh all night."

Whereas the Beatles' early songs were musically satisfying but lyrically rather shallow, with Dylan the lyrics were *everything*. This fascinated Lennon in particular, who first showed Dylan's influence with "I'm a Loser" in late 1964. Lennon's Dylanesque period reached its peak in 1965, with "You've Got to Hide Your Love Away" and several other compositions from *Rubber Soul*, all of them displaying greater lyrical complexity than most of John's earlier compositions. (Lennon even adopted his own version of the Dylan twang as well.) After 1965, Lennon's own talent absorbed almost all traces of Dylan's influence, and he was off and running with a style all his own on *Revolver* and later, but Dylan had been the first to show him what was possible within the confines of rock music.

Correspondingly, Dylan took some influence from the Beatles. Most folk singers in the early 1960s considered rock music hopelessly vacuous and bourgeois, but Dylan, always restless for the next innovative step, saw something more in the Beatles' music. Perhaps he was already plotting his coup at the 1965 Newport Folk Festival, when he shocked his cohorts by appearing on stage with an electric guitar. From then on, Dylan rocked.

Like John Lennon, Dylan began rapidly to move away from the Beatles' influence on him, and the two forces grew apart. In 1966, Dylan's monumental *Blonde on Blonde* included "4th Time Around," a sort of "Norwegian Wood" parody which John Lennon later said made him extremely uncomfortable.

By the time of Dylan's next album, following his July 1966 motorcycle accident and recovery, the Beatles had released *Sgt. Pepper*, introducing a new wave of lush orchestration copied by everyone, including the Stones. Or at least, *almost* everyone. Dylan, ever the individual, came out with *John Wesley Harding*, an album as simple as the plain black-and-white photograph on its cover. It was rumored that he once yelled "turn that off!" when someone put on *Sgt. Pepper* in his presence.

Friendships That Did and Didn't Last

Perhaps Dylan and John Lennon were too much alike to mesh. In "God," from Lennon's first post-Beatles album, *Plastic Ono Band*, Lennon lists Dylan (along with the Beatles and Elvis) as one of the icons in which he no longer believed.

Dylan had a better relationship with another former Beatle, George Harrison. They cowrote "I'd Have You Anytime," the first track on Harrison's *All Things Must Pass*, which also features a cover version of Dylan's "If Not for You." The two later appeared on the stage of New York's Madison Square Garden for the shows on August 1, 1971, that became the *Concert for Bangladesh*. Still later, of course, Dylan and Harrison would join their hero Roy Orbison, along with Tom Petty and ELO's Jeff Lynne (who produced "Free As a Bird" and "Real Love"), in the Traveling Wilburys.

George Harrison maintained his friendship with Bob Dylan, joining him at the concert for Bangladesh. Archive Photos

"Eight Days a Week"

The group originally intended "Eight Days a Week," from *Beatles for Sale* in the U.K. and *Beatles VI* in the U.S., as the title song for their forthcoming film, *Eight Arms to Hold You*. John Lennon had been trying to write a song using the film's title, but "Eight Days a Week," with its more imaginative name, resulted instead. The film became *Help!* (after another Lennon song), and "Eight Days a Week" appeared separately.

"Eleanor Rigby"

Paul McCartney first got the idea for "Eleanor Rigby" while waiting to see his girlfriend, actress Jane Asher, in a play. He was in Bristol, in southwest England, and he happened to notice a store called "Daisy Hawkins." It seemed, he said, like "a nice atmospheric name," and he played around with the phrase "Miss Daisy Hawkins" before settling on Eleanor Rigby instead.

As for the priest in the song, Paul had originally planned to call him Father McCartney, but then John Lennon's friend Pete Shotton pointed out that this would sound as though he were singing about his own father. So instead, the name became Father McKenzie.

No Beatle plays a single note on the recording of "Eleanor Rigby." In fact, McCartney is the only member of the group who appears at all on the song, singing a solo vocal that is double-tracked to produce astonishing harmonies. The music comes from a string octet: four violins, two violas, and two cellos. At that time, Paul was listening to a lot of Vivaldi, and became interested in using strings. Since McCartney couldn't read or write music (none of the Beatles could), George Martin scored the instrumentation for the octet.

Taping of the song concluded on the devilish-sounding date of June 6, 1966—that is, six-six-sixty-six.

In August, just prior to the release of *Revolver*, "Eleanor Rigby" came out as the A-side of one of rock history's more unusual singles—unusual because of the contrast between the two sides. "Eleanor Rigby" / "Yellow Submarine" certainly showed the Beatles' versatility, and the range of their palettes: from the black, brown, and gray (as it were) of "Eleanor Rigby" to the yellow, blue, and green of the companion track.

"The End"

"The End," the last song credited on the cover of Abbey Road—though it is followed by the unlisted "Her Majesty"—includes a sixteen-second drum solo by Ringo Starr, his only one on a Beatles record. After this come guitar solos, respectively, by John Lennon, Paul McCartney, and George Harrison. The three also sing "Love you" twenty-four times.

Brian Epstein

Brian Epstein worked as the Beatles' manager from 1962 until his accidental death on August 27, 1967. Though he is not remembered as the world's greatest businessman, Epstein helped shape the group's style, changing them from the leather-clad rowdies they had been in their Hamburg days. He also helped them obtain a recording contract with Parlophone, and was instrumental in promoting them. Looking at pictures of Epstein with the group, he appears like a grown-up in the presence of four kids; therefore it is hard to believe that he was only five years older than the two oldest members, John Lennon and Ringo Starr.

Epstein came from a wealthy Jewish family in Liverpool, and attended the Royal Academy of Dramatic Arts with future actress Susannah York. He later enlisted in the British Army, but was thrown out for impersonating an officer.

The occasion for his discharge was an absurd incident. One night Epstein, returning to base after being on leave, appeared at the gate wearing his civilian clothes. But since he came from an upper-class family and was dressed accordingly, the gate guard mistook him for an off-duty officer and saluted him. Epstein made no effort to correct this error and later, when his superiors found out about it, they charged him with impersonating an officer.

After leaving Her Majesty's Service, Epstein returned to the family business, the North End Music Stores (NEMS) in Liverpool. The latter was a branch of the Epstein family's furniture stores, and among its customers was Jim McCartney, who purchased a piano there for his son Paul some time in the 1950s.

"What Brings Mr. Epstein Here?"

On October 28, 1961, a young man named Raymond Jones appeared at Epstein's record shop, requesting a copy of the single "My Bonnie" / "The

Relaxing in a hotel room, August 6, 1964, are (left to right) John Lennon, George Harrison, Brian Epstein, Ringo Starr, and Paul McCartney. Archive Photos/Express Newspapers

Saints," recorded by a group called the Beatles on the Polydor label in Germany.

Until that time, Epstein had never heard of the group or the single, which is odd: Being an energetic and highly conscientious businessman, he made it a point to know exactly what the kids were listening to, and he advertised in and wrote a column for *Mersey Beat* magazine, which often featured articles about the Beatles. (Later a couple of girls would tell him that the Beatles were the same group of boys he had yelled at once for hanging around the store, listening to records but not buying anything.)

He questioned Jones about the group, and learned that they were playing locally at the Cavern Club. So he went to see them at the Cavern. The first Beatle to meet him was George Harrison, who was standing in front of the dressing room. Aware of who Brian was, George must have been surprised to see the dapper and impeccably mannered gentleman in the midst of the sweaty, noisy Cavern Club. His first words to his future manager were "What brings Mr. Epstein here?"

After going back to the Cavern several times, Brian decided that he would become the Beatles' manager—a decision which horrified the rest of the Epstein family. But Brian saw something in the group, although even he was sometimes disgusted by their habits.

At his first "official" meeting with the Beatles, only three of them showed up at his office. John arrived, and introduced Cavern Club disk jockey Bob Wooller as his father. George and Pete Best (still the group's drummer at the time) came, but a fourth member seemed to be missing. They waited a half-hour for Paul while the punctual Epstein became more and more annoyed. Finally he told George to call him. George returned from the phone, explaining that Paul was in the bath. Brian exploded: "This is a disgrace! He's going to be very late!" "Late," George replied, "But very clean."

In the early days, Epstein was meticulous, even obsessive, in his efforts to clean up the group's act—so much so that he effectively kept the American press from learning of their Hamburg leather-and-blue-jeans phase until after Beatlemania had subsided. Typical of his concern for the group's image was this footnote to a memo, written June 19, 1962, informing them of upcoming concert dates: "Note that on ALL the above engagements, during the performances, smoking, eating, chewing and drinking is STRICTLY PROHIBITED, *prohibited.*"

But later, on the day when the group finally got its big, big, big break, it would be Brian Epstein who broke with decorum. They were playing in Paris, staying at the exclusive George V Hotel (pronounced *Zhorzh Sank* by those in the know) when they received word that "I Want To Hold Your Hand" had reached Number One in the United States. During the ensuing celebration, someone got a picture of Brian, no doubt inebriated, smoking a cigar, with a chamber pot atop his head.

Bigger Than Elvis

Epstein's first contract with the group, which he drew up himself, was invalid for two reasons: both Paul and George were under twenty-one, and thus under British law had to have their parents' signatures to make the contract binding; and Brian, in his haste and excitement, had forgotten to sign his own name. That was in late 1961, and around that time his management organization, NEMS, received its first proceeds from a Beatles show, at the Dee Estuary in Cheshire: one pound.

Despite these small beginnings, Epstein regularly encouraged the boys by telling them they were going to be "bigger than Elvis." At that stage, the promise seemed absurdly optimistic: they couldn't even get a record company to give them an audition, much less a contract. But Brian kept on believing and encouraging, and at one low point he commissioned Bob Wooller (who he now realized was not John's dad) to perform a special task. While the group was sitting with Brian talking, Wooller came in and informed Brian that Elvis Presley's manager, Colonel Tom Parker, was on the phone.

The little white lie helped keep the boys encouraged; of course, there would come a day when Colonel Tom Parker *was* calling Brian. The two managers and the five stars finally met on August 28, 1965, at Elvis's home in Beverly Hills. By then, Brian's prediction had come true: the Beatles *were* bigger than Elvis—much bigger.

"Everybody's Got Something to Hide Except Me and My Monkey"

The title of "Everybody's Got Something to Hide Except Me and My Monkey" is, at forty-seven letters, the longest of any Beatles song. But before John settled on that name, he had simply called it "Come On, Come On."

Lennon wrote this raucous track, from Side Three of *The Beatles*, in reply to a cartoon he had seen depicting Yoko Ono as a monkey on his back, supposedly taking away his creativity even as her talons ripped his flesh.

According to one account, "Everybody's Got Something to Hide Except Me and My Monkey" features one of only two Beatles performances by George Harrison on fire bell, the other being "Penny Lane."

Fake Beatles

Along with Beatles products and Beatles-related recordings, the Beatles inadvertently spawned another industry: that of fake Beatles recordings.

These were songs that appeared—whether because of the performer's name or the sound of the record—to be by the Beatles, but were not. Sometimes this resemblance was purely accidental, as in the case of a song by the Rolling Stones. Such instances of mistaken identity resulted from rumors started by fans, rather than bogus claims made by the performers themselves. However, these were very much the exception rather than the rule.

The spread of the consumer-protection mentality spawned by Ralph Nader and others was still many years away, and since most of the group's fans were teenagers, they tended to be particularly naïve record buyers. Into such a market came a group called the Beetles in the U.S. Their album, *The Beetle Beat*, looked very much like the cover of *Meet the Beatles*, but it cost about one-fourth as much as the true Beatles album. Several thousand fans forked over allowances and babysitting money for the album, only to learn that it was a scam.

Another group had the audacity to actually use exactly the same name as the Beatles. In 1965 the group, whose lead singer had the last name of Lemon, released a single with a Beatles-sounding title, "That Kind of Girl." (One source says "The Girl I Love.") It later turned out that the group was actually called the Five Shits: at least their punkish band name was ahead of its time.

Another deceptively named group was a duo called John and Paul who, also in 1965, put out a single on the London label, "People Say" / "I'm Walking." Although neither of the songs sounded like the *real* John and Paul, one or both of these often made it onto Beatles bootleg albums.

Psychedelic Confusion
The advent of psychedelia produced two famous records that, though their performers did not tout them as such, were mistaken for Beatles songs. Dudley Moore and Peter Cooke intended "L.S. Bumble Bee" / "Bee Side" as a mere parody of the Beatles and other bands that were moving into the psychedelic scene. However, many people thought that Moore's voice sounded like Lennon's, and the songs, like those of "John and Paul," have often been added to bootlegs.

The second of these two famous recordings was not so much purported to be a Beatles song as it was supposedly a song featuring members of the Beatles. The track, "Sing This All Together," appeared on the Rolling Stones' 1967 album *Their Satanic Majesties Request*. The faces of the Beatles appeared hidden in various places on the album cover, and "Sing This All Together" was rumored to include John Lennon and Paul McCartney on backing vocals. This was untrue, but the mistake is understandable, since Lennon and McCartney had assisted on an earlier Stones single, "We Love You."

Futs, Moles, and Assorted Later Fakes
In 1968, the Moles (true name Simon Dupree and the Big Sound) deposited a demo tape in a London subway station locker. They sent the locker key to a major English music publication with a letter stating that the tape

should be released on the Parlophone label. Although many assumed that the Moles were in fact the Beatles, the record still had poor sales. Simon Dupree and the Big Sound changed their name to Gentle Giant and achieved success in Europe, though they never had much impact Stateside. "We Are the Moles" (Parts I and II) has likewise found its way onto Beatles bootlegs.

A 1970 release made use of what could be called "The John F. Kennedy Effect." In the late 1950s, the name of the young senator was already such a magic word in Massachusetts that when a stockroom worker in a razor factory decided to run for state treasurer, he merely placed his name—John F. Kennedy—on the ballot and got himself elected. So it was for the reggae group John Lennon and the Bleechers, who undoubtedly sold many copies of their Punch Records single, "Ram You Hard," purely on the basis of their lead singer's name.

In 1970 a group called the Futs (one source says "Futz") released a single called "Have You Heard the Word" / "Futting Around," and the mysterious record instantly inspired theories. Some said it was the Beatles' last recording, some said it was John Lennon and the Bee Gees, and others said it was all four Beatles plus all three Bee Gees. The identify of the Futs was never revealed.

Hotlegs and Klaatu shared a history similar to that of the Futs, though in these cases, the perpetrators became known. Hotlegs' February 1971 release, "Neanderthal Man" / "You Didn't Like It Because You Didn't Think of It," supposedly sounded like the Beatles. A few members of Hotlegs would later join 10cc, a group which often made use of Beatlesque harmonies.

In the mid-1970s, when Beatles nostalgia had reached such a point that "Got to Get You into My Life" occupied the Number Seven spot on the U.S. pop charts ten years after its original release, a group called Klaatu issued an album on the Capitol label. Capitol, the company responsible for the release of Beatles albums in America, did little to dispel the rumor that Klaatu were the reunited Beatles. Actually, the album, which contained such songs as "Anus of Uranus," was the work of Canadian session musicians. Klaatu, like every Beatles pretender from the Beatles on, proved more convincing to businessmen than to fans.

In April 1994, Gannett News Service reported a legal dispute between Apple Corps and an Akron, Ohio, rock group called "1964 The Tribute." Essentially this was a cover band like Beatlemania, but operated without permission to use the Beatles' personae.

Families of the Beatles

The four Beatles came from distinctly different family situations, a factor that influenced their strikingly dissimilar personalities.

Ringo's home life was the only one that approximated the media myth of the Beatles' "poverty-stricken" childhoods. He and his mother lived in the Dingle, one of Liverpool's poorest districts. John, by contrast, lived with his aunt and uncle in Woolton, a pleasant middle- to upper-middle class neighborhood near Penny Lane. The financial situations of the McCartney and Harrison families fell somewhere in between the two others.

Three of the eight parents of the Beatles were over forty when their sons were born: Jim McCartney and Harold and Louise Harrison. Paul was the older of two children, George the youngest of four, and John and Ringo were both only children.

George came from by far the most "normal" of the four family situations—i.e., two parents. Each of the other three would experience the loss of a parent during their childhood. Ringo's father left when he was very young, and Paul's mother died when he was a teenager. John saw his father leave when he was five, *and* his mother die when he was seventeen.

Lennon and McCartney wrote several songs about their parents: "When I'm Sixty-Four" (Paul's father), "Julia" (John's mother), and "Let It Be." ("Mother Mary," while also being the Virgin Mary, referred to Paul's mother.)

As for wives: John and Ringo each married early in the Beatles' career together; George at the middle, in 1966; and Paul toward the end, in 1969. All except Paul, who lost his wife, Linda, to breast cancer in 1998, were divorced. Paul and—on their second marriages—John and Ringo all married divorcees who already had children of their own. All four Beatles ultimately married women from other countries: the Japanese-born Yoko Ono; Olivia Arias (Harrison), originally from Mexico; and the Americans Linda Eastman and Barbara Bach (Starr).

George, the youngest Beatle, became the last to father a child, a son named Djani, in 1978. By that time, the first-born Beatle child, Julian Lennon, was already fifteen years old.

Fan Club

The Beatles Fan Club, founded in 1963, had a national secretary named "Anne Collingham" who signed all club material and acted as intermediary between the fans and the Beatles. The funny thing about Anne was that she didn't exist: the name was simply a way of personalizing the P.R. people, secretaries, assistants, and letter-readers that developed as a buffer between the group and its fans.

In July 1969 the Fan Club announced several new chapters: the official Heather Chapter (named after Paul McCartney's stepdaughter), the Fabulous Ring Chapter, the Members of the British Empire Chapter, the Pottie Bird Beatle Chapter, the Walrus Waves Chapter, and the Flying Cow Chapter. Fan Club members were especially fond of George Harrison's mother, Louise, and in September 1970, following her July 7 death, established a Louise F. Harrison Memorial Cancer Fund.

In December 1969 the Fan Club issued a report to all area secretaries, ordering them to ignore "rumors" of the group's breakup. The report stated that "The four, as a group, have a whole new decade in front of them!!!"

First Recording

The first recording by the four Beatles occurred in the fall of 1960 at Akustick Studio, behind Hamburg's Central Station.

The group's manager at the time, Allan Williams, didn't like Pete Best's drumming, so he hired another man to sit in with the group. And . . . well, it just goes to show that some things are meant to be. This other drummer, borrowed from Rory Storme and the Hurricanes, was Ringo Starr, and though it would be two more years before he joined the group, it so happens that he appears on their first recording.

Williams showed less foresight in his choice of vocalist for the recording: instead of using Lennon or McCartney, he hired Lou Walters, or "Wally," also of the Hurricanes.

The group recorded a cover of George Gershwin's "Summertime" (some sources indicate they also recorded "Fever," but this is probably apocryphal), and in all made nine copies of the 78 r.p.m. disc. The other side was a spoken-word advertisement—in German, presumably—for leather goods. Today there is only one remaining copy of the record.

Other Recording Firsts

The first recording of Lennon, McCartney, and Harrison—as the Quarry Men, with John Lowe—was the mid-1958 cover of Buddy Holly's "That'll Be the Day," as well as Harrison and McCartney's "In Spite of All the Danger," that appears on *The Beatles Anthology 1*. (See *The Beatles Anthology* [CD].) They recorded it in Percy Philip's electrical goods shop in Liverpool, and instead of being paid for the record, the boys paid for the privilege of making it.

The group's first *commercial* recordings were with Tony Sheridan, and occurred in Hamburg on or about June 22, 1961. (See **Beat Brothers; Tony Sheridan.**) Finally, the first EMI recording with Ringo as drummer—that is, the first recording of the Beatles as they came to be known, was on September 11, 1962 (*see* **"Love Me Do"**).

"Fixing a Hole"

The first night of recording for "Fixing a Hole," February 9, 1967, was also the first time since they signed with EMI in 1962 that the Beatles recorded somewhere other than the Abbey Road studios—in this case, at the Regent Sound Studio on Tottenham Court Road in London. They did this simply because, as George Martin later recalled, the Abbey Road studios were all booked for the night.

The Regent studio was an inferior facility in all regards, Martin later recalled, with a low ceiling and "boxy" acoustics; therefore it's fortunate that "Fixing a Hole" proved to be one of the simplest recordings on *Sgt. Pepper*. The group finished it in a second session—back at Abbey Road, of course—twelve days later.

"Flying"

"Flying" was the first Beatles song attributed to Harrison-Lennon-McCartney-Starkey. With the exclusion of "Revolution 9," which defies classification, it was the only instrumental released by the group between 1962 and 1970.

On this *Magical Mystery Tour* composition—which for several months carried the working title "Aerial Tour Instrumental"—John Lennon plays the main theme on the mellotron, with George Harrison and Paul McCartney adding guitars. Ringo plays maracas and drums, and joins the other three in the wordless chorus at the end of the song. (Most people think it's only Ringo, because he has the deepest voice. The same is true with "Carry That Weight" on *Abbey Road*, another of the group's rare four-part harmonies.)

John and Ringo created the bizarre sounds that tie the end of "Flying" into the beginning of "Blue Jay Way," using various sound effects and backward tape loops.

"The Fool on the Hill"

"The Fool on the Hill," which precedes "Flying" on *Magical Mystery Tour*, features Paul McCartney on flute and recorder, a wind instrument with a whistle mouthpiece. John Lennon on maracas and Ringo Starr on finger cymbals provide percussion, and George Harrison plays the harmonica. (That is, according to one source; the most knowledgeable of all authorities on Beatles recordings, Mark Lewisohn, refuses to speculate as to who played what because there is no documentation.)

This McCartney composition carries on an ancient literary theme, that of the wise fool. It was a concept expressed two thousand years before by another Paul, the Apostle, who said: "God hath chosen the foolish things of the world to confound the wise." It also appears in numerous novels and poems—and in the earlier Beatles song "Nowhere Man."

France

France was the only country the Beatles toured where they were not overwhelmed by adoring fans. Even the Philippines, where the Beatles could have been killed by demonstrators in 1966, *noticed* them. But when the Fab Four toured France in January 1964, their reception was lukewarm by Beatles standards. Many years later, Paul remembered that they were disappointed to discover that most of their French fans were male.

Only two things of note happened during their visit to France. One was a fistfight that broke out at the Olympia Theater when someone in the Beatles' entourage denied a photographer the opportunity to take exclusive pictures. The other was the announcement, received by the Beatles and Brian Epstein in Paris, that "I Want to Hold Your Hand" had reached Number One on the *Billboard* charts in America.

Of course eventually even the French succumbed to Beatlemania, and "Michelle," with its French chorus, became a big hit in that country in 1965. The French national anthem, the "Marseillaise," appeared at the beginning of "All You Need Is Love." (Not long afterward, Jimi Hendrix would record "The Star-Spangled Banner." A few years later, Queen did a rendition of "God Save the Queen," and of course the Sex Pistols had their own famous song by that title, though it is not actually a version of the British national anthem.) One other Beatles song pays an oblique tribute to things French: "The Sun King," the name by which King Louis XIV was known.

"From Me to You"

John Lennon and Paul McCartney wrote "From Me to You" in the back of a van on the way to a show.

The song followed "Love Me Do" and "Please Please Me" as the group's third British single. In America, where Capitol Records had not yet caught on to the pop phenomenon in Britain, Vee Jay Records released "From Me to You" / "Thank You Girl." This became the first Beatles single to enter the American pop charts (at Number 125) on August 3, 1963.

Germany

Germany was the first foreign country most of the Beatles had ever visited, and they spent a large portion of the years 1960 to 1962 there. They made their first commercial recordings there, tracks which would later appear as "The Beatles with Tony Sheridan." In addition, they recorded their only foreign-language single in German.

(See also **Hamburg; "Komm, Gib Mir Deine Hand" / "Sie Liebt Dich"; Tony Sheridan.**)

"Get Back"

The song "Get Back" began its life with a nationalistic-sounding title: "Don't Dig No Pakistanis Taking All the People's Jobs." This fact, when it came out years later, led to denunciations of Paul McCartney as a racist. In fact he had written the original lyrics as a parody of the nativist British politician Enoch Powell, much as he lampooned Soviet Communism with "Back in the U.S.S.R."

After playing with various absurd lyrics about Pakistanis, Puerto Ricans, and Mohicans, McCartney decided on a Tucson, Arizona, setting. He had visited Tucson recently with plans to buy a farm, and he explained to the others that it was where the popular TV western *High Chaparral* was shot.

On January 23, 1969, the first day of recording "Get Back," the Beatles made ten takes, none of which they used. That was also the first day of work for their new tape operator, Alan Parsons, who would later generate a number of hits with the Alan Parsons Project.

The group recorded and released "Get Back" in two different versions. The studio version came out on a single in April 1969, backed with "Don't Let Me Down," and includes an extra verse not found on the second version. The performance recorded on the rooftop of the Apple offices on January 30, 1969, is of such high quality that its sound is almost indistinguishable from that of the studio version. This second, live version of "Get Back" is the last song on *Let It Be*.

The latter begins with Paul saying "Rosetta, Oh Rosetta." John sings, to the tune of the song they are about to play, "Sweet Rosetta Fart, she thought she was a cleaner, but she was a frying pan." At the end of "Get Back," the audience that had gathered on Saville Row that winter day can be heard clapping; Paul says something that sounds like "Don't smoke"; and John says, "I'd like to say thank you on behalf of the group and ourselves, and I hope we've passed the audition."

"Get Back," which featured Billy Preston on keyboards, was the first Beatles single which prominently featured another recording artist—as opposed to the invisible violinists and cellists on "Eleanor Rigby."

Get Back

Get Back ranks after the Beach Boys' *Smile* as the second most famous album never released.

In January 1969, John, Paul, George, and Ringo got together at Twickenham Film Studios in London to record material for a new album, promoted with the impressive promise, "The Beatles As Nature Intended." The album was to show the group returning to more traditional styles of rock 'n' roll (hence the title *Get Back*), and the accompanying film by the same name would illustrate how the Beatles recorded their songs.

However, things began to go wrong almost from the moment the cameras started rolling on January 2, 1969. The differences among the group members, both artistic and personal, were becoming greater and greater. George and Ringo both walked off the set for a time. Paul, more interested in solo projects than in group ones, had become such a hermit that millions of American fans would soon believe him to be dead. John was too consumed with Yoko Ono to put more than a halfhearted interest in the Beatles.

The group had their picture taken for the cover of *Get Back* in a parody of the cover shot from *Please Please Me*, the group's first album. The four men posed in the same place they had posed six years before, looking down

The Beatles at the time of their breakup. AP/Wide World Photos

at the camera from the balcony of an apartment building; yet instead of the short hair and brown suits in the earlier photographs, all except Paul had long hair and mustaches, and all were dressed in colorful clothing. The two photographs later adorned the covers of *The Beatles 1962–1966* and *1967–1970*.

Songs on *Get Back*

Before the Beatles gave up the project, some radio stations received promotional copies of *Get Back* in mid-1969. The song listing was as follows:

> [Side One]
> "One After 909"
> "Save the Last Dance for Me" [A brief version of The Drifters' hit]
> "Don't Let Me Down"
> "Dig a Pony" [studio version]

"I've Got a Feeling" [studio version]
"Get Back"

[Side Two]
"For You Blue"
"The Walk"
"Teddy Boy" [later released on *McCartney* in April 1970]
"Two of Us"
"Maggie Mae"
"Dig It" [a five-minute version]
"Let It Be"
"The Long and Winding Road"
"Get Back" [a short return to the title track, to close out the album]

Recycled as *Let It Be*

Get Back lay dormant for a year in the midst of legal and artistic quarrels among the Beatles. During this time, the group recorded and released *Abbey Road*, and each of the four men began solo careers. The Beatles left their third and last manager, Allen Klein, with the responsibility of marketing the film and album they had made in January 1969.

Klein saw that they could make more money by blowing the film up from 16 mm to 35 mm and distributing it as the Beatles' "new" full-length motion picture. By this time, though, "Get Back" had acquired the status of an oldie, so the movie and the album (pieced together by Phil Spector) received the title of a newer McCartney composition, *Let It Be*. Instead of "The Beatles As Nature Intended," what emerged a year and a half after the fact sounded more like what John Lennon described as "the Beatles with their trousers off."

"Getting Better"

Jimmy Nicol substituted as drummer when Ringo was sick during the Beatles' 1964 tour of Australia. Whenever any of the Beatles—perhaps wanting to make sure that *he* didn't get sick too—would ask Nicol how he was feeling, he would invariably reply, "It's getting better." Paul remembered this phrase one spring day in 1967 when he was taking his dog, Martha, for a walk. He noticed that the weather was getting better than it had been recently, and he smiled when he remembered Jimmy Nicol. Later that day he called up John and said, "Let's do a song called 'It's Getting Better'."

On the recording of this upbeat *Sgt. Pepper* track, John added the line "It can't get no worse" in reply to each of Paul's *getting betters*. The droning sound heard in the background of "Getting Better" is George Harrison, playing yet another Indian instrument, the tamboura. George Martin comes in at the beginning of the song on piano. However, he is not playing by conventional means: rather than striking the keys, he is hitting the strings directly. The beat of the song becomes irregular in the last two seconds.

In contrast to the song's uplifting message was an event that occurred during recording on March 21, 1967. Lennon came to the Abbey Road studios tripping on acid, and felt so unwell that he couldn't join McCartney and Harrison for vocal overdubs. George Martin, who knew that John was feeling sick but had no idea of the reason why, escorted him to fresh air. There was no question of going out the front door, where they were likely to run into a coterie of waiting fans, so Martin took him up to the roof and left him there. There Lennon remained until his cohorts, aware that he was on acid and that it was a thirty-foot drop to the ground, rescued him.

Also while the group was recording "Getting Better"—but presumably on another night—someone asked George Martin if a brand-new group, recording down the hall at Abbey Road Studios, could stop by and hear the Beatles play for just a few minutes. Martin reluctantly agreed. The new group came in, stood around for a little while, and then left. They were called Pink Floyd.

"Girl"

"Girl," John's bittersweet song from *Rubber Soul*, features a straight-faced backing chorus from Paul and George who are, quite audibly, singing "tit-tit-tit."

John later said that the verse about a man breaking his back and eventually killing himself "to earn his day of leisure" was a reference to the Catholic belief in suffering on Earth in order to assure one's place in Heaven.

"Give Peace a Chance"

"Give Peace a Chance," John Lennon's first solo hit, was credited to Lennon-McCartney as songwriters. It was the first solo single by any of the ex-Beatles, and the first release by the Plastic Ono Band—a group that did not exist.

Lennon had already apprised the media of the non-existence of the Plastic Ono Band prior to the release of "Give Peace a Chance," explaining that the group would consist of "whoever happens to be in the room at the time." The first ad for the band showed a page torn at random from a phone book—the Joneses, in fact—with the legend, "You are the Plastic Ono Band." When reporters came to the press conference announcing the release of the first Plastic Ono Band single in July 1969, they found not Lennon or Yoko Ono behind the lectern, but a set of tape recorders, enclosed in plastic, that played "Give Peace a Chance."

Lennon wrote "Give Peace a Chance" during his and Yoko's ten-day "bed-in" at Montreal's Queen Elizabeth Hotel. He quickly composed the song, which consisted mainly of a chorus and a series of shouted harangues, and ordered a tape machine sent up to his room so that he could record the song immediately. The Lennons requested all those present in their suite at that moment to join in on the chorus. These included Timothy Leary; a Canadian chapter of the Radha Krishna Temple; Tommy Smothers of the Smothers Brothers; comedian Dick Gregory; a rabbi; Petula Clark ("Downtown"); and the New York disk jockey (and onetime self-proclaimed "Fifth Beatle") Murray the K.

"Glass Onion"

In "Glass Onion," from Side One of the White Album, John Lennon paints a sardonic portrait of those who claimed to find "hidden messages" in the Beatles' music by playing albums backward at various speeds and scanning covers for "clues."

"Glass Onion" mentions five Beatles songs: "Strawberry Fields Forever," "Lady Madonna," "The Fool on the Hill" (here Lennon over-dubbed a few notes from a recorder as a parody of the flute in "Fool"), "I Am the Walrus," and "Fixing a Hole." To further confuse aspiring Beatles decon-structionists, Lennon drops a false "clue": "the Walrus was Paul." Of course John himself was the Walrus, inasmuch as that has any meaning at all. He *was*, after all, the one who sang "I Am the Walrus."

Other self-referential Beatles songs are "All You Need Is Love," which quotes from "She Loves You" at the end; "I Am the Walrus," with its reference to "Lucy in the Sky with Diamonds"; and George Harrison's "Savoy Truffle," also on the White Album, which refers to "Ob-La-Di, Ob-La-Da."

"Golden Slumbers"

"Golden Slumbers," from *Abbey Road*, has a longer history than most Beatles songs. Its lyrics are 350 years old, taken from the dramatist Thomas Dekker (1572–1632), who wrote:

> Golden slumbers kiss your eyes;
> Smiles awake you when you rise.
> Sleep, pretty wantons, do not cry,
> And I will sing a lullaby.

Paul McCartney had seen the words, with the original music that accompanied them, on the piano at his father's home. Unable to read music or to remember the original tune, he wrote his own.

"Good Day Sunshine"

Paul McCartney wrote "Good Day Sunshine," on *Revolver*, but apparently he doesn't play a single note on the song. Nor do John Lennon or George Harrison. The recording of "Good Day Sunshine" involves only two instruments: George Martin's piano and Ringo Starr's drums. Martin recorded Ringo's percussion twice, so that a different drum track comes out of the right and left channels in stereo.

"Good Morning Good Morning"

John Lennon took his inspiration for "Good Morning Good Morning," on *Sgt. Pepper*, from a corn flakes commercial he had seen.

The rich horns section on "Good Morning Good Morning" comes from Sounds Incorporated, a Liverpool group featuring three saxophones, two trombones, and one French horn. At the end is the chaos of dogs and horses and lions that closes out the song, each of the creatures larger than—and thus capable of consuming—the one before.

George Martin discovered that the sound of the clucking chicken segues nicely into the guitar note that follows it, beginning "Sgt. Pepper's Lonely Hearts Club Band (Reprise)." This recording "trick" won him kudos from his colleagues in the industry.

(See also ***The Beatles Anthology* [CD].**)

"Good Night"

John Lennon, author of "Good Morning Good Morning," also wrote "Good Night," the last song on the White Album.

Lennon wrote it for his six-year-old son, Julian, and he later said that he had Ringo in mind as the singer from the beginning. In fact Ringo is the only Beatle involved in the recording, his solo vocal backed by a full choir and a thirty-piece orchestra.

The Beatles and George Martin had a sense of humor when it came to the order of tracks on an album. On *Magical Mystery Tour*, "Your Mother Should Know" seems to introduce "a song that was a hit before your mother was born"—but instead of the promised oldie, the next piece is "I Am the Walrus." That sense of humor is even more evident on the White Album, where the earnest "I Will" follows the raunchy "Why Don't We Do It in the Road"; and where "Good Night," with its schmaltzy orchestration, comes directly after the eight-minute assault of "Revolution 9." Thus the White Album ends, not with a bang but a whimper.

"Got to Get You into My Life"

Among George Martin's abilities as a producer was his facility for linking two unrelated songs by a sound which interfaced with both. The most well-known example of this is the clucking chicken at the end of "Good Morning Good Morning," which turns into the opening guitar notes of the *Sgt. Pepper* theme's reprise. Almost as remarkable, however, is the aural association between the final horn blast of "Got to Get You into My Life" and the opening sitar drone of "Tomorrow Never Knows," the last song on *Revolver*.

"Got to Get You into My Life," one of Paul McCartney's finest songs ever, became a hit in the United States in the summer of 1976—almost exactly ten years after its original release. (And this was long before oldies were a popular staple of FM radio.) The single was backed with "Helter Skelter," whose own popularity had been sparked by the broadcast of a TV movie concerning the Manson murders; since it seemed in bad taste to put "Helter Skelter" on the A-side, that honor went to "Got to Get You into My Life."

Great Britain

"I simply adore them." Those were the words, not of a screaming teenage girl, but of the Queen Mother.

Great Britain, a tiny island nation, ruled the world for an entire century between the Battle of Waterloo in 1815 and the beginning of World War I in 1914. After two crippling world wars, however, England's political power declined—yet as the Beatles-led "British Invasion" of the 1960s showed, its cultural influence was still enormous. Soon to follow the Beatles were the Rolling Stones, the Who, the Kinks, the Animals, the Yardbirds, and many other British bands who brought vast sums of revenue into the United Kingdom. (That is, until the cost of funding the British welfare state became prohibitive for rock multimillionaires, "tax refugees" who sought asylum in the United States.)

Though the Beatles did not gain world recognition until 1964, they were already popular in their homeland a year before that. The ten-year-old daughter of the Royal Variety Show organizer begged her daddy to book the group to play before the Queen Mother and Princess Margaret on November 4, 1963, and it was at this prestigious engagement that John Lennon made one of his many famous irreverent statements. Just before the band launched into "Twist and Shout," he announced: "On this number I want you to all join in. Those in the cheap seats can clap your hands. The rest of you can rattle your jewelry."

January 19, 1964, about nine weeks after the Royal Variety Show, began the last week in history that no recording by a British artist appeared on the American Hot Hundred charts.

The Beatles' first trip to the U.S. happened to coincide with a visit by British Prime Minister Sir Alec Douglas-Home. Learning that the group would touch down in Washington, D.C., on February 11, 1964, the day he had originally planned to arrive for a meeting with President Lyndon Johnson, Douglas-Home postponed his trip by a day. When he met Douglas-Home on February 12, Johnson remarked, "I liked your advance party, but don't you feel they need haircuts?"

Beatles and Royals

The lives of the Beatles and the Royal Family often intertwined, sometimes in bizarre ways. An American fan wrote to the Queen in 1964, congratulating her on having the Beatles as subjects. A lady-in-waiting wrote back, explaining that as much as Her Majesty would like to, she could not give out the group's addresses.

Princess Margaret and Lord Snowdon attended a celebration the Beatles held after the premiere of *A Hard Day's Night.* Though dinner would be served later, the two were only staying for drinks. George Harrison was hungry, but Walter Shenson, the film's producer, had told him that they could not eat until "the Royals" left—in other words, there was still *somebody* who outranked the Beatles. Finally George told the Princess, "Ma'am, we're starved, and Walter says we can't eat until you leave." She burst out laughing and said to Lord Snowdon, "Come on, Tony, we're in the way."

A year later, Queen Elizabeth and Prince Phillip were on vacation in Canada when a reporter asked the Prince about the Beatles. Soon afterward, the Canadian press reported that Phillip had said the group was "on the wane." This caused quite a shock back in the U.K., and the London *Evening Standard* conducted a poll in which five out of seven people said that they couldn't believe the Prince had made such a disturbing appraisal. A few days after the miniature scandal broke, Philip sent a telegram to Brian Epstein, explaining that what he had really said was "I think the Beatles are away."

In May 1968, the Queen asked the group to play a show at the London Palladium to benefit the British Olympic teams competing at the Games in Mexico City. But it was a different time, and the Beatles were busy with other things, so they declined Her Majesty's request.

"Her Majesty," of course, is the last song on the last-recorded Beatles album, *Abbey Road*. Cheeky as it is, the song nonetheless seems to show pride in being British. Oddly, the only other Beatles song to mention the British royalty is also on *Abbey Road*—"Mean Mr. Mustard."

Hairstyles

It may be hard for people born in the 1960s or afterward to understand, but the Beatles' hair was once almost as noteworthy as their music. Not their hair when it got to be *really* long, in 1968 and afterward, but their hair in 1964, which at the time was considered so long as to be preposterous.

In 1961 in Hamburg, Astrid Kirchherr influenced the Beatles' adoption of what would become their world-famous hairstyle. Kirchherr's future fiancé, Stuart Sutcliffe, was the first Beatle to have his hair cut in that fashion, popular in France at the time. The rest of the group howled with laughter when they first saw Stuart's hair, but after a while all of them—with the exception of Pete Best—got their hair cut the same way. They didn't know it then, but they had taken the first steps in a tonsorial revolution that would banish the crewcut and the D.A. to oblivion.

In February 1963, Maureen Cleave of the London *Evening Standard*—who later conducted the infamous "We're More Popular Than Jesus" interview with John Lennon—became the first reporter to mention the Beatles' unique hairstyles in print. A year later, when the Beatles appeared in an America still very much in the grip of 1950s machismo, the natives were stunned to see men with the hair of women. One American reporter asked them if he could take two pictures of the group—one with their wigs on and one with them off. John replied that if they were wigs, how did they get dandruff?

Tired of the same old questions from Americans, the Beatles eventually began giving erroneous replies concerning the provenance of their hairstyles. On the *Beatles Story* LP, issued in the U.S., George states that the group's hair was a result of going swimming and not combing it afterward.

On the group's 1966 world tour, a number of unpleasant things happened—events that influenced the decision to stop touring. One of these was an attempt by a woman in Washington, D.C., to hold Ringo down and cut his hair by force.

Hamburg

The Beatles' development took place against the backdrop of four cities in three countries. Liverpool gave them their start; London saw their breakthrough, and New York their triumph. But in Hamburg, on the gloomy North Sea coast of Germany, they became musicians.

The Beatles—John Lennon, Paul McCartney, and George Harrison on guitar, Stuart Sutcliffe on bass, and Pete Best on drums—played three stints in Hamburg: first at the Indra and Kaiserkeller clubs from April to October 1960; then at the Top Ten Club from April to July 1961; and finally at the Star Club in early 1962, just prior to making their first recordings with EMI.

Allan Williams, the group's first manager, got them their German bookings. He also arranged their first recording (see **First Recording**), which took place in Hamburg, as well as their first *commercial* recording, with Tony Sheridan (See **The Beat Brothers; Tony Sheridan**)—which also took place in Hamburg.

In Hamburg, the Beatles met three Germans, two young men and a woman, each of whom would become important to the group: Jurgen Vollmer, Klaus Voorman, and—most significant of all—Astrid Kirchherr, who gave them the hairstyles they would make famous, and who took away their bass player.

Having Just a Little Too Much Fun
John Lennon later remarked that though punk rockers seemed to think that their own antics were very original, the Beatles had been doing the same thing fifteen years before. The group members were encouraged to put on a show for their audiences, and this is exactly what they did.

Except for Pete Best, they all carried on to excess, whipping up their listeners by shouting obscenities from the stage and throwing food and beer at each other and at the crowd. Their audiences, which consisted mainly of gangsters, prostitutes, transvestites, and other inhabitants of the Hamburg demimonde, loved the group—particularly the nasal-sounding loudmouth who was clearly their leader.

Lennon distinguished himself by antagonizing Hamburg audiences with impersonations of Hitler. (This was only fifteen years after the end of World War II.) He was also known to stand on the Reeperbahn, the main street of Hamburg's club district, dressed in nothing but a pair of long woolen underwear, reading the *Daily Express*. At other times he appeared onstage in even more abbreviated forms of dress, such as a pair of shorts and a toilet seat around his neck. He later remarked that anyone could carry on in such a fashion if forced to play for eight hours at a time and survive on little more than speed and beer.

Their first trip to Germany ended when the group, along with Rory Storme and the Hurricanes, destroyed the stage of the Kaiserkeller Club. McCartney and Harrison spent a night in jail, and when the authorities discovered that George was underage, they deported him to Liverpool.

The Top Ten

After playing at Liverpool's Cavern Club for a time, the group returned to Hamburg for a gig at the Top Ten Club. In contrast to the sleazy clientele at the Indra and Kaiserkeller, Top Ten Club audiences were mostly young, affluent existentialists (or "exis"), who were fascinated by the group.

The exis nicknamed John "The Sidie Man," Paul "The Little One," and George "The Beautiful One." They pronounced "Beatles" as "Peedles," a schoolboy colloquialism for penis. Chief among their group were Jurgen Vollmer, who took the photograph that appears on the cover of John Lennon's *Rock 'n' Roll* album; his friend Klaus Voorman, later bass player for Manfred Mann and much of John's, George's, and Ringo's post-Beatles work (as well as the artist for the *Revolver* cover); and Klaus' ex-girlfriend, Astrid Kirchherr.

Astrid, a photographer, posed the scruffy, leather-clad boys against backdrops of huge machinery or gray Hamburg skies, capturing a look of portent in the eyes of three who would go on to conquer the world. Under her direction, they were not just thugs and hooligans; they became *arty* thugs and hooligans. She thus designed an image for the group which they would maintain until Brian Epstein repositioned them as the lovable moptops a year later.

The "moptop" part, however, came from her. Stuart Sutcliffe became the first to let her cut his hair in a French style popular among the exis, and though the others laughed when they first saw his new 'do, they all—except for Pete Best—soon washed out the 1950s grease and adopted the look.

Stuart and Astrid were soon engaged, and he left the Beatles. He had never been a very good bass player, and it was easy enough for Paul to take his place.

One Last Time in Hamburg

On their return to Liverpool, things soon changed for the Beatles as they acquired the manager, producer, and label that would stay with them on their road to fame: Brian Epstein, George Martin, and Parlophone Records respectively. When they traveled to Hamburg for the third and final time, it was not to play dives, as they had before; this time they played their most prestigious venue to date, the Star Club.

But it was also a melancholy time. Stuart died of a brain hemorrhage on April 10, 1962, the day before they returned to Hamburg.

"Happiness Is a Warm Gun"

John Lennon took the idea for "Happiness Is a Warm Gun," which closes out Side One of *The Beatles*, from a magazine he saw the same week Robert Kennedy was assassinated. The publication, a gun magazine, had an article with the apparently unselfconscious title of "Happiness Is a Warm Gun." John used this as a parody on the *Peanuts* cartoon, with its saying, "Happiness Is a Warm Blanket."

Using a technique for which the Beatles became famous, the song is actually three different compositions woven together. The first part describes a girl, who John later said was Yoko Ono, also referred to in other White Album compositions such as "Julia" and "I'm So Tired." After some psychedelic imagery worthy of *Sgt. Pepper*—e.g., "multicolored mirrors on his hobnail boots"—the song goes into the second part, a heroin withdrawal anthem that prefigures Lennon's solo "Cold Turkey." On top of the cry for a "fix" is a classic Lennon non sequitur about the Mother Superior jumping the gun, and then the song slides into its heavy-metal final section, wrapping around the words of the title.

"A Hard Day's Night"

George Martin once said that "A Hard Day's Night" opened up the second phase of the Beatles' musical progression, ending the period from "Love Me Do" onward and beginning a phase that would lead up to *Help!* and the treasures that lay beyond. It also opened a second phase technically: whereas the first two albums had been two-track recordings, this was a four-track, allowing for the addition of more effects.

The song's opening chord has defied identification by musicologists. Wilfrid Mellers described it as a "dominant ninth of F [major]," whereas Tim Riley called it a G major 7th.

A Hard Day's Night (Film)

A Hard Day's Night, released in the summer of 1964, was the first of five Beatles films. It cost the least to make, and is generally considered the best.

Richard Lester was the director, and Alun Owen wrote the script. Owen, a Liverpool writer, spent two days following the Beatles during a trip to Dublin, so that he could record observations of their humor and mannerisms before writing his much-acclaimed screenplay. It was a case of art almost exceeding life; somehow the fictionalized Beatles of *A Hard Day's Night* were more themselves than the real ones.

When United Artists originally approved the movie's budget in late 1963, the Beatles were popular in Europe but unknown beyond its shores. Therefore UA, fearing that the group's popularity would have already waned by the time of the film's release, invested only £250,000 ($600,000) in the project. The executives overseeing the project hoped the soundtrack would make back the money they lost on the film.

As it turned out, the soundtrack album went gold, like virtually every piece of vinyl released by the Beatles between 1964 and 1970. As for the film itself, it received two Academy Award nominations, and 15,000 prints were made and distributed to theaters and movie houses around the world. One of these prints wound up in a California time capsule, to be opened in 1,000 years. Within a relatively short time, United Artists' $600,000 yielded over $13,500,000, a 2,250 percent return.

The title of *A Hard Day's Night* came from "Sad Michael," a piece from John Lennon's *In His Own Write*, published earlier in 1964. Lennon had borrowed the phrase from Ringo, who used it to describe a particularly grueling tour. As a film title, it won out over considerably less imaginative names suggested by people involved in the making of the film: *Moving On*, *Let's Go*, and *Beatlemania*.

The film's director, Richard Lester, had built his reputation making wacky comedies, and his style meshed well with the Beatles' own humor. Lester would become the only director to do more than one Beatles movie, going on to make *Help!* with a vastly higher budget but a less interesting

The Beatles attend the London premiere of A Hard Day's Night. *John, his back to the camera, is accompanied by wife Cynthia.* Archive Photos/Express Newspapers

script. He also directed *How I Won the War* (starring John Lennon), the film referred to in "A Day in the Life."

Among the extras on "A Hard Day's Night" was a thirteen-year-old Phil Collins, who in the 1980s would attain superstardom as the lead singer of Genesis, and later as a solo artist.

A Hard Day's Night (LP)

The *Hard Day's Night* soundtrack was the first Beatles album to contain entirely Beatles-written songs, since all previous albums had included at least one cover. It was also the *only* album consisting entirely of Lennon-McCartney compositions, because each subsequent release would contain at least one Harrison or Starkey song.

Of course, the above refers only to *British* albums. At that time, Capitol Records in the U.S. still engaged in the regrettable practice of repackaging British releases. In the case of *A Hard Day's Night*, Capitol removed a number of the songs from the British version and farmed them out to other albums, then padded the remainder of the soundtrack with George Martin's incidental music from the film. Though Martin was a fine composer, those pieces were mainly string instrumentals of Beatles tunes such as "I Should Have Known Better."

The only advantage to the U.S. release (and this only mattered at the time) was that it came out two weeks ahead of the British one, on June 26 as opposed to July 10, 1964.

George Harrison, Lead Guitarist for the Beatles

Born: February 25, 1943, at 12 Arnold Grove, Wavertree, Liverpool, his parents' home.

Family: Father, Harold Harrison, bus driver; Mother, Louise Harrison. Youngest of four children: two brothers (both born July 30, one in 1934, one in 1940) and one sister.

Schools: Dovedale Primary (attended the same year as John Lennon, although they did not meet); Liverpool Institute (where he met Paul McCartney, who introduced him to Lennon).

Married: Patti Boyd, model, whom he met during the filming of *A Hard Day's Night*, on January 21, 1966. Divorced 1977; married Olivia Arias, Dark Horse Records secretary, in 1978.

Children: One son, Djani, by Olivia, born August 1, 1978.

In the early days, John, Paul, and Ringo each had qualities that made them stand out, but George had none; ultimately, however, his very lack of a "trademark" itself became a trademark. Hence his nickname "The Dark Horse," which he would later use for a solo album and an ill-fated record company. Quiet, brooding by nature, sincere to a fault—a tendency evident in his often plainspoken manner, and in his later devotion to Hinduism—Harrison developed a reputation as the most serious-minded of the Beatles.

Most major groups have had someone in the George Harrison role—the less flamboyant, more solid member who forms the backbone of the

George Harrison and wife Patti Boyd attend the premiere of Yellow Submarine, *July 18, 1968.* Archive Photos/Popperfoto

ensemble. Most of the time, it's the bassist, whether Bill Wyman of the Rolling Stones (along with equally low-key drummer Charlie Watts); John Entwistle of the Who; or John Paul Jones of Led Zeppelin. In Harrison's case, though, the Dark Horse would ultimately come out as a leading contender.

First among the Beatles alphabetically, Harrison was the last chronologically, and perhaps because he was the youngest, it took him longer to develop his own distinct identity. This identity first emerged when Harrison took the lead by introducing the others to Eastern mysticism. After the debunking of the Maharishi and transcendental meditation (TM), George embraced mainstream Hinduism, whereas the others reverted to various Western forms of unbelief; but in the meantime, India exerted a strong pull on songs from "Norwegian Wood" to "Hey Jude." And by the time of the Beatles' last album, George would pen two of the strongest compositions on *Abbey Road*: "Something" and "Here Comes the Sun." A year later, he would come out with one of the greatest post-Beatles solo efforts, *All Things Must Pass*.

Louise Harrison

George got his first guitar for £3 ($7), purchased from a schoolmate when he was thirteen years old. He practiced until his fingers bled, and his mother Louise would often stay up with him till late at night, coaching and encouraging him.

Louise would prove to be the most helpful of all the future Beatles' parents: She let her son and his friends practice in her home many a time when they had nowhere else to go. Later, she would win the adoration of the Beatles' fans by answering their mail personally, a labor that required the writing of 200 letters a week. On George's birthday in 1964, the Harrisons received 30,000 cards and letters.

Mrs. Harrison explained that she was used to writing many letters, since she'd had several pen pals for a number of years. One of these was in Australia, and Mrs. Harrison, over a period of time, sent her many pictures of her children as they grew up. When the Beatles toured Australia in 1964, pictures of George as a little boy began turning up in newspapers there—contributed by the woman who had been saving them since he was a lad.

Journey to the East

George's fascination with India began on the set of *Help!* The set decorators, charged with creating an exotic backdrop for the film, had left a sitar lying around, and George picked it up. He soon became interested in learning how to play it, and got in contact with Indian sitar master Ravi Shankar. Shankar, along with the instruments he and his band played, were virtually unknown in the West—but that was about to change in a big way.

So, too, George's life began to change. He learned from Shankar about the religion of India and the concepts of *karma* and *maya* and other words he had never heard before. (The fact that karma is today a household word can be attributed to Harrison, who more than any other person influenced the interest in Eastern mysticism that first flourished in the late 1960s.) As evidence of the changes taking place in George, he and his wife Patti began regularly having dinner with their cleaning woman, Margaret. It may have been an ostentatious show of his freedom from status-consciousness, but he was apparently sincere.

In 1974, George went to Washington, D.C., where Jack Ford, a Harrison fan, introduced the former Beatle to his dad, the president of the

United States. George and Jerry exchanged buttons: Harrison's *Om* for Ford's *WIN* (Whip Inflation Now.) Two years later George met Secretary of State Henry Kissinger, and gave him a copy of his favorite book, *Autobiography of a Yogi* by Paramahansa Yogananda.

All Lawyers Must Sue

In later years his music, most of which concerned itself with his religion, would seem preachy to fans, and his Hinduism would spark almost as much criticism as Bob Dylan's conversion to Christianity in the late 1970s. But with *All Things Must Pass* in 1970, Harrison managed to bring together his music and his message in almost flawless harmony.

This, the first three-record album of the rock era, included "My Sweet Lord," one of the most oft-interpreted solo compositions by any of the former Beatles, with twenty-three cover versions in the first seven years after its release. "My Sweet Lord" was, prior to Paul's 1978 "Mull of Kintyre," the only ex-Beatle single to reach Number One in Britain.

However, all its success notwithstanding, the song caused its author more problems than any of his career. The owners of the rights to "He's So Fine," the Chiffons' hit from the early 1960s, noticed alleged similarities between their tune and Harrison's, and in 1975 they took him to court on charges of "unconscious plagiarism." George even played guitar for the judge to demonstrate how he wrote his songs, but to no avail: he was fined $400,000.

His battle became the basis for "This Song," from his album *Thirty-Three and a Third*. George later remarked that the song he had actually been thinking of while composing "My Sweet Lord" had not been "He's So Fine," but the Eddie Hawkins Singers' "Oh Happy Day."

A decade or so later, in the age of "sampling," when M. C. Hammer built songs around whole compositions by Rick James or Prince, the "My Sweet Lord" case might have been laughed out of court. For that matter, there have been plenty of other instances of similar-sounding compositions that never resulted in a courtroom battle: Aretha Franklin's "Spanish Harlem" and the Eagles' "New Kid In Town," for instance.

But Harrison was not the only singer caught in a legal squabble—John Lennon, for instance, had an imbroglio of his own over "Come Together." The Doors nearly got sued because "Hello, I Love You" sounded a lot like the Kinks' "All Day and All of the Night." And even in 1997, the Verve got sued for an unauthorized sampling of the Rolling Stones' early hit "Time Is On My Side" on their "Bittersweet Symphony." Mick Jagger and Keith Richards had nothing to do with the lawsuit, having long since lost control of those early songs to former manager Allen Klein—who was also the Beatles' manager in their last days as a group.

World's Greatest Guitarist—Burt Weedon

As the youngest Beatle, George seemed most comfortable in the background, a trait he carried with him even into his solo career. At about the time he released *All Things Must Pass*, he was sitting at a cafe with Eric Clapton when a waitress approached him and said, "You are the one, aren't you? You are a group, aren't you?" George pointed at Clapton and said, "No, I'm not. He is, though. That's the world's greatest guitarist—Burt Weedon."

Probably Harrison invented "Burt Weedon" on the spot; or perhaps it was a running joke between him and Clapton, like the title of a famous song they cowrote (see **Eric Clapton**). Of the four ex-Beatles, George seemed the most inclined to make and keep friendships with other superstars—not just Clapton, but Bob Dylan and others.

Harrison and Dylan, along with Roy Orbison and fellow Orbison devotees Tom Petty and Jeff Lynne, formed the Traveling Wilburys in the late 1980s. After Orbison's death, the other members of this, perhaps the most super of all supergroups, continued to put out albums. Once when musical comedian "Weird Al" Yankovic hosted a show on MTV, he referred to the Beatles as "George Harrison's group before he was in the Traveling Wilburys."

"Hello Goodbye"

"Hello Goodbye" is the only song from Side Two of the *Magical Mystery Tour* LP that was also included in the film.

The upbeat finale of the song, which has been likened to a South Sea island tribal dance, was ad-libbed in the studio. Paul plays bongos and conga drum on this portion.

The Beatles shot a "video" of "Hello Goodbye," showing them in their *Sgt. Pepper* uniforms performing the song while women dressed in Hawaiian hula skirts danced. It resurfaced in the 1995 *Beatles Anthology* TV special.

"Help!"

As he indicated in an interview shortly before his death, John Lennon considered "Help!" one of his best compositions. It was an honest song, he said—in it, he was singing about his true self, and not hiding his feelings.

Maureen Cleave, the reporter to whom he later explained that "We're more popular than Jesus," had asked him why he never wrote songs that contained words with more than one syllable. So he wrote one. But when he showed her the lyrics to the new song, full of such words as "self-assured," "appreciate," and "independence," she remained unimpressed.

Help! (Film)

Help!, the Beatles' second movie, cost twice as much to make as *A Hard Day's Night*. Whereas the first one had been shot in black and white, this one was in color; and whereas *A Hard Day's Night* had taken place in dreary old England, this film took the group to the beaches of Bermuda and the ski slopes of Austria. Yet almost everyone, including both critics and fans, considered *A Hard Day's Night* a better motion picture.

John Lennon himself later said, "[*Help!*] didn't work. It was like having clams in a movie about frogs." And Paul, reminiscing in the *Beatles Anthology* TV special, suggested one possible factor in the film's lack of an "edge": the Beatles were stoned throughout the entire shooting of it. Of course, it would be another two years after *Help!* before they would begin to speak openly of such things, but they were red-eyed and silly just the same. Paul recalled how once during the shooting in Austria, a scene called for him and Ringo to run—so they kept on running till they were out of sight, at which point they lit up a joint.

But there was also a certain clear-headed financial wisdom guiding the direction of the film, and the Austrian and Bahamian settings were far from coincidental. The Beatles and Walter Shenson, the film's producer, had invested in a Bahamian company, and wanted to show that they were an "asset to the [Bahamian] business community." However, they banked their money in sterling, and when Prime Minister Harold Wilson devalued the pound in 1967, the Beatles and Shenson lost £80,000 (almost $200,000.)

Haphazard *Help!*

The film, originally to have been entitled *Eight Arms to Hold You*, was "Respectfully dedicated to the memory of Mr. Elias Howe, who in 1846 invented the sewing machine." If John Lennon didn't write this dedication, it was certainly in the style of his irrelevance- and non sequitur-based humor, which he displayed in works ranging from the essays of *In His Own Write* to songs such as "I Am the Walrus."

Perhaps the best thing to emerge from *Help!* was George Harrison's infatuation with the sitar. George Martin had used the ancient Hindustani

The Beatles pose in the Swiss Alps for a scene from Help!, *their second movie. Note the third leg behind George.* AP/Wide World Photos

instrument to give an "exotic" feel to the background music in the film, and Harrison began playing around with the sitars he found on the *Help!* set.

The style of *Help!*, along with *A Hard Day's Night* to a lesser extent, would become the basis for *The Monkees* TV show and the group that sprang from it, both of which debuted in 1967.

Help! (LP)

The soundtrack of *Help!* is a classic example of how much got lost from Beatles albums between their release in Britain and their appearance in the U.S. The only flaw in the British album is that it's missing one song from the film soundtrack, "She's a Woman," later included on the British *Rarities*. But the American *Help!* is a different case altogether.

To begin with, the cover clearly states that this is a Beatles album, yet only half the songs on the record are Beatles compositions, the remainder being incidental music from the film played by the George Martin Orchestra. Only seven of the fifteen Beatles songs from the British album were used, the other eight being siphoned off to four other albums between December 1964 and June 1966. To add further insult to injury, the American album was listed as a "deluxe set," giving the record company an excuse to charge more for it.

On the cover, the Beatles hold their arms up in different, seemingly random, configurations, but in fact they are spelling out H-E-L-P in semaphore. Someone at Capitol decided to move the pictures around for the U.S. cover, so instead they spell out H-P-E-L. Also, the American cover gave the last Beatles song on the album the questionable title of "You're Gonna Loose that Girl."

"Helter Skelter"

"Helter Skelter," a name now synonymous with some of the most gruesome murders in history, was in actuality a (comparatively) innocent song about a playground slide, using sexual innuendoes and double meanings such as "coming down fast." Somehow Charles Manson took "Helter Skelter" as a signal for racial war, and seven people died before his "Family" had played out his interpretation of the song.

In one early take on July 18, 1968, the song ran for twenty-seven minutes, eleven seconds—the longest Beatles recording, released or unreleased. The album version, recorded on September 9, had a much shorter running time, but was no less bizarre. The song features the first (and perhaps only) recorded performance by John Lennon on saxophone, while road manager Mal Evans plays the trumpet. One of George Harrison's contributions cannot be heard: while Paul McCartney was singing, he ran around the studio holding a smoldering ashtray over his head. At the end of the song, Ringo—not John, as is popularly believed—shouts, "I've got blisters on my fingers!"

Coincidentally, in 1968, the same year as the release of the song, British author Patricia Moyes published a children's mystery named *Helter Skelter*.

"Her Majesty"

"Her Majesty," the last song on the last album the Beatles recorded, *Abbey Road,* seems as though it was added on at the last minute. And in a sense it was, though it was the first song recorded. Since Paul McCartney lived closest to the Abbey Road studios, he was the first to arrive on July 2, 1969, the first day of recording for what would be the final album. He did the song in three takes, and planned to include it in the medley he was building with five other of his songs, along with three of John Lennon's.

But when it came time to assemble the tracks on July 30, "Her Majesty" seemed out of place between "Mean Mr. Mustard" and "Polythene Pam"; therefore Paul told tape operator John Kurlander to throw it out. But Kurlander's professionalism wouldn't allow him to do so, and instead he tacked it on twenty seconds after "The End." When Paul heard the acetate, he liked it, and so it stayed—a characteristically irreverent finale to what might otherwise have been the pompous epigram that concludes "The End."

"Here Comes the Sun"

George Harrison wrote "Here Comes the Sun," the composition that opens up Side Two of *Abbey Road,* in an attempt to cheer up all four of the Beatles.

The group was entangled in the squabbles documented by Paul McCartney in "You Never Give Me Your Money" when Harrison "played hooky" from the Apple offices one day and went to Eric Clapton's house in the country. There he picked up a guitar and began strumming it. Something about the unusually clear weather on that day must have inspired him, because he later said that "Here Comes the Sun" was the first thing that came out.

"Here Comes the Sun" played a tiny part in the 1972 presidential campaign, when Democratic presidential candidate George McGovern quoted it in one of his speeches.

"Hey Bulldog"

One of the Beatles' only direct contributions to the movie *Yellow Submarine* was a film of them recording John Lennon's "Hey Bulldog."

Originally this was to have been a promotional clip of the group working on "Lady Madonna," but "Hey Bulldog" happened to be the song that they were doing on that day—February 11, 1968—so "Hey Bulldog" it was. It only appeared in British versions of *Yellow Submarine*, however. Incidentally, this "video" was the first film shot by the newly created Apple Films.

"Hey Jude"

In a 1976 poll, readers of the American fan magazine *Survey* voted "Hey Jude" their second-favorite Beatles song after "A Day in the Life."

Considered by many to be Paul McCartney's best composition, "Hey Jude"—the Beatles' first release on the newly formed Apple label—became the group's biggest-selling single. The song spent nine weeks at Number One on the American charts, longer than any Beatles single, and became the Number-One song of 1968 in the U.S. Within just a year, it sold over five million copies, and in the first eight years after its release, it had the most recorded cover versions of any Beatles song other than "Yesterday" and "Something"—thirty-nine.

"Hey Jules/John/Jude"

Paul started out writing this song for Julian Lennon, whose parents John and Cynthia were in a middle of a divorce. McCartney recalled later that he was driving out to see Julian and his mother when a song began to form in his head. He called the tune "Hey Jules," and he hoped it would cheer up the six-year-old Julian.

Julian's dad was enthusiastic about the song when Paul played it for him, a notable fact since Lennon often had caustic things to say about McCartney's compositions. But this time, John was thrilled, and he especially liked what Paul thought was a throwaway line: "The movement you need is on your shoulder." John pointed out that lyric, and Paul responded that of course he would replace it when he found a better phrase, but John was emphatic that it was the best line in the song.

The true subject of "Hey Jude" seems not to have occurred to Lennon; in fact, he thought it was about *him*. Then again, perhaps it was really about

McCartney himself, who at the time was in the midst of his own breakup—with his girlfriend of almost five years, Jane Asher.

Hey Jude(n)

According to one story, late one night in the summer of 1968, McCartney appeared in front of the by-then vacant Apple Boutique—the first failed incarnation of Apple Records—and spray-painted the name of his forthcoming song on the front window in gigantic letters.

The next day, many Londoners who saw the words got the wrong message. This was 1968, and the memory of World War II was still plenty fresh—as fresh as the memory of Vietnam in 1990s America. To people forty years old and older, "Jude" seemed close to the German *Juden*, or Jew. Just three decades before in Germany, events such as *Kristallnacht*, when hordes of Nazi thugs smashed up the windows of Jewish-owned shops, were frequent. Likewise it was common to see *Juden* painted across the front of a store or synagogue.

Who had written *Hey Jude* on the window of the Saville Row boutique? Was there a new generation of young Nazis on the loose? For a few days, there was a minor controversy over the apparently taunting anti-Semitic slogan. But then the Beatles released their new single.

At least, that's the legend. In fact it's unlikely that McCartney in 1968 could have gone around in London undetected, and unassailed by mobs; but it makes a good story.

How Long?

"Hey Jude" may well be the original "rock epic," a form perfected in the 1970s with such masterworks as Led Zeppelin's "Stairway to Heaven," "Funeral for a Friend" by Elton John (whose first album includes a song called "Hay Chewed" that doesn't sound a thing like "Hey Jude") or Lynyrd Skynyrd's "Free Bird." As different as these compositions are, they share certain characteristics: length (six minutes or more); a series of changes in melody line; and a buildup from a soft beginning to a strong, prolonged ending.

The song starts with Paul accompanying himself on piano, and as it progresses, more and more instruments join him. In the background is a forty-piece orchestra, a larger number of musicians than on any Beatles song other than "A Day in the Life." Thirty-nine of the musicians can be heard clapping their hands and singing "na-na-na-na" with the group; one of them walked out of the studio, saying, "I'm not going to clap my hands and sing Paul McCartney's bloody song."

At seven minutes, eleven seconds, "Hey Jude" at that time was the longest song issued as a single by any group. About the only artists who could get away with this type of excess were the crown princes of the era: Bob Dylan and the Beatles. Dylan had previously set the record with the six-minute "Like a Rolling Stone."

"Hey Jude" ends with the longest fade-out of any Beatles recording except perhaps "I Want You (She's So Heavy)," another seven-minute behemoth. George Harrison's "Isn't It a Pity (Version One)," from *All Things Must Pass*, lasts just one second less than "Jude." "Isn't It a Pity" also uses the same tune as the "Hey Jude" fade-out, which is fitting, given the source of the "Hey Jude" chorus: Paul said it was influenced by the droning chants and mantras he'd heard in India.

Hey Jude

Hey Jude, also called *The Beatles Again*, was released in the U.S. in February 1970. Though not an *album* as such, it brought together six tracks that had never appeared on an LP in either the U.S. or Britain: "Rain," "Lady Madonna," "Hey Jude," "Revolution," "Don't Let Me Down," "The Ballad of John and Yoko," and "Old Brown Shoe." "Can't Buy Me Love" and "Paperback Writer," which had appeared on the British *Collection of Beatles Oldies*, saw their first U.S. album release on *Hey Jude* as well.

For some reason, "I Should Have Known Better," from *A Hard Day's Night* six years earlier, wound up on *Hey Jude*. Similarly inexplicable is the absence of "The Inner Light" or "You Know My Name (Look Up the Number)," both of which saw release a decade later with *Rarities*.

The cover photograph is from the Beatles' last photo session together, on August 22, 1969, at John Lennon's home.

"Hey Jude" / "Revolution"

"Hey Jude" / "Revolution" became the Beatles' biggest-selling single, and like their classic double A-side, "Penny Lane" / "Strawberry Fields Forever," it placed the talents of McCartney and Lennon in sharp juxtaposition. The single marked a new phase in the Beatles' career as a group, and just as the earlier record had heralded the upcoming *Sgt. Pepper*, this one served as advance notice for the White Album.

"Hey Jude" / "Revolution" was also the inaugural release for Apple Records, along with "Those Were the Days" by Mary Hopkin, "Thingumybob" by the Black Dyke Mills Band, and "Sour Milk Sea" by Jackie Lomax. During National Apple Week—August 11–18, 1968—the Beatles had the four records packaged together in a special boxed set called *Our First Four*, and sent them to the Queen, the Queen Mother, Princess Margaret, and the Prime Minister. The Queen Mother wrote back to say that she was "greatly touched by this kind thought from the Beatles" and "much enjoyed listening to these recordings."

"Hey Jude" was already a long song at 7:11, and together with "Revolution," the single clocked in at a staggering 10:33—half of a typical album side.

Given the great interest in alleged "secret messages" left by the Beatles in their songs, it is interesting that not even Charles Manson, who built an entire eschatology around the White Album, noticed what could have been interpreted as a Biblical reference in the title of this single. Manson observed the similarity between the name "Revolution" and that of the Bible's last book, Revelation, but he does not seem to have noticed that the next-to-last book of the Bible is Jude.

"Honey Don't"

Ringo sings the Beatles' cover of Carl Perkins' "Honey Don't," which appears on *Beatles for Sale* (U.K.) and *Beatles '65* (U.S.). Perkins—of "Blue Suede Shoes" fame—witnessed the recording of both "Honey Don't" and another of his songs, "Everybody's Trying to Be My Baby," the latter sung by a longtime Perkins fan who had once performed under the name "Carl Harrison."

George was far from the only Perkins devotee in the Beatles ranks: eighteen years later, Paul McCartney invited Perkins to play on a song for McCartney's *Tug of War* LP.

How I Won the War

The 1967 film *How I Won the War* received a tepid response from critics and fans alike—and that very fact helped to ensure its immortalization. It was the movie that a crowd of people turned away from in the second verse of "A Day in the Life."

John Lennon starred in this antiwar comedy directed by Richard Lester, who had also made *A Hard Day's Night* and *Help!* to considerably more

John rests on the set of How I Won the War *in Almeria, Spain, in 1966.* Archive Photos/Popperfoto

critical acclaim. Lennon played Private Gripweed, a soldier in the English army, and recorded the title song under the name "Musketeer Gripweed and the Third Troop."

Lennon made the film during the respite between the end of touring in August 1966 and the recording of "Penny Lane" / "Strawberry Fields Forever" toward the end of the year. During that time, he began to wear his glasses in public for the first time, as he would continue to do for the rest of his life; also, while he was waiting around on the set between takes, he began working on "Strawberry Fields."

How I Won the War marks the first appearance of a Beatle in a motion picture without the other three.

I

More Beatles song titles begin with the letter *I* than with any other letter of the alphabet, most of these being forms of the personal pronoun followed by a declarative statement.

Thirty-two songs released between 1962 and 1970 start with *I*, and of these, thirteen with the *word* "I." (Or fourteen, since the American version of *Let It Be* lists "Dig a Pony" as "I Dig a Pony.") Six more begin with "I'm," four with "I'll," and two with "I've." All this seems to reveal a certain self-absorption, best expressed in the title of the last song the Beatles ever recorded, "I Me Mine."

"I Am the Walrus"

John Lennon's sinister string of non sequiturs, "I Am the Walrus," was due to appear in the upcoming *Magical Mystery Tour* film during the holiday season in 1967, so the group released it in November as a "taster" on a single with "Hello Goodbye" as the A-side. It was yet another case of two songs—one heavy, one light—ironically juxtaposed on a single. The group had done this before with "Yellow Submarine" / "Eleanor Rigby," and would do it again with 1970's "Let It Be" / "You Know My Name, Look Up the Number."

The title comes from one of John's favorite authors at the time, Lewis Carroll. As demonstrated in *Alice in Wonderland*, Carroll had a talent for the absurd and surreal, which gave him a whole new generation of readers in the psychedelic era. Lennon would not be the only songwriter of the 1960s inspired by Carroll: Grace Slick and Jefferson Airplane wove *Wonderland* imagery throughout their "White Rabbit." By 1982, when Elvis Costello's "Beyond Belief" mentioned Alice and the looking glass, the use of Carrollian imagery had become a recognized fixture of relatively more cerebral rock music.

In one of Carroll's poems, a walrus and a carpenter have a symbolic discussion "of many things... why the sea is boiling hot—and whether pigs have wings." Lennon later said that he had written the song about the walrus because he had thought the walrus to be the hero in that passage. However, he learned—too late—that Carroll had intended the carpenter to be the hero, and the walrus the villain. Nonetheless, as Lennon said, "I Am the Carpenter" wouldn't have sounded right.

Deconstructing "the Walrus"

As for the lyrics themselves, and any attempt one might make to extract any sense from them, Lennon himself said that he didn't know what it all meant. Like Bob Dylan, who had once exerted an enormous influence on his songwriting, he was not using words and phrases for their literal meaning, but for the feeling they created.

Lennon does many wonderful things with language in the song, including his use of nonexistent words such as *snied* and *texpert*. This was a technique he would resurrect a couple of years later with the Latin-inspired dream speech of "Sun King."

Outside of some internal rhyme such as "choking smokers . . . joker," the song is virtually bereft of rhyme. This in itself is quite an achievement— one that even Dylan seldom managed—primarily because rhyming lyrics are important to maintaining the listener's awareness of the song's beat. Lennon, on the other hand, had succeeded before with "Tomorrow Never Knows" and "Strawberry Fields Forever" (which uses only occasional rhymes), and did so now with "Walrus," each time creating a song in which the rhythm was strong enough that it did not need rhyme to reinforce it.

In the lyrics, Lennon makes a reference to "Lucy in the sky," another instance of self-reference in a Beatles song (*see* **"Glass Onion"**).

The BBC's censors took an interest in the lines mentioning "porno-graphic priestess" and "naughty girl you let your knickers down." These sex-ually charged images got "I Am the Walrus" banned from British radio.

"Semolina" is a coarse flour, and "pilchard" is a fish of the sardine fam-ily. As for the reference to Edgar Allan Poe ("Man you should have seen them kicking . . ."), it has been suggested that Lennon was commenting on attempts to deconstruct his own writing. In any case, Poe and Edmund Lear, mentioned by last name in "Paperback Writer," are the only writers referred to directly in Beatles songs. Poe also appears on the cover of *Sgt. Pepper*.

Bury My Body

The sound at the beginning of "I Am the Walrus," which Lennon created on a mellotron, was supposed to resemble a police siren of the type used in Britain, growing louder as it comes closer to the listener.

According to legend, Lennon wanted to include a snippet of radio in the song's long fade-out, and he simply turned on the radio to discover that the BBC was broadcasting Shakespeare's *King Lear*. (Sir John Gielgud played the title role in this production, though he does not appear in the part on "I Am the Walrus.") In the fade-out, Shakespeare's words from the death scene—Act IV, Scene VI, lines 246-255—come into the foreground:

246	*Oswald*: Slave, thou hast slain me. Villain, take my purse:
	If ever thou wilt thrive, bury my body,
	And give the letters which find'st about me
	To Edmund, Earl of Gloucester; seek him out
250	Upon the English party. O untimely death!
	Death! [he dies]
	Edgar: I know thee well, a serviceable villain,
	As duteous to the vices of thy mistress
	As badness would desire.
	Gloucester: What, is he dead?
255	Sit you down, father; rest you

When the "Paul Is Dead" affair became news a couple of years later, those words—written over 350 years before—would become central pieces of evidence in the investigation.

The chorus at the end of "I Am the Walrus" falls into two parts, both sung by the Michael Sammes Singers. The eight men sing "Oompah, oompah, stick it to your joompah," and the six women sing "Got one, got one, everybody's got one." The Sammes Singers also provided the "Ho-ho-ho, hee-hee-hee, ha-ha-ha!" heard earlier in the song.

"I Feel Fine"

Long before Jimi Hendrix emerged on the scene, "I Feel Fine" marked the first use of feedback on a major rock song. It's only a few seconds of hum just before the opening riff, but in 1964, it was revolutionary.

People didn't know what to think of it: some thought that their copies of the single were damaged, and a rumor went around that the Beatles had recorded the sound of a humming bee and amplified it onto the record. (They would not use prerecorded sound effects until two years later, on *Revolver*.) In fact it was simply feedback, produced by overloading the preamps to create a vibrating sound.

"I Feel Fine" closes with a second or two of what sounds like barking dogs. This was Paul McCartney—a devoted dog owner—playing around in the studio.

"I Me Mine"

George Harrison based the tune of "I Me Mine" on a piece he heard an Austrian marching band playing on television late one night. A decade later, he would name his autobiography after the song.

Producer Phil Spector stretched "I Me Mine," originally little more than a fragment, for *Let It Be*; the much shorter version on *The Beatles Anthology 3* represents its true length as recorded, before the introduction of Spector's studio tricks.

Made without John Lennon on January 3, 1970, "I Me Mine" was the last song recorded by the Beatles. (Some might say it was the last song for twenty-four years, when the same three gathered to do "Free As a Bird.") It was also, along with "Across the Universe" and "The Long and Winding Road," the occasion of the last Beatles *recording session*—that is, for overdubs of previously recorded material. On April 1, 1970, Spector gathered a group of orchestral musicians to lay down the lush backing for those three songs; Ringo was the only Beatle present.

"I Saw Her Standing There"

"I Saw Her Standing There" is the first song from the Beatles' first album, *Please Please Me*, a record they completed in a single day—February 11, 1963.

When a band is about to play a song, usually someone will "count off" so that everyone is in sync. This may be the drummer clicking his sticks together, as in the studio recording of AC/DC's "Back In Black" (1980); or it may be a group member counting off the numbers *one-two-three-four*, as Paul McCartney does at the beginning of "I Saw Her Standing There." Either way, it's fairly unusual to include the count-off in the actual recording—and it was certainly unusual in 1963, when the Beatles did it.

There are people who claim that if you listen closely, McCartney says, "One-two-three-fuck!" Maybe if you listen closely enough, you will hear that, but that doesn't make it so. Again, this was early 1963, and the Beatles were still very much in the position of trying to gain acceptance: it would be several years before they would start pulling little pranks like the inclusion of "tit-tit-tit" in the chorus of "Girl."

When John Lennon joined Elton John onstage at Madison Square Garden on November 20, 1974, he announced that "We thought we'd do a number by an old estranged fiancé of mine, called Paul." Then John and John launched into an exciting, though mangled, version of "I Saw Her Standing There." It would turn out to be the last live show Lennon ever did.

"I Wanna Be Your Man"

Lennon and McCartney wrote "I Wanna Be Your Man" for the Rolling Stones. The two had stopped by a club where the Stones were playing, and Mick Jagger and Keith Richards told them they needed a song.

There they were: the Glimmer Twins (as Jagger and Richards would come to be known), and the Nurk Twins—a lesser-known name under which

Lennon and McCartney had performed. While Jagger and Richard sat at one table, Lennon and McCartney went off to another and wrote "I Wanna Be Your Man." Years later, Jagger would still profess admiration over the way the pair could come up with a ready-made tune.

The song became the Stones' first hit, reaching Number Twelve on the British pop charts in early 1964. The Beatles later recorded it with Ringo on lead vocal, releasing it in November 1963 on *With the Beatles* in Great Britain, and in January 1964 on *Meet the Beatles!* in the U.S.

"I Want to Hold Your Hand"

To Americans, "I Want to Hold Your Hand" symbolizes the arrival of Beatlemania in America. And well it should, since the song was the Beatles' first Number One single in the States. The group had released four singles before this one—"Love Me Do," "Please Please Me," "From Me to You," and "She Loves You"—yet they had failed to crack the U.S. market. Now, with the fifth single, that was about to change.

The single sold five million copies worldwide, a fraction of its total sales, since it was distributed through a dozen different LPs in various countries over the years following its release. "I Want to Hold Your Hand" is second only to "Hey Jude" as the Beatles' biggest-selling single.

But things looked different in January 1964, when John Lennon said that *if* the single managed to even penetrate the U.S. charts, it would only be due to Americans' "sympathy for Britain." The day after he said this, the song entered the *Billboard* charts. Eleven days later, it had sold a half-million copies, and received a gold record certification two weeks after that, on February 3, 1964.

"I Want to Tell You"

When George Harrison was writing one of his three *Revolver* tracks, the hard-rocking "I Want to Tell You," he had a hard time coming up with a name. Asked its title by George Martin, he said "I don't know"—which became the working title. Later, recording engineer Geoff Emerick dubbed it "Laxton's Superb," a type of apple.

The Beatles receive Gold Records for both "I Want to Hold Your Hand" and Meet the Beatles *in February 1964.* Archive Photos/Popperfoto

"I Want You (She's So Heavy)"

John Lennon wrote "I Want You (She's So Heavy)," which closes out Side One of *Abbey Road*, for Yoko Ono. That in itself hardly distinguishes the song, but other things do.

"I Want You (She's So Heavy)" contains half of its entire lyrical content—words which Lennon sings over and over and over and over in the recording—within the title. In all, there are only twelve distinct words in the entire composition—*bad-baby-driving-heavy-I-mad-me-she's-so-want-yes-you*—which, when strung together, sound like an encyclopedia of 1960s cool-speak. Regarding the sparse wording, Lennon explained to *Rolling Stone* editor Jann Wenner: "When you're drowning, you don't say 'I would be incredibly pleased if someone would have the foresight to notice me drowning and come and help me.' You just scream."

"I Want You" is, at 7:49, the Beatles' longest actual song—as opposed to another Lennon composition, "Revolution 9," charitably called an "instrumental."

The recording contains George Harrison's only Beatles performance on a white-noise generator. This creates a roar that builds hypnotically along with the music, louder and louder, until suddenly—everything stops. Lennon had first used the surprise ending in "Strawberry Fields Forever," in which the music seems to end, only to return. He and McCartney played around with this idea several times throughout their careers as Beatles, but perhaps nowhere in the group's catalogue is a surprise ending used with quite as much jarring effect as here.

"I Will"

"I Will," as almost anyone would agree, is a nice song, classic Paul McCartney—sweet that goes just to the edge of saccharin. The fact that it comes just after "Why Don't We Do It in the Road" on the White Album, thus providing an ironic juxtaposition between the latter's raw sexuality and its own pristine cuteness, saves the song from seeming cloying. The two tracks together also illustrate the versatility of McCartney's songwriting.

But the most interesting aspects of "I Will" relate to its recording—not simply the fact that it took sixty-seven takes before McCartney was satisfied, but also the other events taking place in the Abbey Road Studios on the day the Beatles did most of the work on the song, September 16, 1968.

In between takes, Paul recorded various snippets and ad libs, "Can You Take Me Back" being the only one that ever saw release. More curious was the fact that earlier that day, before the Beatles got to the studio, personnel at Abbey Road began making a recording of all the "title lines" from Beatles songs released to date—e.g., the line "she loves you" from "She Loves You," and so forth. Though the reasons for this are unclear, author Mark Lewisohn—always a reliable authority—noted that the project was assigned the same job number, for accounting purposes, as the White Album.

Thus, Lewisohn speculated, it is possible the group intended to include this undoubtedly bizarre-sounding collection of all their song titles as part of the album—which was, after all, entitled *The Beatles*. One wonders, though, what line the recording engineers chose for "Tomorrow Never Knows," which does not contain a "title line."

"I'm Down"

"I'm Down" did not appear on an album in the U.S. or Britain until *Rock 'n' Roll Music* in June 1976; before that, it had only been on a single, as the B-side of "Help!"

In the recording, made on June 14, 1965, Paul McCartney does an impressive throat-wrenching vocal in the style of Little Richard, whose "Long Tall Sally" (also covered by the Beatles) this song resembles. But what's most impressive about Paul's work on that day in the Abbey Road Studios was what it illustrates about his versatility: in the course of recording "I'm Down," he also managed to lay down the vocal track for a song in an entirely different style, "I've Just Seen a Face"—and then recorded "Yesterday."

"I'm Looking Through You"

"I'm Looking Through You," from *Rubber Soul*, marks Ringo Starr's first recorded performance on a nonpercussive instrument, the Hammond organ.

Paul McCartney began writing "I'm Looking Through You" after an argument with his girlfriend, Jane Asher. Jane had decided to go to Bristol to act in a play, something Paul didn't want her to do, and there followed a period of separation which most likely influenced the writing of "You Won't See Me" as well. At the end of their breakup, Paul went to see her in a play in Bristol and, while there, got the idea for what would become "Eleanor Rigby."

There is a slight variation between the British and American versions of "I'm Looking Through You." The British one has an ordinary beginning, but the American version features two false starts.

"I'm So Tired"

"I'm So Tired," from Side Two of *The Beatles*, musically resembles another John Lennon composition from the same album, "The Continuing Story of Bungalow Bill": for instance, the line "went out tiger-hunting with his elephant and gun" in the latter sounds like a drawn-out version of the part in "I'm So Tired" where Lennon sings "I wonder should I call you." Lennon himself once admitted that he had a few riffs that he really liked, and which he repeated often.

"I'm So Tired" is the insomniac's anthem, especially because the protagonist is not happy to be awake, burning his candle at both ends: he would like nothing more than to sleep, only he can't. John Lennon considered it one of his best White Album songs. Like many of his compositions from this period onward, he wrote this one about Yoko Ono, reflecting an obsession that made it difficult to sleep.

At the end of the recording, Lennon chants some gibberish that "Paul is Dead" theorists interpreted as "Paul is dead man, miss him, miss him." Directly after this chanting, a high voice—perhaps Yoko's—emits a wordless sound that lasts for perhaps a quarter of a second, and then Paul McCartney's guitar begins "Blackbird."

"I'm the Greatest"

John Lennon wrote "I'm the Greatest," which Ringo Starr recorded for his November 1973 album, *Ringo*.

The title, of course, refers to Muhammad Ali's trademark statement, and the lyrics refer to *Sgt. Pepper*. The song's music resembles elements of "Being for the Benefit of Mr. Kite!," "Revolution," "Cry Baby Cry," "I Want You (She's So Heavy)," and "Golden Slumbers."

In 1969, with the breakup of the Beatles imminent, three Beatles briefly considered forming a group called "The Ladders," consisting of John Lennon on rhythm guitar, George Harrison on lead guitar, Klaus Voormann on bass, and Ringo Starr on drums. Though the idea for the Ladders quickly died, that same lineup plays on "I'm the Greatest," along with Billy Preston on organ.

"In My Life"

John Lennon wrote "In My Life" first as a poem before he composed any music. Lennon had wanted to mention places he had known in his life, and originally planned for the song to include references to Liverpool sites such as Strawberry Fields and Penny Lane. But when he realized that an excess of name-dropping would clutter the song, he trimmed it down.

The recording of "In My Life" appears on *Rubber Soul*. The "Elizabethan"—as it's been called—piano piece in the middle of the song was played by George Martin.

India

The Beatles actually made *two* trips to India. The second and more famous one, of course, was their visit to the Maharishi's ashram in February 1968; their first time in India was July 1966, on the heels of their ill-fated excursion to the Philippines.

Besieged by a crowd of 600 in New Delhi on their first trip, the group managed to make it to a music store, where they purchased sitars. In January 1968, George Harrison spent five days recording in Bombay, during which time he taped the instrumentation for "The Inner Light" as well as his *Wonderwall Music*. (See **Sitar; Maharishi Mahesh Yogi**.)

"The Inner Light"

"The Inner Light," the B-side of "Lady Madonna" in 1968, was the first George Harrison song released as a single by the Beatles. It was also the last of three Indian-inspired pieces by Harrison, which began with "Love You To" in 1966 and continued through "Within You Without You" in 1967. None of these three songs uses any rock 'n' roll instruments, or features any Beatle except George.

Harrison recorded "The Inner Light" at the same time as his first solo album, the *Wonderwall Music* soundtrack. Both took place in a Bombay studio that wasn't soundproofed, and according to Harrison, one can hear taxis going by in the background if one listens closely.

The basis for the lyrics of this song is much older even than the 350-year-old poem that Paul McCartney used for "Golden Slumbers." The words of "The Inner Light" were taken from the writings of the philosopher Lao-Tzu (c. 604–c. 531 B.C.), whose work formed the basis for Taoism: "One may know the world without going out of doors / One may see the Way of Heaven without looking through the windows / The further one goes, the less one knows."

This, not merely one of Harrison's best, but one of the Beatles' best songs, proved especially hard for collectors to obtain prior to 1979. Eleven years after its release, it was available on only one Beatles album in the entire world, Spain's *Por Siempre Beatles*; in 1979 and 1980, however, it became available to British and American listeners respectively on the *Rarities* albums.

Instruments

In their more than seven years recording together, the Beatles made count-less innovations in their uses of various types of instrumentation. "Classical" instruments such as cellos, violins, and harpsichords received their first and greatest pop exposure through the group, not to mention such Indian instru-ments as sitars, tablas, and tambouras.

And though they hired many session musicians—no Beatle plays on "Eleanor Rigby" or "She's Leaving Home," for instance—the Beatles them-selves played a wide variety of instruments ranging from steel guitar to flute to washboard. This of course was in addition to their standard lineup of George Harrison on lead guitar, John Lennon on rhythm guitar, Paul McCartney on bass guitar, and Ringo Starr on drums.

In some cases, the band member played an instrument repeatedly, and it became as much a part of his work as his ordinary role. John Lennon, for instance, performed on the acoustic guitar in more than a quarter of the 215 Beatles songs released between 1962 and 1970. George Harrison's Beatles career on the piano, by contrast, lasts the duration of one note—the final one on "A Day in the Life."

Among the instruments played at one time or another by group mem-bers, in addition to the ordinary lineup, were steel guitar, twelve-string lead guitar, banjo, sitar; six-string bass, Arco string bass, fuzz bass, double bass; piano, Steinway piano, harpsichord; organ, Hammond organ, harmonium, clavioline; electric piano, mellotron, synthesizer, white noise generator; sax-ophone, flute, flugelhorn; harmonica, tamboura, recorder, comb and paper; xylophone, firebell, cowbell; washboard, tambourine, maracas, bongos, claves, conga drum, timpani, African drum, tabla, finger cymbals, loose-skinned Arabian bongo, anvil, castanets, and packing case. (The latter report-edly occurred on "Words of Love.")

Israel

Israel's government rejected a 1964 proposal from Brian Epstein for a Beatles show in that country. Government officials said that security would be too costly, and besides, the music would be harmful to Israeli youth.

Prime Minister Golda Meir received an acorn from John and Yoko Lennon during their 1969 "Nuts for Peace" campaign. Mrs. Meir said that she didn't know who John and Yoko were, but if the acorn was being sent in the name of peace, she was all for it.

"It's Only Love"

"It's Only Love," from the British *Help!* and the American *Rubber Soul*, was originally called "That's a Nice Hat." Released a full year before "Tomorrow Never Knows," this song may have constituted John Lennon's first reference to his new experiences, as the song begins with the words "I get high."

"I've Just Seen a Face"

"I've Just Seen a Face" shares the same history as "It's Only Love": both were on the British *Help!* and American *Rubber Soul*, and both had working titles entirely different from their later name—"Auntie Gin's Theme," in this case.

Japan

In the LP era, the Japanese wing of EMI released all the pre-*Sgt. Pepper* Beatles albums in both their British and American versions. Hence Japan had more different albums by the Beatles—thirty-one in all—than any country.

The Japanese concert program for the group's 1966 tour was meticulously prepared, with information about each song, its American and British release, its lead vocalist, etc. Brian Epstein found the program such a valuable information source that he kept a copy of it on his desk for reference.

"Julia"

John Lennon named one of his most powerful White Album compositions, "Julia," after his mother. Julia Lennon, abandoned by her husband, was killed in a car accident when John was seventeen years old. There is also another figure present in "Julia," indicated by the haunting intonation of the phrase "Ocean Child," which in Japanese is *Yoko Ono*.

Lennon took the opening line of "Julia" from the writings of Lebanese mystic and author Kahlil Gibran.

"Kansas City/Hey-Hey-Hey-Hey!"

Sometimes referred to simply as "Kansas City," the song "Kansas City/Hey-Hey-Hey-Hey!" is actually two compositions, the first by Jerry Lieber and Mike Stoller, the second by Richard Penniman—a.k.a. Little Richard. The Beatles turned it into a single song, which appeared on *Beatles for Sale* in Britain and *Beatles VI* in the U.S.; nonetheless, it was in essence the group's only medley prior to the later song-cycle experiments that culminated with the second side of *Abbey Road*. (See also **"Boys"** / **"Kansas City."**)

"Komm, Gib Mir Deine Hand" / "Sie Liebt Dich"

The Beatles did not record their only foreign-language single as a heartfelt tribute to the people of Germany, the country where they had cut their teeth as musicians. That's the official line, and it sounds nice, but it's not true: in fact the single was a calculated marketing maneuver pushed on them by others.

Convinced that German fans would never respond to a song in English, the West German branch of EMI persuaded Brian Epstein and George Martin that the Beatles needed to record in German. So they made the record—in Paris. There was no need to redo the music; they simply sang the songs again in their German versions, which had been written by translators.

Of course it's impossible to make rhymes match up perfectly when moving between languages: hence though the title "Sie Liebt Dich" is a literal translation of "She Loves You," "Komm, Gib Mir Deine Hand" means "Come Give Me Your Hand" rather than "I Want To Hold Your Hand."

As it turned out, fans all over the world responded to the Beatles with or without being able to speak English, so this was their only foreign-language single. The Beach Boys later followed suit with a German version of "In My Room" called "Ganz Allein," or "All Alone."

"Lady Madonna"

Paul McCartney based the tune of "Lady Madonna" on an old song called "Bad Penny Blues."

In its back-to-the-basics style, "Lady Madonna" marked a shift away from psychedelia. Bob Dylan had already set the tone in 1968, with the release of his minimalist *John Wesley Harding* to a world still swooning from *Sgt. Pepper*. Now the Beatles followed suit, and "Lady Madonna" helped usher in a return to basics in music, fashion, and lifestyles.

From "Lady Madonna" onward, simplicity would be the name of the game, just as complexity had been in 1966 and 1967. With the exception of a few White Album and *Abbey Road* compositions, the group's songs would use simple lyrics—for example, "Why Don't We Do It in the Road"—and simple music, as in "The Ballad of John and Yoko."

"Lady Madonna" / "The Inner Light"

The Beatles released "Lady Madonna," backed with "The Inner Light," in March 1968 on the Capitol label in America and the Parlophone label in Britain. This was the last such single: When the group came out with "Hey Jude" / "Revolution," in August, the record bore the Apple logo.

This single marked a critical turning point, and "Lady Madonna" and "The Inner Light" make an interesting combination because the latter shows where the group had been, whereas the former points where they were going. "The Inner Light" would become the last Beatles song to use Indian instrumentation, and one of the very last to employ mystical imagery or a transcendental message in its lyrics. It was, in effect, the last Beatles song of 1967, just as "Lady Madonna" would become the first song of 1968.

John Ono (Winston) Lennon, Rhythm Guitarist for the Beatles

Born: October 9, 1940, at 6:30 p.m. in Oxford Street Maternity Hospital, Liverpool.

Family: Father, Alfred Lennon, sailor; Mother, Julia Lennon. Raised by his Aunt Mimi and Uncle George Smith. Grew up as an only child, though in fact he had a half-sister, Julia Baird.

Schools: Dovedale Primary; Quarry Bank High School; Liverpool Art College.

Married: Cynthia Powell, at Mount Pleasant Registry Office in Liverpool, in 1963. Divorced November 8, 1968; married Yoko Ono, artist, in Gibraltar on March 20, 1969.

John Lennon with son Julian and Yoko Ono, December 11, 1968. Archive
Photos/Express Newspapers

Children: Two sons: John Julian, by Cynthia, born 1963; and Sean Taro
Ono, by Yoko, born October 9, 1975, Lennon's thirty-fifth birthday. Also a
stepdaughter, Kyoko.

Died: 11:07 p.m., December 8, 1980, at Roosevelt Hospital, on the corner of 59th Street and 9th Avenue in New York City. Death caused by multiple gunshot wounds delivered at close range to his lungs, arm, and legs by Mark David Chapman outside the Dakota Apartments in New York.

To many minds, John Lennon was half of the Beatles in himself. Though part of the group's unique charm in the early 1960s was that they had no "front man," unlike most groups from the previous decade such as Bill Haley and the Comets, Lennon was the unquestioned leader. Eventually his leadership would become less important, not only to him but to the rest of the group, but in the early days it was crucial.

John was the dynamic one, the visionary, the motivator. Not long before his death in 1980, Lennon recalled a "gag" that he led in the early days of the Beatles, whenever the collective spirit had begun to lag and the group was flirting with depression. In the dressing room, when no one else was around but the four of them, he would ask, "Where are we going, fellows?" They would answer, in pseudo-American voices, "To the top, Johnny!" Then he would ask them, "Where is that, fellows?" And they would say, "To the toppermost of the poppermost!" To this, John would answer "Right!"

Lennon was inspiring, choleric, acerbic, disagreeable, enchanting, an exhorter, a poet, a mystic, an anarchist, a cartoonist of the mind, lovable, revolting, sexy, political, apolitical, a hypocrite, a genius, a father, a lover, a pinup, an adolescent, a rebel, a follower, restless, peace-loving, violent, a hero, a victim.

Alfred and Julia

Like most rock stars of the 1960s, John Lennon was born during World War II—not afterward, meaning that he was *not* a "Baby Boomer." Or as Lennon put it in his book *In His Own Write*, he came into this world when "the Nasties" were bombing Liverpool.

His parents, Alfred and Julia Lennon, gave him the middle name of Winston after England's Prime Minister. Alfred—or Freddie, as he was called, was a sailor, and his role in the boy's upbringing would be minimal. He disappeared for years, then returned at the end of the war, when John was five years old.

At that time, Freddie announced that he was on his way to New Zealand, and wanted to take his son with him. Given the opportunity to decide, John almost elected to go with Freddie, but chose at the last minute to stay with Julia. It was a decision that would have far-reaching consequences: had John Lennon moved to New Zealand, it is hard to imagine how he ever would have met Paul McCartney.

Actually, John did not really live *with* Julia, but rather with Julia's sister Mimi and Mimi's husband George Smith. Julia would sometimes come to see John, and when she did it was like a visit home from college by a fun-loving older sister. They would go to movies and shows, and she would buy him candy; then she would disappear for months. In the meantime, Uncle George and Aunt Mimi took care of the boy, ensuring a degree of normalcy that would have been missing from his life if he had stayed with either of his biological parents.

A Lad of Diverse Talents

One early indication of John's creative talent was "Sport and Speed Illustrated," a book of stories, cartoons, and drawings that he created when he was seven years old. At the end of "Sport and Speed" he wrote the message, "If you liked this, come again next week. It'll be even better."

At around the same time, his teachers at Dovedale Primary in Liverpool began noticing strange things in the young Lennon's English compositions. The boy, who had severe myopia, often mixed up words in his compositions, substituting ones similar in appearance, sometimes with hilarious results. His nearsightedness thus influenced him toward word-play, which in turn gave him a remarkable ability with puns, a facility he would put to use with his books *In His Own Write* and *A Spaniard in the Works*. Critics have noted the same connection—physical myopia leading to imaginative language—in the life and work of James Joyce.

Nearsighted he may have been, but John was far from inactive. At age ten—the year before he drew the pictures that adorn the cover of his solo *Walls and Bridges* album—he won a swimming certificate for the Beginner's Event, a twenty-five yard course. The Liverpool Association of Schoolmasters gave him the award, and it would be a long time before Lennon again received any favorable recognition by teachers.

His third-year report card at Quarry Bank High School read, "Hopeless. Rather a clown in class. A shocking report. He is just wasting other pupils' time." Another report was even more succinct: "Certainly on the road to failure."

One of his prime confidantes from the earliest days, who became a member of his first band and would remain a close friend long after Lennon became famous, was Pete Shotton. Together, they created all kinds of trouble for their schoolmasters at Quarry Bank. But there was no question who had the dominant role in their friendship: John was always the leader, and he always attracted a group of followers.

He had a way of winning other boys' allegiance by his ability to take charge and do daring things that everyone else was afraid to do. At one church picnic when he was a little boy, John and his gang spied a group of monks, sitting quietly together. The grave old men inspired awe in the boys, and just to show his friends that he wasn't afraid of a bunch of monks, John dressed up as one and went to sit with them. The boy—if there is any truth to his legend, which sounds a bit like a ripoff of the story about the boy Jesus and the old men of the temple—talked with the monks while his gang, amazed at his bravery, rolled on the ground with laughter.

Learning to Play

While at Quarry Bank, John's uncle George gave him his first musical instrument—a harmonica, which a bus driver taught him to play. The boy quickly became interested in music, and stole a guitar from another boy at school. However, he returned it a few days later when he realized that he didn't know how to play it.

Julia Lennon had moved to a house near George and Mimi's, and she taught John the first two guitar chords he ever learned. But she did it on a four-stringed banjo, so when he first began playing guitar, his impulse was to ignore the two bass strings. The first song he learned to play was "That'll Be the Day" by Buddy Holly.

When John was seventeen years old, Julia was killed by a drunk driver—an off-duty policeman. No charges were ever brought. Lennon would later name his son Julian after his mother, and wrote the White Album song "Julia" for her.

Bitterness over his mother's death, combined with his interest in rock music, did little to improve John's performance in school. The principal of Quarry Bank, who nonetheless saw Lennon's potential, wrote this on the report card that John took with him to art school: ". . . I believe he is not beyond redemption and he could really turn out a fairly reasonable adult who might go far." Little did the principal know to what degree Lennon would live up to the Quarry Bank motto, which is translated from the Latin as "From this rough metal we forge virtue"—or, more symbolically, "Out of this rock you will find truth."

"The Guitar's All Right . . ."

"The guitar's all right," Aunt Mimi would tell John, "but you'll never make a living at it." When Queen Elizabeth awarded him the MBE (see **MBE**) in 1965 as recognition for the millions of pounds he had brought into the British economy, John gave it to Mimi for safekeeping. But before he did, he had the medal placed on a large plaque engraved with her famous words: "The guitar's all right, but you'll never make a living at it."

On the Beatles' mid-1964 Far East Tour, Aunt Mimi went with her nephew and the rock band she had once detested. Crowds in Hong Kong parted for her, chanting "John Mama, John Mama." She told an Australian

TV man that John had been bad at math in school, so the reporter asked him how he was able to count all the money that he had made. John explained, "I don't count it, I weigh it."

Lennon never had much of a concept of money, and the transition of the Beatles to the highest-paid act in the world did little to change this. He was exceedingly generous, purchasing a new home for Mimi and a super-market for Pete Shotton, his old Quarry Bank friend, at a cost of £20,000 ($50,000.) In the late 1960s, Lennon even bought an island off the coast of Ireland, called Dorinish, for a group of hippies to use as a commune.

The Return of the Father

Understandably, Lennon's generosity did not extend to his father, Alfred Lennon, who conveniently resurfaced in 1964. Freddie was working as a dishwasher when a woman told him about "I Want to Hold Your Hand," say-ing—according to his own account—that the singer sounded like him, "only not as good."

After trying unsuccessfully to contact his son, the elder Lennon went to the press, and the story immediately hit the tabloids that the Beatle had forsaken his poor, dear father now that he was rich and famous. Under pres-sure, John gave the old man a few pounds, though he had nothing to say to him. They had a few strained meetings, and that was it.

Freddie Lennon managed to secure a recording contract, and released a single, "That's My Life" / "The Next Time You Feel Important," on December 31, 1965. He earned a tidy sum from interviews as well, in which he managed to make it seem as though he, and not John, were the real star.

To hear Freddie tell it, the transatlantic ship on which he briefly worked in the 1940s could not have left the dock unless he were there to assure that all went well—an amazing claim, since as a steward he had noth-ing to do with actually sailing the ship. He also suggested that John had inherited his musical talent from him, and that John had always loved him more than he did his mother.

During this period, Freddie married a twenty-two-year-old woman, and at age sixty-five fathered a child. Presumably, then, Julian Lennon has an aunt or uncle a few years younger than he.

Meets Yoko

As a teenager, John's idea of the "perfect woman" had been Brigitte Bardot. But when he met his perfect woman on November 9, 1966, she was not at all like the French actress.

Lennon's friend John Dunbar had invited him to visit his Indica Gallery in London for a preview of a show the next day by a Japanese avant-garde artist named Yoko Ono. One of her exhibits was an apple, priced at £200, or $500. To John, this kind of massive put-on indicated a sense of humor as deep as the cosmos itself: somebody could pay £200 just to watch an apple rot.

Of course theirs was not the first famous relationship to begin over an apple, but one wonders: Was this *the* apple—the one that inspired Apple? Certainly there was something symbolic about the apple rotting, inasmuch as John meeting Yoko was one of the principal events that spelled the beginning of the end for the Beatles. Likewise it is worth noting that November 9, 1966, was the day when Paul supposedly died: once again, there is truth in the myth.

Dunbar introduced them, and instead of saying "Hello," Ono handed Lennon a card that said "Breathe." He liked that, too—but most of all he liked the fact that she wasn't a Beatles fan. In fact, she claimed she'd never even heard any of the Beatles' songs, which is about like saying one has never heard of Europe.

Two Virgins

Yoko, the daughter of a wealthy Japanese financier, was seven years older than her future husband. She had attended Sarah Lawrence College, which lists among its other famous alumni Linda Eastman, later Linda McCartney.

Some eighteen months passed between the first meeting of John and Yoko and the night when they consummated their relationship, an event that they commemorated with the recording of the *Two Virgins* album.

On that first night together—probably May 19, 1968—John's wife Cynthia was away, and he invited Yoko over to his house. They made a recording of what they called "Unfinished Music," a series of sounds in the style of his later "Revolution 9." After that, they made love and took photographs of themselves—front and back—with no more clothing on between them than John's necklace.

It may seem prurient to discuss these details, but John and Yoko certainly did. In fact, they chose to release the recordings as an album, with the nude pictures on the cover. Not surprisingly, Parlophone Records wanted nothing to do with it; therefore Lennon and Ono had to find other distributors for their album, *Unfinished Music No. 1—Two Virgins*. In Britain, it came out under Track Records, owned by the Who, and in the U.S. on the Tetragrammaton label.

The latter trademark seems odd in this context, since the Tetragrammaton is the term for the four-letter designation (*YHWH*) used by the ancient Israelites to signify the name of God. Certainly there was nothing reverential about *Two Virgins*, and the authorities were not amused by the cover, even though the record came packaged in brown paper.

The Naked Saint

It was the kind of unlistenable album that would have surfaced briefly on college radio, then died quickly . . . only it was John Lennon, and on the cover he was showing off—as he called it—"me prick" to the whole world. (Like most European men, by the way, Lennon was not circumcised, a fact evident from the infamous picture.)

Two Virgins began a period of Lennon-Ono nudity that did not earn them much sympathy from the "Blue Meanies" of the Establishment. Police in New Jersey seized 30,000 copies of *Two Virgins*, and the British government impounded 4,200 erotic lithographs of the couple. The latter came in sets of fourteen, which sold for $1,000.

As for Sir Joseph Lockwood, head of EMI, he was simply flabbergasted—from a marketing standpoint. "If you must have a naked man on the cover," he demanded, "why didn't you use Paul instead?"

Around this time, Yoko made an avant-garde film called *Self-Portrait*, a forty-two-minute study of John's penis. According to Ono, "the critics wouldn't touch it"—the film, that is.

Underneath the *Two Virgins* cover picture was a rather bizarre inscription:

> When two great saints meet it is a humbling experience.
> The long battle to prove he was a saint.
> —Paul McCartney

"Saint," however, was not the word that most people now used to describe John Lennon. His young female fans in particular felt betrayed, and one of them—under the name Rainbo—recorded a song called "John You Went Too Far This Time." Rainbo would later go on to fame under the name Sissy Spacek.

The British authorities, who had always had a look-the-other-way policy toward the Beatles, suddenly changed their attitude entirely, and on October 18, 1968, Scotland Yard policemen busted Lennon for possession of hashish. Then Yoko, pregnant with the child they planned to name John Ono Lennon II, had a miscarriage.

In early 1969, John and Yoko released their second collaboration, *Unfinished Music No. 2—Life with the Lions*. By now, the Beatles not only had a label of their own, Apple, but a subsidiary called Zapple, and *Life with the Lions* would become one of only two records bearing the Zapple label. The record itself, yet another series of beeps and squawks, had a much less controversial cover than its predecessor, though this one was certainly disturbing. It showed a haggard-looking John and Yoko in Yoko's hospital room just after her miscarriage.

A White Wedding

Under Yoko's influence, John became fascinated with the use of the color white. Although, contrary to the popular wisdom, the Beatles *never* intended to use the nude Lennon-Ono picture on the cover of their double album, John may have been the force behind the cover of the White Album.

Lennon held an exhibit of "White Art," entitled "You Are Here," at the Robert Fraser Gallery in London in July 1968. One of the objects at the exhibit, for instance, was a huge circular canvas, completely white except for the tiny letters reading "you are here." A group of amused art students left a rusty bicycle as a "contribution" to the exhibit. Lennon, apparently unaware of the sarcasm behind this gesture, promptly added it to the other works on display.

John stayed fascinated with white. On the cover of *Abbey Road*, more than a year after the art exhibit, he was photographed wearing a completely white suit. And in the meantime, he had a white wedding of sorts. John and Yoko were married on March 20, 1969, not so much for moral purposes as for the sake of staging an "event." The ceremony took place in a small chapel in Gibraltar, and the "two virgins" wore white. Yoko had on a white minidress, white wide-brimmed hat, white socks, and white tennis shoes, and the groom wore a white jacket, off-white pants, and white tennis shoes.

As Nicholas Shaffner pointed out in *Beatles Forever*, the Lennons did the opposite of the commonly accepted ritual, having a private wedding and a public honeymoon. Since they had already shared their first night together with the world, presumably there wasn't all that much left to hide. The happy couple honeymooned in public, and John recorded the entire saga on "The Ballad of John and Yoko."

Then, to provide the planet with further information about their nuptials, in November of that year the Lennons released their third (and mercifully last) piece of "Unfinished Music," the *Wedding Album*.

Wedding Album did not do as well as either of its two predecessors. *Life with the Lions* hit Number 174 on the U.S. *Billboard* charts, whereas *Two Virgins*, largely on the merits of its unique cover, soared all the way to 124th place before disappearing from sight. *Wedding Album*, which spent three weeks on the Top 200 Albums Chart (as compared with eight weeks apiece for the other two), never made it above Number 178.

The album itself, packaged along with press clippings, a plastic piece of wedding cake, and a copy of their marriage certificate, featured on Side One twenty-two minutes of the Lennons repeating each other's first names. Side Two consisted of the couple in their Amsterdam hotel room, talking to reporters and ordering food from room service. Yoko can also be heard saying the word "Peace" over and over while John fiddles with his guitar, playing portions of the tune that would turn into "Because."

John and Yoko display their marriage license. Archive Photos

Nuts for Peace and Other Curiosities

"The Ballad of John and Yoko" mentions fifty acorns tied in a sack. In June 1968, the couple planted two acorns at Coventry Cathedral in England "for peace." They called these "living art sculptures," naming one acorn "John by Yoko Ono," the other "Yoko by John Lennon, Sometime in May, 1968." Fans stole the acorns within a week after their planting, so the Lennons had two more buried, this time with a twenty-four-hour guard posted at the site.

On these two acorns, John and Yoko founded their "Nuts for Peace" campaign, which would come into full bloom soon after their wedding. Among the tenets of the "Nuts for Peace" ideology was that soldiers should be forced by worldwide agreement to take off their pants before going into battle. Another idea called for a new calendar: 1970 would become Year One A.P. (After Peace).

To inaugurate this new era of peace, John and Yoko collected fifty acorns and sent them to world leaders. An elderly woman sent the newlyweds two acorns that she had been saving for forty years.

On April 22, 1969, John had his middle named changed from Winston to Ono. This ceremony took place on the roof of the Apple Building on Saville Row in London. Lennon explained that since his wife had had to accept his surname, it was only fair that he adopt hers.

Around that time, the producers of a musical entitled "Jesus Christ," planned for St. Paul's Cathedral in London, asked John to play the title role. Lennon responded that he would only appear if Yoko could play Mary Magdalene. As it turned out, neither of the Lennons ended up performing in the show.

The End

Less than an hour before midnight on December 8, 1980, John Lennon was shot by Mark David Chapman in front of the Dakota Apartments. A lawyer later explained that Chapman "understood Lennon's words, but did not understand their meaning." On the way to Roosevelt Hospital, a policeman asked John, "Do you know who you are?" He could no longer talk, so he just nodded.

On the night of December 9, all across the world people held vigils in his honor. At Onkel Po, an exclusive jazz club in Hamburg, the city where Lennon's musical abilities had matured, "Starting Over" was played before the evening show. This was the first time that a rock song had ever been played before a performance there, and the audience stood in silent tribute. On the other side of the Wall that night, DDR-1, the station in East Berlin, broke its ban on rock 'n' roll and played one and a half hours of Beatles music.

It was fitting that the celebration of John Lennon's life should take place on December 9. Lennon was born on October 9, 1940—he later told

Jann Wenner that he was born in the ninth month of the year, which proved that counting was not among his talents—and one of his first songs was "One After 909." He met Yoko on November 9, 1966, released "Revolution 9," and in 1969 changed his name to John Ono Lennon—meaning that, as he pointed out, he and Yoko Ono Lennon would have nine Os between them. His "Number Nine Dream" reached Number Nine on the U.S. Billboard charts, and his son Sean was born on the same day of the year as he, October 9. Finally, Lennon died in a hospital with a nine-letter name on the corner of 59th Street and 9th Avenue.

Another eerie coincidence came to light on June 25, 1985. Mark Lindsay, scheduled to play John in NBC's *John and Yoko: A Love Story*, was fired from the picture when Yoko learned that Lindsay—born Mark David Chapman—happened to have the same name as the man who had killed her husband. Therefore she had him replaced with another Mark, Mark McGann.

The Lennon-McCartney Partnership

In 1971, during the worst days of squabbling among the former Beatles, John Lennon said in an interview with *Rolling Stone* that he and Paul McCartney had quit writing songs together in 1962. However, in his 1980 *Playboy* interview, he rescinded his earlier statement, saying that they had written many songs "Together, in the same room."

Although they began writing separately in 1965, the two wrote many songs together even to the end. Increasingly, however, Lennon and McCartney collaborations began to take on the form of "We Can Work It Out" or "A Day in the Life," in which one wrote the verses and the other the bridge. Even *Let It Be* features a true Lennon-McCartney song, "I've Got a Feeling," though by that point their differences in style make the song sound as if it were actually two separate compositions joined together. And in fact it is: Paul's "I've Got a Feeling" and John's "Everybody Had a Good Year."

The Momentous First Meeting
One of the world's greatest artistic partnerships began on the afternoon of July 6, 1957, at St. Peter's Church, Woolton Parish, Liverpool. This date has been the subject of dispute, and accounts have varied from June 15, 1956 (as stated in the group's authorized biography) to some time in 1958. It took Beatles authority Mark Lewisohn, who tirelessly pored over back issues of the *South Liverpool Weekly News* until he found an advertisement for a performance by the Quarry Men at Wooton Parish, to determine the correct date.

Some time before 8:00 p.m., the Quarry Men, who had played a show earlier that day in the back yard of the church, were setting up their instruments for a show in the church hall. It was then that former Quarry Men tea-chest bass player Ivan Vaughan introduced a friend from the Liverpool Institute, fifteen-year-old Paul McCartney, to the group's leader. Despite the fact that they were in church—few people have commented on the significance of the place where Lennon and McCartney first met—John Lennon happened to be drunk.

The younger boy told Lennon, almost seventeen, that he played guitar and sang. Then he proved it by belting out Eddie Cochran's "Twenty Flight Rock," and "Be Bop a Lula" by Gene Vincent. Several things impressed Lennon: the fact that Paul's voice reminded him of Little Richard's; the fact that he could tune a guitar (none of the Quarry Men could, and they had to pay a man to do it for them); and his ability to remember lyrics, which Lennon never could do. Paul even wrote down the words to the two songs he'd sung, and gave them to John. After a few weeks' consideration, Lennon sent his friend Pete Shotton round to see McCartney and invite him to join the group.

So momentous was this meeting for the future of music and culture that a whole book has been written about it, *The Day John Met Paul: An Hour-by-Hour Account of How the Beatles Began* by Jim O'Donnell (New York: Hall of Fame Books, 1994). The event was also parodied in the 1984 mock rockumentary *Spinal Tap,* when Nigel Tuffnel and David St. Hubbins recalled their own first meeting as schoolboys at a place called "Squatney."

In their early days as songwriters, Lennon and McCartney would write "Another original by John Lennon and Paul McCartney" at the top of a page before writing a song—this at a time when those names meant nothing to the world of music. They composed 100 songs together in their first year, many of which were accidentally thrown away years later. "Love Me Do" and "One After 909" were the only ones from this original crop ever recorded and released by the Beatles.

"Let It Be"

According to John Lennon, Paul McCartney's quasi-religious "Let It Be" was inspired by Simon and Garfunkel's "Bridge over Troubled Water"; in fact the latter song came out later.

The reference to Mary in "Let It Be," though it suggests the mother of Jesus, also indicates Paul's mother Mary, who died when he was in his early teens.

The Beatles released the song in two different versions. Version 1 came out as a single in 1970, backed with the bizarre "You Know My Name (Look Up the Number)." It appears also on *The Beatles 1967–1970* album. Version 2, longer than the first one, came out on the album of which it is the title track.

Let It Be

In a poll conducted by leading music critics and published in *Rock Critics' Choice: The Top 200 Albums,* all but one of the Beatles' true albums—as opposed to collections of singles—from *Rubber Soul* onward earned a top-twenty slot. The one exception was *Let It Be.*

Considered by most to be the Beatles' worst album, this was the only LP by the group not fully produced by George Martin, though Martin's absence is far from the only reason for this most dismal of discs.

After the excesses of earlier years, the Beatles intended to get back to their rock 'n' roll roots. Hence the original name of the project, *Get Back,* touted with the promise "The Beatles As Nature Intended." The making of the album would culminate in a concert, and a film would cover everything from the beginnings in the studio to the grand finale onstage.

Not one element of it—album, film, concert—turned out quite as they intended. The album was a mishmash, the concert a relatively minor affair, and the film the documentary of a group's breakup. It didn't even end up with the intended title, since by the time of its release the song "Get Back" was ancient history. So they called it *Let It Be,* and the title, with its implication of "leave it alone," took on an ironic significance.

The "Rooftop Concert"

With the exception of "Across the Universe" and "I Me Mine," the Beatles recorded *Let It Be* during the month of January 1969. After rehearsing in front of the cameras at Twickenham Studios in London for two weeks beginning on January 2, the group cut the album in the basement studios at Apple Records and ended with the "Rooftop Concert," an impromptu live performance on the roof of Apple Records, on January 30. During those four weeks, the group made twenty-four hours of music and ninety-six hours of film, leaving twenty-three and a half hours of music and ninety-four and a half hours of film unreleased. Much of the music appeared on bootleg albums during the next twenty-five years, and a few songs saw legitimate release on *The Beatles Anthology 3* in 1995.

The Beatles perform on the roof of the Apple Building on Saville Row, January 30, 1969.
Archive Photos/Express Newspapers

As for the "Rooftop Concert," the group had been unable to agree on a concert setting, so they settled on the low-key live performance documented in the film. Without prior notice to the public, the Beatles appeared on the roof of the Apple Building on Saville Row and performed five numbers: "Dig a Pony," "I've Got a Feeling," "One After 909," "Don't Let Me Down," and "Get Back." This performance takes place near the end of the film, as a crowd gathers on the street below, traffic slows to a standstill, and the police come in to stop the commotion. Except for "Don't Let Me Down," all of these live recordings appear on the album.

Spector Exhumes *Get Back*

As the Beatles lost interest in *Get Back*, the music lay dormant. Then in January 1970, Phil Spector, the American producer noted for his work in the early 1960s and for his "Wall of Sound" techniques—who incidentally accompanied them on their first trip to the U.S. in 1964—was asked to sift through the recordings and make an album out of them. The result was, to say the least, uneven.

There are raw, live-in-the-studio recordings such as "Get Back" or "For You Blue," while at the other end of the spectrum there are the four songs to which Spector added lush orchestral overdubs: "Across the Universe," "I Me Mine," "Let It Be," and "The Long and Winding Road." Finally, there are assorted "throwaways" such as "Maggie Mae" and "Dig It." The first song on the album, "Two of Us," promises the old Beatles that fans had known and loved, but *Let It Be* seldom delivers. It is a hodgepodge, an album that mentions farts and wet dreams along with the lofty visions of "Across the Universe" and the title track.

But Spector's poor work on *Let It Be* should be considered in light of several mitigating factors. The Beatles had already more or less broken up by the time he went to work on the album, and they didn't want to be bothered with it any more. Spector had the job of turning some of the Beatles' most lackluster output into a real album, and it wasn't an enviable task. Finally, on the night of the film's premiere, Spector and George Harrison began work on what would become both men's masterwork—Spector's as a producer, Harrison's as a musician—*All Things Must Pass*.

In spite of the fact that *Let It Be* fell far below the mark for a Beatles album, it was still good enough that in 1970 it won the Grammy Award for Best Original Score for Movie or TV.

With a Bang, Not a Whimper

In Britain, *Let It Be* originally came out in May 1970 along with a booklet full of color photos and dialogue from the film. November saw the album's rerelease in Britain, this time with a lower price and no booklet. The booklet, never available in America, became a major collector's item.

As for the Beatles, they went out with a bang rather than a whimper: even though *Let It Be* was the last album they released, it was not the last they recorded. In the summer of 1969, six months after making the music for what would become *Let It Be*, they recorded *Abbey Road*, a last hurrah.

* * * * *

Let It Be Song List

Title	Composer	Time
Side One		
Two of Us	McCartney	3:33
Dig a Pony*	Lennon	3:55
Across the Universe	Lennon	3:51
I Me Mine	Harrison	2:25
Dig It	Harrison-Lennon-McCartney-Starkey	0:51
Let It Be	McCartney	4:01
Maggie Mae	Trad., arr. by Harrison-Lennon-McCartney-Starkey	0:39
Side Two		
I've Got a Feeling	Lennon-McCartney	3:38
One After 909	Lennon	2:52
The Long and Winding Road	McCartney	3:40
For You Blue	Harrison	2:33
Get Back	McCartney	3:09

*"I Dig a Pony" on the U.S. version.

Liverpool

Chartered in 1207, Liverpool is a city of some 500,000 people perched on an estuary of the Mersey River—hence the name "Mersey Beat" for the music pioneered by the Beatles and propagated by lesser groups such as Gerry and the Pacemakers. People from New York are New Yorkers, and Dubliners come from Dublin, but "Liverpoolers" are known as Liverpudlians—or, in slang, "Scousers," a term coined in 1959.

In the 1980s, the City Public Relations Office of Liverpool began offering a Beatles Souvenir Pack, with a Beatles map of the city showing the birthplaces and childhood homes of all four, the schools they attended, and the places where they played their first concerts. The site of the Casbah Club, owned by former drummer Pete Best's mother, is there, as is the location of the Cavern Club on Mathew Street, long ago torn down. Included also are the Strawberry Field Salvation Army Home and Penny Lane. Information about such tours is available on the World Wide Web.

Aside from the Beatles and people associated with them (such as Brian Epstein), Liverpool has produced another famous—albeit fictional—citizen. The city was the birthplace of the prostitute immortalized in one of erotic fiction's early classics, *Fanny Hill*.

London

After Liverpool and Hamburg, London was the most important city in the early history of the Beatles.

Beatlemania began in the British capital in October 1963 (see **Beatlemania**), and in that month, the London *Times* first mentioned the group. Like its New York namesake, the *Times* is a prestigious paper whose attention can make a person's career. In its first Beatles-related story, the *Times* reported that forty policemen had been called out to control a crowd of fans attempting to buy tickets to the group's November 23 date in Newcastle.

But the much-maligned William Mann holds the *Times'* chief claim to fame in Beatles lore. In late 1963, Mann wrote a piece on the Beatles for the newspaper in which he praised the boys for "pediatonic clusters" in "This Boy" and "Aeolian cadences" in "Not a Second Time." Despite the fact that none of the Beatles had ever been to college or learned how to read music, Mann noted their use of "major tonic sevenths and ninths" and "flat submediant key switches." Many years later, John Lennon said that he still didn't know what an Aeolian cadence was, but he suspected it was some sort of tropical bird.

"Long Long Long"

"Long Long Long," the delicate and somewhat spooky melody by George Harrison that closes out Side Three of the White Album, is a religious piece rather than a love song.

By then, Harrison had clearly become quite serious about Hinduism; Paul McCartney was not, and he had a bottle of Blue Nun wine sitting on the Hammond organ he was playing. When he hit a high note, the bottle began to rattle. The sound is audible in the song's final buildup, just before the ghostly voice comes in and sings a wordless finale.

"Love Me Do"

"Love Me Do," recorded September 11, 1962, was the Beatles' first release through EMI/Parlophone, and their first recording with George Martin as producer. It was also one of the first songs Lennon and McCartney wrote, and as such it bears the imprint of their hero Buddy Holly, with a similarity between the main riff and that of Holly's "I'm Gonna Love You Too."

And of course "Love Me Do" was the first song recorded by the final configuration of the Beatles: Lennon, McCartney, Harrison, *and* Ringo Starr. But there's more to it than that.

When the group auditioned for Martin, Pete Best was still their drummer, but Martin wasn't impressed with Best's drumming. Since none of the other Beatles considered Best a team player anyway, they let him go, and brought in the former drummer for Rory Storme and the Hurricanes, Ringo Starr. But George Martin had never heard Ringo's drumming, and he had no intention of letting him audition on valuable studio time, so he brought in Andy White, a studio drummer.

Ringo later said that at the time he was afraid the other three might be trying to get rid of him, just as they had done to Pete. But he realized this wasn't so when they asked Martin if they could record another version of the song, with Ringo on drums. Therefore there are two versions of "Love Me Do." In the more common one, released on *Please Please Me* in Britain and *The Early Beatles* in America, White plays drums, with Ringo on tambourine. The other, more rare version, with Ringo on drums, appeared on the original "Love Me Do" / "P.S. I Love You" single in October 1962, and later came out on the American *Rarities* album.

"Love Me Do" reached No. 17 on the British charts, the worst performance of any Beatles single in Britain from then on.

"Love You To"

"Love You To," one of George Harrison's three *Revolver* compositions, seems to have been arbitrarily named. After all, the lyrics do not mention the title, which in any case should be "Love You *Too*." The working title of this, the first of three Beatles songs using only or primarily Indian instruments, was "Granny Smith"—like the apple. Given the working title of "I Want to Tell You" (see that entry), it appears that the apple concept was floating around the Beatles for a long time.

"Lucy in the Sky with Diamonds"

In spite of its surreal imagery and the fact that its initials are "LSD," John Lennon insisted that one of his most popular *Sgt. Pepper* tracks, "Lucy in the Sky with Diamonds," had nothing to do with drugs.

Lennon got the idea for the song, he said, from a painting his son Julian had done in school. The painting showed a girl against a black background with stars, and when Dad asked Julian who she was, the boy said she was his schoolmate "Lucy, in the sky, with diamonds."

The opening notes come not from a harpsichord, but from a Hammond organ whose sound Lennon and George Martin had altered.

In 1974, a team led by American paleoanthropologist Donald C. Johansen found the remains of a human female who had lived some 3.5 million years before in what is now the Afar region of Ethiopia. They named this "first" human Lucy after "Lucy in the Sky with Diamonds."

LSD (Lysergic Acid Diethylamide)

LSD may not be the subject of "Lucy in the Sky with Diamonds," but its use undoubtedly aided the already-creative mind of John Lennon in producing the song's striking imagery. By the time he wrote "Lucy" in early 1967, he had tripped plenty of times, and had made it a habit—as regular a habit as such a thing can be.

Discovered in 1938 by Albert Hoffman in Switzerland, the drug was still legal in the mid-sixties when Lennon and the others were taking it. By temporarily altering aspects of the brain's chemistry, particularly the presence of serotonin (which aids in filtering out background noise and focusing the attention on particular objects), LSD induces in users a sense that they have gained a glimpse of something beyond ordinary reality.

A Trip to/from the Dentist

Lennon and George Harrison were the first Beatles to do acid, in early 1965. (That's right—not 6 or 7, but 5!) John and his wife Cynthia, along with George and Patti Harrison, had gone to the house of a dentist friend of theirs, and were all having coffee when the dentist told them that they had better not leave. The four, thinking he was trying to get them into some sort of bisexual orgy, got out of there in a hurry. They were about to have one of the most memorable nights of their lives.

The Lennons and Harrisons went to a club located high up in a building. On the elevator ride to the top, they began noticing that the lights looked different, and that things didn't sound the way they normally should. The elevator ride seemed like it lasted for hours, and they thought they were trapped; so when the door opened, they felt relieved.

But now they were in the club with flashing lights and laughing faces. The four sat down at a table and tried to calm themselves. Someone came over and asked if he could sit by John, who told him, "Alright, as long as you don't talk to me."

Somehow they got home in George's car. Back at the Harrisons', Patti said she wanted to get out and play football. Eventually everyone went to bed except for John. He later recalled that he felt as though the living room were a submarine, with him guiding it. He also did a drawing that showed four faces saying "We all agree with you!"

Three years later, he may have been referring to this incident in "Revolution 9," where somewhere among the mishmash of sounds a voice—probably his—can be heard describing a visit to a "bloody dentist, only he wasn't a dentist."

And They All Turned On

The next day John and George discussed what had happened, and John said he liked it. They got Ringo to turn on, and finally Paul. John later said that he was sure "Got to Get You into My Life" was about tripping.

Just as all four later tried Eastern religion, but only George stuck with it, John continued with LSD after the others gave it up. Yet though he was the last to try it, the garrulous Paul characteristically became the first to admit to his use of the drug, in *Life* magazine in May 1967.

This occurred the same month that *Beatles Monthly* magazine gave a free subscription to a fan who wrote in to say that she was very happy that the Beatles hadn't gotten "mixed up in this drugs business. . . . I know if Paul took drugs I'd be worried sick, but I know he's too sensible."

"Maggie Mae"

"Maggie Mae," from *Let It Be*, was the only song released by the group after June 1965 not written by any of the Beatles. It was an old traditional Liverpudlian ditty, arranged by Lennon, McCartney, Harrison, and Starkey. Lime Street, mentioned in the thirty-nine-second piece, is Liverpool's "red-light district."

Like "One After 909," this smutty Liverpool tune is among both the Beatles' first and last songs. Not only is "Maggie Mae" on the group's swan song album, but on July 6, 1957, the day when Lennon and McCartney met, the Quarry Men may have performed it—oddly enough, at a church picnic.

Magical Mystery Tour (Film)

Part of the Beatles' charm lay in their naïveté, which allowed them to do things that others claimed could not be done. Sometimes, however, this naïveté proved more a liability than an asset, as with *Magical Mystery Tour*, their hour-long film for television shown just after Christmas 1967 on BBC-TV in Britain.

The Beatles themselves directed *Mystery Tour*, their third film, and they must have figured that, just as they'd broken all the rules in the studio, they could do the same behind the camera. The critical difference, however, was that they *knew* the rules of music before breaking them.

So they started off merrily, not bothering with anal-retentive details such as continuity. They wouldn't even allow themselves to be confined by the strictures of a script.

Four (or Five) Magicians—But No Plot

Certainly they didn't have anyone to stop them. Brian Epstein, the only "grown-up" who had much influence over their general affairs—though he was only thirty-two, just five years older than John—had died in August of that year. Therefore with no one to keep their various manias in check, nothing could dissuade the Fab Four . . . except perhaps their own fickle attentions. Even Paul, who had originated the idea of the film, grew bored with it partway through. During the tedious editing portion, when professionals tried to make sense of the Beatles' slapdash home movie, the group stood in the cutting room, singing songs with a toothless old bum from Soho who balanced a bottle of port on his head.

And a home movie was all it ever was, a pointless and plotless story of "four (or five) magicians" wandering aimlessly about the English countryside. The group had hoped to join elements of the Keystone Kops and Ken Kesey's Merry Pranksters (immortalized in *The Electric Kool Aid Acid Test* by Tom Wolfe), bringing together a bunch of oddball characters—including themselves—on a bus tour. It would all be very zany and impromptu-seeming, along the lines of what Richard Lester had achieved with their first two films.

The operative here is "impromptu-*seeming.*" In fact, every scene of *A Hard Day's Night* and *Help!* had been carefully crafted, every "spontaneous" moment scripted. It takes a lot of effort to seem effortless, as Michael Jordan or any other virtuoso can attest.

Inasmuch as there was any script at all, it came from whatever happened to be the desires of the moment. John, for instance, shot a scene of himself feeding spaghetti to a fat lady, which was based on a dream he'd had. At that point in the Beatles' career, dream-fulfillment seemed an appropriate metaphor. They were at the top of their game, a sensation well-expressed in Lennon's own "Baby You're a Rich Man."

It didn't seem that they could do anything wrong.

A Box Best Left Unopened

The Beatles' film aired on Boxing Day 1967. (At the 1997 MTV Music Video Awards, the Spice Girls—by then EMI's hottest property, as the Beatles had once been—told Kurt Loder that their film would come out on Boxing Day, to which the nonplussed Loder replied, "Yeah, that's a big holiday here too.") The day after Christmas, Boxing Day has nothing to do with boxing, but with *boxes*—of gifts, traditionally given to the poor on this day. It is also a major film-release date: hence the release of *Magical Mystery Tour* and, exactly three decades later, the Girls' *Spice World*.

Suffice it to say that *Magical Mystery Tour* is almost as banal and dreary as *Spice World,* the only difference between the relative importance of the groups involved. Had it been broadcast in color, *MMT* might have stood a chance; but in black and white, as the BBC showed it, the lack of visual stimulation forced viewers to confront the fact that—as Gertrude Stein said of Oakland—there was no *there* there.

The critics pounced. They had waited for the Beatles to make a mistake, and now they tore into *Mystery Tour* with relish: "chaotic," "appalling," "blatant rubbish." *MMT* became—to use a few anachronisms—the *Heaven's Gate*, the Sony Betamax, the USFL, the Edsel of the Beatles' career.

Opinions have mellowed with time, but not much. Originally the group had intended the film for release in the U.S., but after the bad reviews they shelved their plans.

Magical Mystery Tour (LP)

Nineteen sixty-seven is unique among all Beatles years in that the group released its entire output from that year on just two albums, *Magical Mystery*

Tour and *Sgt. Pepper's Lonely Hearts Club Band*. Compare this with 1964 or 1965, in which Capitol Records released four Beatles albums each, as well as numerous singles.

Actually, *Magical Mystery Tour* was not really an *album,* but a collection of assorted material. Side One contains the six songs from the *Magical Mystery Tour* film—music which fared much better with critics and fans than did the movie itself. "I Am the Walrus," from the film, came out as the B-side of a single. The A-side, "Hello Goodbye," is on Side Two, along with the contents of two other previously released singles: "Penny Lane" / "Strawberry Fields Forever" and "All You Need Is Love" / "Baby You're a Rich Man."

Minus the last four songs mentioned, *Magical Mystery Tour* came out as a double EP (extended play) in Britain on December 8, 1967. In the U.S., the entire album appeared as an LP in November 1967—one of the only times when American fans got something better than their British counterparts did. Finally in 1976, *MMT* came out as an LP in Britain.

The costumed figures on the cover of the album are John (the Walrus) in the foreground, with the Eggmen (from left to right—Paul, George, and Ringo) standing behind him.

* * * * *

Magical Mystery Tour Song List

Title	Composer	Time
Side One:		
Magical Mystery Tour	McCartney	2:48
The Fool on the Hill	McCartney	3:00
Flying	Harrison-Lennon-McCartney-Starkey	2:16
Blue Jay Way	Harrison	3:50
Your Mother Should Know	McCartney	2:33
I Am the Walrus	Lennon	4:35
Side Two:		
Hello Goodbye	McCartney	3:24
Strawberry Fields Forever	Lennon	4:05
Penny Lane	McCartney	3:00
Baby You're a Rich Man	Lennon-McCartney	3:07
All You Need Is Love	Lennon	3:57

Maharishi Mahesh Yogi

Devotees supposedly don't call him "the," but he is known as *the* Maharishi Mahesh Yogi to most of the world.

Born in India in 1911 as Mahesh Brasad Warma, he got his degree in physics and worked in a factory. Then in his thirties he came under the influence of Swami Brahmananda Saraswati, Jagadguru, Bhagwan Bahnkaracharya of Jyotir Math. That's all one name—but fortunately the mentor was commonly known as Guru Dev. (As in "Jai guru deva om," from "Across the Universe.")

In 1956, Warma adopted the title Maharishi, or "great sage," and after Guru Dev died, he moved to Los Angeles and started the Spiritual Regeneration League. In the process, he established a cultic offshoot of Hinduism called Transcendental Meditation, or TM, which is based on the use of meditation to achieve inner peace. Finding little success in America, the Maharishi moved to London, and again, nothing much happened for him . . . until August 24, 1967.

On that date, he was conducting what a London newspaper ad claimed would be his final lecture before he retired to "a life of silence." Presumably this was the equivalent of furniture stores that hold perpetual going-out-of-business sales; either that, or after Patti Harrison introduced him to her husband and his bandmates, retirement didn't look so good after all.

Going to See the Plan in Bangor

The Maharishi invited the Beatles to his Spiritual Regeneration League Center in Bangor, Wales, and a day after meeting him, they were on their way. On the train to Bangor were the four Beatles, Paul McCartney's girlfriend Jane Asher, Patti Harrison, Maureen Starkey, and Mick Jagger. Despite the fact that the authorities had held up the train so that all the Beatles' party would be able to make it—a courtesy normally reserved only for royalty—Cynthia Lennon didn't make it on board because the police refused to believe she was really John's wife.

The trip to Bangor was the first excursion the group made without their manager, Brian Epstein, or their assistants, Mal Evans and Neil Aspinall. But they were so accustomed to going places with other people to look after them that they had long ceased to carry their own money—a habit common to royalty and semi-royal figures such as John F. Kennedy.

While in Bangor they went to a Chinese restaurant with Jane, Patti, Maureen, Jagger, and biographer Hunter Davies, and upon finishing the meal, they realized that no one had enough cash to pay. They were used to being in London, where no one would have *expected* them to pay, but the

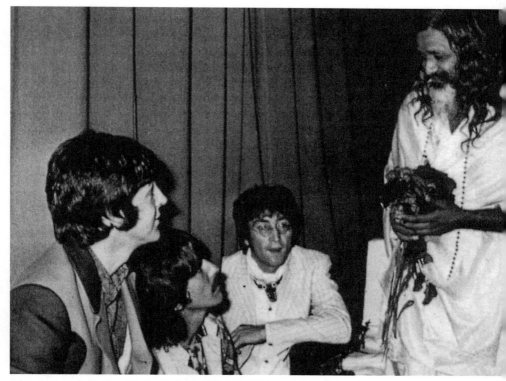

Paul, George, and John with the Maharishi Mahesh Yogi. Archive Photos

proprietors of a Chinese restaurant in northwestern Wales weren't exactly "with it," and they did expect them to pay. After a few minutes of searching, George discovered that he had some money stashed in his sandal, and the group paid the bill.

The Beatles cut their stay in Bangor short when they learned that Brian Epstein had died of an accidental overdose of sleeping pills. The Maharishi offered them comforting platitudes, which John Lennon shared in the utmost of seriousness with a TV reporter at the time. The guru tried to convince them to stay and finish the course in Bangor, but they rushed back to London.

It was a significant turning point for the group: they had just lost the man who helped get them where they were, and now they were about to accept the guidance of a new teacher.

Disillusionment in Rishikesh

The Beatles made arrangements for themselves and their significant others to attend the Maharishi's meditation school, an ashram or spiritual retreat in Rishikesh, India. The group took off for India on February 21, 1968, leaving a single, "Lady Madonna" / "The Inner Light," to tide the world over in their absence.

Studying with them in Rishikesh were actress Mia Farrow, Mike Love of the Beach Boys, and Donovan, as well as Ms. Farrow's sister and an unnamed American businessman. The last two were immortalized, respectively, in Lennon's songs "Dear Prudence" and "The Continuing Story of Bungalow Bill."

For the group members, it was a wonderful opportunity to get away from the pressures of their careers, and amidst the breathtaking mountain scenery, they felt their energy return. Pretty soon they were writing songs again, composing the bulk of what would become the White Album. And it wasn't long before they tired of the Maharishi and his ashram.

None of the four Beatles stayed for the entire six-week course. Ringo, who had brought several cases of baked beans in case he didn't like the food, left first, saying that the place reminded him of Butlin's, a British holiday camp. Paul stayed long enough to grow a beard, following Mike Love's example—as did the other two—but he soon departed as well.

Now the two more extroverted, fun-loving Beatles were gone; the two more serious and introspective ones took longer to see the light. John tried to involve himself as much as possible in life at the ashram, and even wore a turban for a while, but said that it made him want to make "cripple faces." He became disillusioned with the Maharishi when he learned that the alleged holy man's interests in Mia Farrow were not exactly of a spiritual nature. When confronted with this, the Maharishi offered only evasive answers, so John decided that he'd had enough. This left only George, who bade farewell to the Maharishi and Transcendental Meditation (but not to orthodox Hinduism) soon afterward.

John later told a journalist that on their way to the airport from the ashram, his and Cynthia's taxi broke down. With the sun about to set, they were stuck on a highway in the middle of a foreign country, a crowd beginning to gather around their cab. Somehow the Lennons were able to hitchhike to the airport in Delhi, but John later said he felt at the time that the Maharishi had put a spell on them as punishment for leaving his ashram.

Lennon's "Sexy Sadie" is a scathing attack on the man he dubbed the "Maharoonie."

Charles Manson

Critic William Mann in 1963 became the first major figure to see things in the Beatles' music that weren't really there (see **London**), but he was not the last. It was a phenomenon that arose from the diminishing of Christian belief in the West as a whole: People were looking for their gods elsewhere, as John Lennon noted in his infamous "We're more popular than Jesus" comments. Whatever the cause, many found something more than mere entertainment in the Beatles' music; it became instead a form of enlightenment.

In no instance was this misguided belief system more sinister than in the case of Charles Milles Manson. Manson, who often referred to himself as "Man's Son" (i.e., the Son of Man, as Jesus was called), claimed god status not only for the Beatles, but for himself. Because of hidden messages he claimed to have received from the White Album, seven adults and one unborn child died.

A 5'2" Messiah with Bad Teeth

Ironically, Manson's very early life was not unlike that of John Lennon. He lived for a time with a strict aunt and uncle, and his mother—who was more like a fun-loving older sister—dropped in occasionally to see him. Born "No Name Maddox," Manson was raised in Ohio, Kentucky, West Virginia, and Indiana, during which time his mother stayed with a man named Manson long enough for the boy to adopt his name.

He spent half his life prior to 1967 in reform schools, jails, and prisons. While in prison after a series of armed robberies and other crimes, Manson learned to play guitar and heard about a group with a hit song called "I Want to Hold Your Hand." He believed he could produce better music if given a chance, and began writing songs. In fact, the Beach Boys' *20/20* album (1969) contained "Never Learnt Not to Love," cowritten by Manson and Dennis Wilson; and still later, in 1993, Guns 'n' Roses cut his "Look At Your Game, Girl."

Also while in prison, Manson absorbed various "ideas" from Nazism, Satanism, and the perverse "Process Church" faith of Robert DeGrimston. (The latter's adherents later included David "Son of Sam" Berkowitz.) The semiliterate Manson also claimed to have been influenced by Friedrich Nietzsche, though this is unlikely, and selectively read certain apocalyptic passages in the Bible, particularly the Book of Revelation. It was certainly a motley array of notions, even more strange when combined with the lyrics of the Beatles, as it soon would be.

Upon his release from prison at age thirty-three in 1967, Manson began forming his "Family," most of whom were women. Despite the fact that he was only 5'2" and had bad teeth, Manson exerted a Svengali-like magnetism over a certain type of disaffected young girl, and he used his female adherents to attract men to the growing cult with promises of unlimited sex.

The Family traveled all over the state of California, and earned the dislike even of hippies, who rejected Manson's credo: "Wrong is right." For more than a year, the members of the Family immersed themselves in drugs, orgies, and an occasional robbery, but this all changed when Manson heard the White Album.

The Hidden Meaning of the White Album

To Manson, the Beatles were using the White Album as a means of conveying information to him about a massive racial war called "Helter Skelter," which *he* would bring about. The five songs he considered most significant were "Blackbird," "Piggies," "Helter Skelter," "Revolution 1," and "Revolution 9."

Long oppressed by the Piggies (rich white people), blacks (the Blackbird) would "rise [the actual lyric is *fly*] into the night" and slaughter their oppressors. This would bring on Helter Skelter, a war like the Armageddon depicted in Revelation.

Not surprisingly, since he admired Hitler, Manson believed that blacks were inferior to whites. Therefore once they defeated the Piggies, they would need him and his Family to show them what to do with the world. Manson would make them slaves again, and he and his Family—who he equated with the 144,000 spoken of in Revelation 7:4—would rule and reign.

As Manson saw it, the Beatles knew what was about to happen. On "Revolution 1," while apparently telling him to count them out, they were subliminally instructing him to count them in (see **"Revolution 1"**), and on "Revolution 9" they approximated Helter Skelter in aural form. *Revelation 9* spoke of four long-haired angels, who Manson knew were the Fab Four. During Helter Skelter, Manson, the Beatles, and the 144,000 would flee to a labyrinth that he claimed lay beneath Death Valley; there they would wait until the war was over, and emerge to establish world control.

Manson was eager for these things to come about, and when John Lennon in "Revolution 1" asked to "see the plan," he knew Lennon was addressing *him*. In fact the album is rife with songs expressing a desire for completion through another person, who Manson believed to be himself; thus in "I Will," "Don't Pass Me By," "Yer Blues," "Long Long Long," and particularly "Honey Pie," he heard pleas directed toward himself. The latter song, according to Manson, indicated that Christ had returned to the Earth and was living in Hollywood. The Beatles loved Jesus, but were too lazy to go and find him, so they begged him to sail across the Atlantic to be with them.

Manson and a few of his girls went so far as to attempt to contact the Beatles at Apple through phone calls and letters, none of which received a reply.

Manson became impatient for Helter Skelter to begin, and in spite of their coy behavior, he knew that the Beatles were ready too. But, he decided, the Blackbird needed a little help. If several rich white people were murdered, with militant slogans painted in their blood, the police would attribute the killings to Black Panthers or a similar group. Whites would bring massive reprisals against the black community, and the backlash would cause Helter Skelter to "[come] down fast."

Helter Skelter Comes Down

Late on the night of August 8, 1969, Charles "Tex" Watson, Patricia Krenwinkel, and Susan "Sadie Mae Glutz" Atkins carried out Manson's orders. They shot, stabbed, and beat to death Sharon Tate, actress and wife of director Roman Polanski, along with her unborn baby; Jay Sebring, hairdresser; Abigail Folger, coffee heiress; Voytek Frykoswki, Ms. Folger's friend; and Steven Earl Parent, student.

The next night, Manson ordered the murders of two more rich "Piggies": Leno LaBianca, grocery owner, and his wife Rosemary, herself a successful businesswoman. After stabbing their victims dozens of times, Watson, Krenwinkel, and Leslie Van Houten fed the LaBianca's dogs because they did not believe in cruelty to animals. Police found the words "Political Piggy," "Pig," "Rise," and "Helter Skelter" written in blood at the scenes of both crimes.

One White Album song had a special, ironic significance for the Manson Family. Manson had renamed Susan Atkins "Sadie Mae Glutz" long before "Sexy Sadie," and when he first heard the song, he took it as further confirmation that he and the Beatles were in sync. But in the end, his Sadie, just like the one in the song, "laid it down for all to see." With the police still desperately searching for leads, she landed in jail on auto-theft charges, and during this time she bragged about her escapades to a couple of fellow prisoners. The two women notified the authorities, who soon arrested Manson and the others.

Still, without the brilliant work of prosecutor Vincent Bugliosi— who told the story of the murders, investigations, and trial in his best-selling *Helter Skelter*—it is unlikely that Los Angeles County would have been able to obtain a conviction. The connection with the White Album, which established "motive," was just too bizarre, too tenuous, for most people to readily accept. In fact, perhaps the toughest part of Bugliosi's job was convincing the jury that Manson believed he had received his "instructions" from a record album. To this end, he introduced the White Album as evidence.

It was the longest trial in American history up to that time, and—until the O. J. Simpson case eclipsed it a quarter-century later—the most famous and scandalous trial of L.A. history. Manson, Watson, Krenwinkel, Atkins, and Van Houten received death sentences, commuted to life imprisonment after California abolished the death penalty. Never once, in the long months of investigation before Susan Atkins talked, did the LAPD consider the scenario that Manson had claimed would be their first supposition: that the murders were racially motivated, committed by black revolutionaries.

Six Degrees of Sinister

A bizarre footnote to this story links its principal characters in an eerie confluence of events. In 1967, the year that Manson began forming his Family and the Beatles reached the apogee of their career, Sharon Tate's husband, Roman Polanski, directed the first major film on the subject of demonic possession. *Rosemary's Baby* starred Mia Farrow, and was partially filmed in the Dakota Apartments in New York City.

The next year, Farrow attended the Maharishi's meditation school in India along with the Beatles, at which time they wrote most of the songs for the White Album. Manson—on the basis of a bizarre misinterpretation of the White Album—would cause the murder of Polanski's wife in 1969. Eleven years after *that,* John Lennon was living in the Dakota Apartments when he was shot by another deranged Beatlemaniac.

Marijuana

Although they did not actually try it until 1964, the Beatles first encountered marijuana more than two years before.

The group—Lennon, McCartney, Harrison, and Pete Best at that time—were in London in January 1962 for an audition with Decca Records, the first of many unsuccessful record company tryouts. The four were walking down Charing Cross Road when they met two men smoking a strange-smelling substance, which they offered to share. The boys fled.

Bob Dylan introduced the Beatles to the wicked weed in 1964, and they began to use it regularly—even, according to legend, on the day they received their MBEs (see **Bob Dylan**). Supposedly they sneaked into the loo at Buckingham Palace and had a toke, but in the *Beatles Anthology* TV special, Paul said they only smoked a cigarette. That's certainly a lot easier to believe: Meeting the Queen of England would already be a strained enough affair without pot-induced paranoia.

According to John Lennon, the group's use of marijuana as a "mind-expanding" drug reached its peak with *Rubber Soul*.

George Martin

In the fifty-two weeks of 1963, a George Martin-produced record was Number One in Britain for thirty-seven of those weeks. No other producer has ever equaled that feat.

Martin produced all of the Beatles' albums except *Let It Be*, in the process earning himself a reputation as perhaps the greatest producer of the 1960s. Without Martin, *Sgt. Pepper* would not have been the masterwork it was: His musical training gave the Beatles' creativity the cohesiveness and sense of direction that it needed.

None of the Beatles could read written music. Paul McCartney learned a bit during the production of "Eleanor Rigby" in 1966, but his was at best a passing knowledge. George Harrison learned just enough Indian notation, which is not at all like its Western counterpart, in order to transcribe such compositions as "The Inner Light" for the Indian musicians who worked with him. In the main, however, the group members had to rely on Martin to help them realize their visions for songs ranging from "Yesterday" to "I Am the Walrus."

Martin, a Royal Air Force pilot during World War II, played a variety of instruments. These included the oboe—listed in the *Guinness Book* as the world's most difficult instrument—which he had learned from the mother of Paul McCartney's future girlfriend, Jane Asher. His musical experience made him a natural as a producer, but EMI chose to put him behind the controls at Parlophone, one of its least successful labels. There he produced comedy records for Spike Milligan, Peter Sellers, and others. If he had not had such a relatively obscure position, however, he might not have been paired up with the insignificant group that signed on with EMI in 1962.

The Fifth Beatle

As it turned out, Martin and the Beatles were made for each other, and together they would have some of their best years. The staid, conservative and always elegant Martin could not have contrasted more with the group in terms of outward appearances, however. When he and the Beatles first

The Beatles and friends at the George V Hotel in Paris, 1963. (Left to right): *Mrs. George Martin, Ringo Starr, George Harrison, Paul McCartney, Brian Epstein, John Lennon, and George Martin.* Archive Photos/Frank Driggs

met, he showed them around the studio where they would record "Love Me Do," and afterward told them, "Let me know if there's anything you don't like." George quipped, "Well, for a start, I don't like your tie."

Also in 1962, Martin took John Lennon out to dinner at an expensive restaurant. During the meal, the waiter brought mange-tout peas (sugar peas), which John had never seen before. Martin explained what they were, and suggested that Lennon try them. John replied, "Alright, but put them over there, not near the food."

On the night of *Magical Mystery Tour*'s release, before they knew it would be savaged by the critics (see **Magical Mystery Tour [Film]**), the Beatles held a costume party to celebrate the film's opening. Martin and his wife Judy came dressed as Prince Phillip and Queen Elizabeth, and Martin later said that he heard someone say, "My God! I didn't think they'd get *them!*"

"Maxwell's Silver Hammer"

"Maxwell's Silver Hammer," by Paul McCartney, was one of John Lennon's least favorite McCartney compositions. The song appears not only on *Abbey Road,* but in the film *Let It Be* as well. It is probably the only song by a major rock artist that uses a hammer struck against an anvil as part of its percussion, and it is one of only a few Beatles songs with a four-part harmony—on the last line.

MBE (Member of the Order of the British Empire)

The Order of the British Empire system, established by King George V in 1917, created the first order of knighthood in British history that could be awarded to men *or* women. It has five classes, with Knights and Dames Grand Cross (GBE) at the top, and Member of the British Empire (MBE) at the fifth level.

Citing the healthy boost that their record sales had given the British economy, George's granddaughter, Queen Elizabeth II, honored the Beatles with the award of MBE on June 12, 1965. Allegedly the boys sneaked a quick joint before going in to see the Queen, though this is unlikely (see **Marijuana**). In any case, at that point they were pretty much perpetually stoned anyway. When she asked them how long they had been together, Ringo replied "Forty years."

Several war heroes returned their MBEs when they found out that "vulgar nincompoops" (as one of them called the Beatles) were receiving the same award.

Almost two years after the awards, the Beatles dusted off their MBEs and pinned them to the uniforms they wore on the cover of *Sgt. Pepper's Lonely Hearts Club Band.*

In November 1969, John Lennon returned his MBE as a protest against the wars in Vietnam and Biafra and, he said, because of the bad airplay his single, "Cold Turkey," had gotten. The medal wound up in a palace drawer, and Lennon later expressed regret that he had reduced the impact of his protest by mentioning "Cold Turkey" along with considerably more important issues.

In the 1990s, Paul McCartney got a leg up on the others when he became a full-scale knight—*Sir* Paul McCartney.

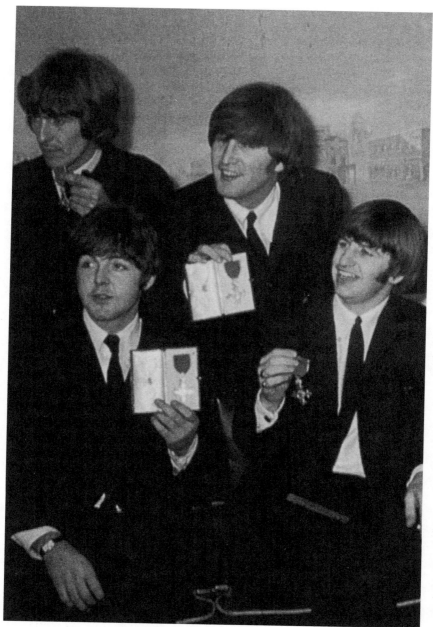

The Beatles display their MBEs in 1965. Archive Photos/Popperfoto

James Paul McCartney, Bass Guitarist for the Beatles

Born: June 18, 1942, at Walton Hospital, Liverpool.

Family: Father, Jim McCartney, factory worker; Mother, Mary Mohin McCartney, nurse. One younger brother, Michael, a musician who later performed under the name of Mike McGear because he didn't want to capitalize on his brother's fame.

Schools: Stockton Wood Primary, Joseph Williams Primary, Liverpool Institute.

Married: Linda Eastman, photographer, on March 12, 1969 (died April 1998).

Children: One stepdaughter, Heather, by Linda's first marriage; two daughters, Mary and Stella; and one son, James.

In spite of the fact that he had the most ready-made "girl appeal" of the four Beatles, Paul McCartney was always much more than a pretty face. With the Beatles and afterward, he played a variety of instruments in addition to the bass—itself not his original instrument, since he only took it over when Stu Sutcliffe left the band—and on his *McCartney* and *McCartney II* albums, in fact, he played *all* the instruments.

As a songwriter, he penned the Beatles' most successful single, "Hey Jude," and the most-recorded song in history, "Yesterday," with 1,186 cover versions between the time of its release in 1965 and January 1, 1973. He gained a listing in *The Guinness Book of World Records* as World's Most Successful Songwriter, with 43 million-selling songs for the Beatles or Wings between 1962 and January 1, 1976. He received the first Guinness Award for Most Honored Composer and Performer in Music in October 1979, and earned the *Guinness Book* entry for Most Gold Records (63—42 with the Beatles and 21 with Wings). He also has had the most songs in the American Top Ten, 89 in the twenty-year period between January 1964 and January 1984.

Music in the Gene Pool

Paul was the only Beatle with a musical parent. His father, Jim McCartney, played in a ragtime band, the Masked Melody Makers, in 1919, when he was just seventeen years old. This being long before the era of political correctness, the group started out wearing blackface masks, colored with a cheap dye. But they were so hot by halftime of their first show that the heat caused the dye to run down their faces. After that, they dispensed with the masks.

Newlyweds Paul and Linda McCartney pose with Heather, Linda's daughter from a previous marriage, at Kennedy Airport on March 17, 1969. AP/Wide World Photos

In the early days of cinema, before the "talkies," movie theaters often employed bands to provide a musical backdrop for films. Jim Mac's Jazz Band, a later Jim McCartney group, played at the first local showing of *The Queen of Sheba*. Unsure of what to play when, they winged it. During a chariot race scene, they struck up "Thanks For the Buggy Ride," and when the queen was dying they went into "Horsy Keep Your Tail Up."

Realizing that there was not much money for beginners in show business, Jim turned to more stable means of employment. He married at age forty, and he and his wife Mary had a son, Paul, within a year.

Getting Around Father

From earliest childhood, Paul displayed a talent for hiding his true intentions—usually behind a smile. When whipped by his parents, he would show no emotion; later on, though, he would go into their bedroom and make a tiny rip at the bottom of their lace curtains.

Jim McCartney wanted his young son to join the Liverpool Cathedral Choir. But Paul had no interest in music or singing, so he deliberately strained his voice until it broke. As a grown man, he would deliberately strain his voice so that he *could* sing "Oh! Darling" the way he wanted it to sound.

When he was a teenager, Paul had already become quite a flashy dresser, much to his father's dismay. Jim got sick of seeing his boy in impossibly tight pants ("drain-pipes," they were called, a popular teddy boy style at the time), so he ordered Paul to submit all new trousers for his approval. Once Jim had okayed a pair of pants, Paul would go out and have them tailored the way he wanted them.

Grief As a Catalyst

McCartney was close to his parents, and became the only Beatle to write a song both for his father ("When I'm Sixty Four") and his mother ("Let It Be"). The reverential tone of "Let It Be" is fitting, because it memorialized a woman who existed by then only in memory: Mary McCartney had died from breast cancer when Paul was fourteen. The same disease, in fact, would claim his wife, Linda, the other most important woman in his life, more than forty years after the loss of his mother.

As with John, whose own mother died about a year after Paul's did, his grief proved to be a catalyst for musical development. The first instrument Paul learned to play was the trumpet, and when he was in his early teens, his family acquired a piano. Jim McCartney bought it from the North End Music Stores, whose owners' son, Brian Epstein, would one day become the Beatles' manager.

Also in his early teens, Paul bought his first guitar for £15 ($36), and at first he thought there was something wrong with him because he couldn't learn any of the chords. But then he realized that since he was left-handed, he was holding the instrument the "wrong" way. So he simply reversed all the strings, and everything went all right after that. Later, McCartney's left-handedness would give the Beatles a unique appearance onstage, with two guitars pointing one way and one pointing another.

Like the young George Harrison, who practiced until his fingers bled, Paul practiced guitar constantly—even on the toilet. By now he and George, who he knew from school at Liverpool Institute, had joined the Quarry Men, a skiffle group led by John Lennon. Britain's Elvis Presley of skiffle (so to speak) was Lonnie Donegan, whose "Rock Island Line" started the craze, and Paul saw Donegan do something that had a tremendous impact on his ideas of how the fans should be treated.

At age fourteen, Paul went to see the performer during lunch hour. Donegan was late in arriving, and when he got there he wrote notes for all the factory girls, explaining that he was the reason they were late getting back to work. From this incident, Paul later said, he learned that a performer must always respect and honor the people who buy his work.

Later, even at the height of the Beatles' fame, Paul had a reputation for being the most friendly toward the fans. And just as John Lennon lived up to his school's motto, so McCartney fulfilled that of his own: "Not for ourselves only but for the good of the world."

A Favorite of the Girls

By the time Paul was twenty, Jim McCartney had already gotten so used to his son's topsy-turvy life that he would nonchalantly edge his way through the crowds of screaming girls at the Cavern Club and bring Paul his dinner.

In May 1963, Paul was very nearly killed. He and the others (all except John) were vacationing at the summer home of the father of their Hamburg friend Klaus Voorman, in the Canary Islands. Paul swam out too far, got carried away by the tide and, though he somehow made it back to shore, could easily have drowned. Later that year, McCartney caught gastric flu, and this time the fans got involved: the November 13, 1963, *Daily Mail* headlines read "Teenagers Weep for the Beatle with a Temperature."

In 1963 Paul met and started dating Jane Asher, the daughter of a wealthy London doctor. He even lived for a while in her parents' home, and it was there, at the Ashers' piano, that Lennon and McCartney wrote "I Want to Hold Your Hand."

Jane Asher's mother had, many years before, taught the young George Martin how to play the oboe. And her brother Peter performed in the duo Peter and Gordon, who scored a hit with Lennon and McCartney's "World

Without Love" in the early 1960s. Later on Peter Asher became a producer for James Taylor, Linda Ronstadt, and others.

As with everyone around the Beatles, Jane found herself a celebrity, not for her acting, but for her boyfriend. A letter he wrote to her was framed in a $1,200, twenty-three-karat gold frame and displayed in a Cleveland department store, that city's *Plain Dealer* reported in 1965. And since she advertised Breck Shampoo on television, many of Paul's female fans began using Breck too.

Those same fans kept an almost constant vigil outside his house in the Cavendish district of London. McCartney's home became a favorite gathering place for fans, not only because Paul was the most watchable Beatle, but also because of its proximity to Abbey Road Studios, where the Beatles did most of their recording. One of the girls later recalled, "We told him once that we could see him from the back of the house, sitting on the loo. [British slang for toilet.] We stood him on a flowerpot to show him we were telling the truth."

They also discovered where he kept his house key, and they often made "tours" through his home while he was away. But they seldom took anything of value, and then only a shirt: just being inside Paul McCartney's house was a big enough prize. Paul usually stopped to chat with them if he had time. Once, when he forgot his gate key, one of the girls showed him how to open the gate by kicking it a certain way.

Casting a Long Shadow

During the last days of the Beatles, the unhappy period he documented in "You Never Give Me Your Money," Paul called up the chairman of EMI, Sir Joseph Lockwood, to discuss a problem. "Sir Joe," as the Beatles called him, wielded enormous power, and was used to having other people cater to him. But it was a measure of the Beatles' power that in Paul's case, Sir Joe asked him to wait just a minute, then got into his Rolls Royce and rode over to McCartney's to discuss things personally.

In 1969, while visiting Portugal, Paul wrote a song for the bandleader at the hotel where he was staying. The song, "Penina," performed by Carlos Mendes, came out in America and Britain for the first time on the 1979 album *The Songs Lennon and McCartney Gave Away*.

Paul's career has overlapped those of several other well-known performers. During the Beatles era, he played on songs by Badfinger, Donovan, the Beach Boys, and James Taylor. (In the latter case, on "Carolina in My Mind" from Taylor's first album.) Also around that time—long before their mid-1970s successes—he sang and played bass and drums on "My Dark Hour" by the Steve Miller Band. In the 1980s, he performed with Stevie Wonder and Michael Jackson; and later with Elvis Costello. On *Flaming Pie* in 1997, he teamed up with Steve Miller again, this time with Miller as the guest.

A longtime admirer of Buddy Holly, McCartney for a time owned the rights to Holly's songs, along with the rights to the "Ramblin' Wreck from Georgia Tech" fight song.

Losing Linda

McCartney referred to Tucson, Arizona, in "Get Back," it is said, because he had gone there some time in 1968 to consider buying a ranch. He apparently did own a ranch in the Tucson area, and it was there that his wife Linda died of breast cancer thirty years later.

In an ironic twist for someone whose own "death" had been the cause of rumors during the late 1960s, the death of Paul's wife stirred up talk. A spokesperson originally said that she had passed away in Santa Barbara, California, and when the true place of death was revealed, this raised suspicions. As it turned out, the family was only trying to get some privacy.

According to Paul's own statement, in their entire married life, he had only spent one night apart from Linda.

"Mean Mr. Mustard"

John Lennon wrote "Mean Mr. Mustard," from Side Two of *Abbey Road*, after he read in the paper about a "mean guy" who hid his money somewhere on his body—only in real life it wasn't up his nose.

The song features Paul McCartney on fuzz bass guitar for the first time in almost four years. He had last played the instrument on "Think for Yourself" from *Rubber Soul*.

"Michelle"

Paul McCartney wrote "Michelle," one of his most popular *Rubber Soul* tracks, for the daughter of an American millionaire. John Lennon helped him with the "I love you" chorus, which Lennon said was inspired by Nina Simone's "I Put a Spell on You."

Part of "Michelle" is in French, one of the first uses of a foreign language on a pop song by an English-speaking group. *"Ma belle"* translates as "My beautiful [one]," and *"Sont les mots qui vonts tres bien ensemble"* means "These are words that go together well." Not surprisingly, the song reached Number One in France.

"Mother Nature's Son"

Paul McCartney wrote—and apparently played all instruments on the recording of—"Mother Nature's Son," from Side Three of the White Album.

The impetus for the song came from a lecture by the Maharishi on the subject of nature. After hearing the same lecture, John wrote "I'm Just a Child of Nature," which he later recorded and released under the name "Jealous Guy" on his solo *Imagine* album more than three years later.

Movies

The Beatles made five films: *A Hard Day's Night* (1964), *Help!* (1965), *Magical Mystery Tour* (1967), *Yellow Submarine* (1968), and *Let It Be* (1970). These involved a variety of categories: in order, there were two features—one black-and-white, one color; a TV movie (or maybe just an overblown home movie); a cartoon; and a documentary.

In contrast to their string of hit albums, only two of these were really successful: the first, a low-budget black-and-white romp, and the next-to-last, a color-drenched psychedelic cartoon. Their involvement in these projects ranged from almost total creative control in *Magical Mystery Tour,* the biggest failure, to virtually no involvement at all in *Yellow Submarine*—the biggest success. Likewise *Yellow Submarine* was the film most removed from reality, in contrast to the least favorite of most fans, *Let It Be.*

All but one of the films involved the Beatles in some sort of alter ego. Of these, *A Hard Day's Night* was closest to the reality, but still a far cry from it, as the group went through all sorts of misadventures before playing a big show that marked the culmination of the film. Pyrotechnics dominated *Help!*, with a contrived tale about a stolen ring and a storyline that used plenty of James Bond-style techniques as the boys raced around the world to escape from a bloodthirsty tribe.

If *Help!* suffered from too much script, *MMT* had too little. By now the group's alter-ego presentation had evolved into the psychedelic era, but it didn't work. *Yellow Submarine,* the most fantastic story of all—involving a fairytale battle with the Blue Meanies in Pepperland—came much closer to capturing the psychedelic spirit. The only movie in which the Beatles appeared as themselves, bereft of fictional alter ego, was *Let It Be,* which is remembered with even more distaste than *Magical Mystery Tour.*

Ringo, the central figure in the first three movies, was the only Beatle who went on to appear in a number of films. Clearly the Beatles were not cinematic superstars, but neither were Elvis or Bob Dylan, as their forays into acting proved.

Movies Never Filmed

In addition to these movies, as with albums and concerts, the Beatles had several plans for motion pictures that never materialized.

In 1965, a few months after *Help!*, someone suggested that the Beatles play conventional dramatic roles in a Western based on a book called *A Talent for Loving*, by Richard Condon (author of *The Manchurian Candidate*), but the group members decided against it because they were not sure enough of their acting skills to play dramatic roles. In fact, the Beatles never did make a drama, leaving behind two comedies, two fantasies, and a documentary.

After going with Jane Asher to see *A Man for All Seasons*—which won the 1966 Academy Awards for Best Picture, Best Actor, and Best Director— Paul McCartney had ideas for a love story and a film portraying Liverpool during the Depression. Also during 1966, the Beatles briefly considered playing the Three Musketeers.

In 1967, the group discussed several different projects: *Shades of a Personality*, which played on the oft-cited comparison of the Beatles to parts of the same person; and *The Lord of the Rings*, a reinterpretation of J. R. R. Tolkein's book. Stanley Kubrick briefly considered the project, but nothing came of it—although fans speculated that John would play the snakelike Gollum; Paul, the hobbit Frodo; George, Gandalf the Wizard; and Ringo, Sam, Frodo's uncultivated but trustworthy servant.

The group dropped two other 1967 proposals due to the devaluation of the subject matter. One—an idea that didn't last long enough to receive a title—would have featured the Maharishi in its starring role. The other, also unnamed, was to be a *Magical Mystery Tour* sequel, an idea they dropped once *MMT* bombed.

"Norwegian Wood (This Bird Has Flown)"

"Norwegian Wood," from *Rubber Soul*, was the first Beatles composition on which George Harrison tried out his new instrument, the sitar.

John Lennon, who wrote the song, said he deliberately used cryptic lyrics so his wife wouldn't realize he was describing an affair he had once had. There is a subtle suggestion that the protagonist, waking up and realizing the girl had left, burned down her apartment.

Bob Dylan parodied "Norwegian Wood" with "4th Time Around," from *Blonde on Blonde*. Lennon later said that Dylan's takeoff made him a little self-conscious.

"Ob-La-Di, Ob-La-Da"

In 1968, Jamaican singer Jimmy Scott was performing in London night-clubs with his Ob-La-Di, Ob-La-Da Band. For his ska-influenced White Album track, Paul McCartney appropriated the name, which Scott had not copyrighted.

Slightly altered, the title reappears in George Harrison's "Savoy Truffle" on Side Four. This reference may have been sardonic, because both Harrison and John Lennon had gone on record as despising McCartney's song. Their antipathy may have had something to do with the excruciating process of recording the track: much of the group's recording time during the first half of July 1968 was devoted to this three-minute, ten-second song.

"Oh! Darling"

In his *Abbey Road* song "Oh! Darling," Paul makes use of his Little Richard-style voice, previously heard in the Beatles' cover of the latter's "Long Tall Sally," as well as McCartney's own Little Richard-influenced "I'm Down." To make his voice sound just right this time, Paul screamed himself hoarse for several days.

"One After 909"

John Lennon and Paul McCartney, or Lennon alone—he later claimed sole authorship—wrote "One After 909" in 1959. (Sometimes the title is shown as "The One After 909.") The Beatles recorded it at a March 1963 Parlophone session, as captured on *The Beatles Anthology 1,* but the group did not release a recording of it until *Let It Be* in 1970. Thus this composition, as well as the Beatles' cover of the old Liverpool dittie "Maggie Mae," could be considered one of the group's first and last songs.

"Only a Northern Song"

"Only a Northern Song" is one of two Harrison compositions on the *Yellow Submarine* soundtrack, half the Beatles' contribution of new material to that project. Among four lackluster songs, this one is a standout—i.e., particularly bad.

Not surprisingly, Harrison wrote the song (whose title refers to the Beatles' music publishing company, Northern Songs, Ltd.), in one hour. What *is* surprising, though, is *when* the Beatles recorded this dog: in April 1967, during the sessions for their finest work ever, *Sgt. Pepper's Lonely Hearts Club Band*. In fact, it was actually considered for a spot on the album, between "Fixing a Hole" and "Being for the Benefit of Mr. Kite!" Fortunately, "Getting Better" won out.

The "Paul Is Dead" Phenomenon

Thomas Jefferson, Daniel Boone, Mark Twain, Harry Houdini, Ernest Hemingway, Bette Davis, and Paul McCartney had one thing in common: all were rumored to be dead in their lifetimes. Such rumors elicited Twain's famous quip: "Reports of my death are greatly exaggerated."

In most cases, the presumption of death originated in America, a land also noted for adherents to an opposite type of legend, one involving a dead superstar—most notably Elvis—who is supposedly alive. Thus the urban legend surrounding the alleged death of Paul McCartney was an almost entirely Stateside event, though the rumor may have begun with a British newspaper story.

It has been said that in November 1966, an English paper reported that McCartney had been involved in a car accident after he left Abbey Road Studios late one night. Of course, if this story even existed, it would have been superseded within hours by the "news" that McCartney was alive and well.

Whether or not it began there, it certainly didn't end there.

The "Story" Breaks

Other possible seeds of the "Paul Is Dead" phenomenon include a thesis by an Ohio Wesleyan University student and a humorous article in an Illinois University newspaper. However, it was Russ Gibb, DJ at WKNR-FM, a progressive rock station in Detroit, who became the Homer of this modern myth by assembling the misinformation into a sort of narrative.

On October 12, 1969—nearly three years after the alleged British newspaper account—Gibb claimed he had received an anonymous phone call, instructing him to search for "clues" by listening to some Beatles songs backwards, and carefully studying the fade-outs of others. When he and his listeners did this, they found the "evidence" (shortly to be discussed in more detail) overwhelming.

Soon the rumor spread around the nation, and investigating the death of Paul McCartney became another fad, like hula hoops and Nehru jackets. The search for clues became a sort of holy quest, highlighting the accuracy of John Lennon's statement that the Beatles were more popular than Christ. F. Lee Bailey, already a famous lawyer and showman a quarter-century before the O. J. Simpson case, presided over a solemn televised "trial," in which Beatles manager Allen Klein and others sought to prove that McCartney was alive, while Gibb and his followers claimed otherwise. Astrologer Jeanne Dixon announced that Paul was still alive, but hardcore adherents of the "Paul Is Dead" cult simply ignored her, as they did anyone who disagreed with their belief.

Of all people, they one they trusted least was Paul McCartney himself, who according to their scenario was a stand-in for the *real*, dead, Paul.

The Death of Paul McCartney

The myth went more or less like this. On November 9, 1966, the "stupid bloody Tuesday," Paul left the Abbey Road Studios in anger after an argument with the other three.

At this point, the story is already in trouble, since November 9, 1966, was a Wednesday. It is, however, interesting that the scenario called for that particular date, because—*in real life*—John Lennon met Yoko Ono on November 9, 1966. So something really did happen in that twenty-four-hour period which helped lead to the dissolution of the Lennon-McCartney partnership. Only it wasn't the death of Paul.

In any case, Paul got into his Aston Martin, a replica of which is sitting on the doll's lap on the cover of *Sgt. Pepper*, and drove away. Supposedly decapitated in an accident later described in "A Day in the Life," he was Officially Pronounced Dead on Wednesday morning at five o'clock.

With beautiful circular reasoning, the latter "fact" is proven not only by the reference to that day and time in "She's Leaving Home," but by the "O.P.D." patch on the alleged Paul McCartney's left arm on the inside cover of *Sgt. Pepper*. Realists contended that this meant "Ottawa Police Department," a reasonable guess since the patch bears the coat of arms of Ontario, the province in which Ottawa is located.

Actually, this too was slightly off the mark, according to George Martin (see **Canada**). In any case, the Paul-Is-Dead stalwarts had a handy answer for anything that did not conform to their theory: The presence of seemingly contradictory information just showed how sinister and thorough the cover-up really was. But clues still slipped out for ardent students to detect them; hence George Harrison points to the phrase "Wednesday morning at five o'clock" on the back cover of the album, and in the same picture, McCartney's back is turned.

But if Paul was dead, then whose back was it? The answer was simple: Since the other three couldn't exactly tell the world that Paul was dead, they conducted a secret Paul McCartney lookalike contest, which a William Campbell won. By a fortunate coincidence, Campbell not only looked like Paul, but he had equal and similar musical ability as well.

Adherents of this theory did not have any explanation as to how the Beatles—who could not go out of their doors without being swarmed by crowds—could conduct such a contest without anyone knowing about it. And anyway, to nitpick thus would have been to miss the point. The "Paul Is Dead" cult was not about providing explanations; it was about searching for *clues*.

Premonitions of Death

Even though Paul wouldn't die for another year, the clues began in 1965. That was when *Help!* came out, showing Paul on the inside cover without a hat—supposedly a death symbol in some country or other. Along with "Help!" and "Ticket to Ride," the songs communicated a sense of loss or need: "The Night Before," "You've Got to Hide Your Love Away," "I Need You," "Another Girl," and "You're Gonna Lose That Girl."

In their next U.S. release, "Yesterday," Paul announced that he was "not half the man I used to be / There's a shadow hanging over me." In December 1965, "We Can Work It Out" / "Day Tripper" proclaimed on the A-side that "Life is very short," and on the B-side referred to a "Sunday driver . . . taking the easy way out."

Rubber Soul, with its funereal cover, offered more evidence. "Norwegian Wood" bears the cryptic subtitle "This Bird Has Flown," and in the following track Paul explains that "You Won't See Me." In "I'm Looking Through You," he continues that theme with the line "Love has a nasty habit of disappearing overnight." Even more significant is the message "The only difference is you're down there," with an added inflection in his voice on the last two words. John sings "some are dead" in his song about people he has known, "In My Life." Lennon closes the album with "Run for Your Life," saying "I'd rather see you dead . . . / You better keep your head. . . ."

June 1966 saw the release of *"Yesterday" . . . and Today* with a cover that showed the Beatles grinning and clutching slabs of meat and severed dolls. Though the group had to quickly withdraw this cover from circulation, the second version held no less sinister connotations in the eyes of Beatles detectives. The photo shows Ringo, George, and John gathered around Paul, who sits inside a coffinlike trunk with a sad look on his face. To top it off, the first song on the album is called "Drive My Car."

Two months later, the cover of *Revolver* showed Paul looking away while John and Ringo appeared to be watching him. Lennon sings, in "She Said She Said," about someone who claims to "know what it's like to be dead," and McCartney opens "Got to Get You into My Life" with the line "I was alone, I took a ride."

Officially Pronounced Dead

Up to this point, the Beatles had been acting as prophets, predicting the future. And then, during the six-month interval between *Revolver* and "Penny Lane" / "Strawberry Fields Forever," the accident itself occurred. This would help to explain the group's longest period of silence between 1962 and 1970: They'd been busy burying Paul and training his successor, William Campbell.

Campbell got up to speed quickly, writing a song every bit as good as anything McCartney had done so far—"Penny Lane," in which he refers to his decapitated predecessor with the phrase "every head he's had the plea- sure to know." The song also refers to a "mac," and in the fade-out of "Strawberry Fields Forever," John utters a garbled message which sounded like "I buried Paul." (He claimed it was "Cranberry sauce.")

Sgt. Pepper's Lonely Hearts Club Band began a series of albums that would keep the grave diggers busy searching in earnest. The album cover itself constituted a veritable encyclopedia of hidden messages. To begin with, the motley crowd is assembled behind a grave, on which are flowers arranged in the shape of Paul's bass guitar. According to designer Peter Blake, some fans even saw in the guitar strings the word PAUL? with a ques- tion mark, as though to say IS HE DEAD?

To the right of the "S" in "BEATLES" is what could be a small replica of an automobile—standing on end, in flames. Paul has an extended hand over his head, a symbol of death, and he holds an oboe, the only one of the four Beatles' instruments not featured in a marching band. (Actually, it was not an oboe, but a *cor anglais*, which is similar to an oboe but lower in pitch.) On the back cover, he is the only Beatle not facing the camera, and the hands of the others spell out "L-VE," with Paul being the missing letter "O." (He was also the only member of the group without an "O" in his name.) At shoulder level to Paul are the words "too late—when they pass away."

Lennon sings "climb in the back with your head in the clouds" on "Lucy in the Sky with Diamonds," and Campbell/McCartney sings (in "Getting Better") "Me hiding me head in the sand." The protagonist of "Good Morning, Good Morning" has "Nothing to do to save his life." But most significant is "A Day in the Life," in which the Beatles spell it all out in the first verse: "He blew his mind out in a car / He didn't notice that the lights had changed."

537-1038

Another cryptic single, "Hello Goodbye" / "I Am the Walrus," came out in November 1967. The A-side introduces obvious "here today-gone tomorrow" conjecture, but it was the B-side that held the most significance for Beatles scientists.

The Walrus sits in an English garden waiting for the van to come, a van which must have been the black one—a hearse?—later shown on the cover of *Abbey Road*. Somebody claimed that "Goo goo goo joob" were the last words uttered by Humpty Dumpty before he jumped to his death in James Joyce's highly experimental novel *Finnegans Wake*. "I Am the Walrus" closes with a death scene from Shakespeare—including the words "Bury my body"; "Death!"; and "What, is he dead?" After that, a voice says some sort of gibberish. Supposedly, when played backwards, this became the voice of John Lennon explaining that he had buried Paul McCartney. And in fact—switching to the real world for a moment—if one listens carefully, the gibberish does seem to contain a word sounding very much like "luaP."

On the cover of *Magical Mystery Tour*, the Walrus wears black, as well he might, since the word "walrus" in Greek means the same as "corpse." On the inside cover, next to the title of "I Am the Walrus" is the subtitle "'No You're Not,' Said Little Nicola." This, along with the line "I am he as you are he" and later references in "Glass Onion," seemed to confirm the belief that the Walrus was Paul.

Also on the front cover is the word "BEATLES" spelled out in starry letters. When fans turned the cover upside-down, the word became a phone number: 537-1038. The number, which they assumed to be Billy Shears's, had to be in London; in actuality it belonged to an unlucky British journalist who could not get a decent night's sleep because of all the calls he got from kids in America. (George Martin later described "sinister" 3 a.m. phone calls from kids asking him if Paul was really dead.)

The booklet included with the album showed Paul sitting in front of a sign that said "I WAS," with two flags draped over his head as in military funerals. On page twenty-three, he appears wearing a black carnation, while the others have on red ones. The title track of *Magical Mystery Tour* says "Dying to take you away," and "Fool on the Hill" has the line "Well on his way, head in the clouds. . . ."

Miss Him, Miss Him

In the lower right-hand corner of the lyrics sheet/poster that came with the White Album, Paul has skeleton hands reaching out behind him. Another picture, almost in the middle of the poster, shows him with his arm raised, looking as if he's about to expire, with a ghoulish-looking figure behind him, about to pounce. In another picture two inches to the left of this one, it looks as though the other three Beatles are pushing an unwilling Paul off of a building. And in the upper left-hand corner of the poster, he floats in a bath-tub as if dead.

As for the music, "I'm So Tired" ends with a line of gibberish that supposedly translates to "Paul is dead man, miss him, miss him" when played backwards. "Don't Pass Me By," like "A Day in the Life," spells it out: "You were in a car crash / And you lost your hair." Or was it "head"? "Cry Baby Cry" mentions a seance, and afterward McCartney (or Campbell) sings "Can you take me back?" Naturally "Paul Is Dead" enthu-siasts, like Charles Manson, found plenty of meaning in "Revolution 9." The words "Number nine, number nine," when played backwards, became "Turn me on dead man" to some ears. "Revolution 9" also includes the sound of a car crash.

On the cover of *Yellow Submarine,* John's hand is extended over Paul's head. (Though these were cartoon drawings, this still seemed like a signifi-cant death symbol.) And why does George sing "We are dead" in "It's All Too Much"?

Crossing *Abbey Road*

This brings events to the point at which, in the view of the "Paul Is Dead" faithful, the scandal broke. It was fitting, then, that the story should return to the place where it supposedly began when Paul left the studio in a fit of anger three years before: Abbey Road. The cover of that album proved to be the single most important piece of evidence in the entire "Paul Is Dead" investigation, a treasure trove of clues.

John, dressed in white, leads the procession of four across the road. They are going to a funeral, and he plays the part of "the Minister" while Ringo, dressed in black behind him, is "the Undertaker." At the back is George, in blue jeans because he's "the Grave Digger," leaving Paul to fill the unpleasant role of "the Corpse."

"The Corpse" is out of step with the others, barefoot (as the British bury their dead), with his eyes closed. He carries a cigarette in his right hand, though Paul was left-handed. The license plate behind him says "LMW 28IF," which could only mean that "Linda McCartney Weeps" because her husband would have been twenty-eight IF he had lived. (In actuality, he would have been twenty-seven, but in Asia people add an extra year to their age for the nine months they spent in the womb.)

On the back cover, the "O" in "ROAD" is chipped. Like the missing "O" in "LOVE" from the *Sgt. Pepper* back cover, this one seemed significant because Paul was the only Beatle without an "o" in his name. Also on the back cover, the shadows to the right of the word "BEATLES" form the shape of a slanted skull.

And that was just the cover; the music had even more clues. On "Come Together," Lennon sings that "One and one and one is three," suggesting that now there were only three Beatles. The alleged Paul sings, in "Oh! Darling," that "I nearly broke down and died." On Side Two, "You Never Give Me Your Money" mentions getting in a car and driving away, and the song ends with the chorus "One-two-three-four-five-six-seven / All good children go to heaven."

The Death of "Paul Is Dead"

Capitol Records made no effort to deny the rumors of McCartney's death for the simple reason that all this nonsense was good for business. *Sgt. Pepper* and *Magical Mystery Tour*, both two years old, shot back up the charts as amateur sleuths purchased new copies for further study.

But "Paul Is Dead" had already peaked by the time *Let It Be* hit the record shops in May 1970. There were still a few stray clues for those who cared—the title track sounded funereal, and there was latent significance in "The Long and Winding Road." In fact, what was really dead was "the Beatles" as a group. Peter Doggett suggested in his study of the group's last two albums that the "Paul Is Dead" phenomenon represented a sort of eruption in the collective unconscious, a reaction to the awareness of the Beatles' impending breakup.

Did the Beatles deliberately plant any of the clues? Probably not at first, but it's quite possible that they played around with a few "clues" of their own around the time of the White Album. Certainly John's "Glass Onion" would suggest a desire to fool the unwary.

What is really interesting about the whole phenomenon, though, is what it says about the modern world. It resembles the spontaneous hysteria that occurred in response to Orson Welles's *War of the Worlds* radio broadcast in 1938, when people all over the country hid in fear from the invading Martians. In both cases, technology did not prevent the mass confusion, but rather abetted it.

(See also **Web Sites** for information on "Paul Is Dead" in cyberspace.)

"Penny Lane"

Penny Lane is a street in Liverpool, and even though Paul McCartney wrote the famous song named after it, John Lennon was the one who lived near there as a little boy.

"Penny Lane," which came out as a single in February 1967 with "Strawberry Fields Forever" on the other side, marked the beginning of a new era for the Beatles. Appropriately enough, *The Beatles 1962–1970* albums are divided so that the second volume begins with these two songs.

Paul, who had been going to classical concerts at the urging of his girlfriend, Jane Asher, got the idea for the trumpet obligato in "Penny Lane" from Bach's "Brandenburg" concertos. Since he could not read or write musical notation, he hummed this portion for George Martin, who wrote down the notes for the musicians.

When "Penny Lane" first went out to radio stations in the U.S. and Canada, it contained an extra seven notes from the piccolo trumpet at the very end of the song, but all subsequent releases of the single had that extra loop trimmed off. Original copies of this version—which first appeared on an album as part of *Rarities* in the U.S.—brought as much as $150 in the 1980s.

A Hidden Message

Whereas most of the hidden messages fans claimed to find in Beatles songs simply weren't there—or at least, they weren't intentional—"Penny Lane" contains a pair of innuendoes planted by the song's composer. Yet most fans have missed these entirely.

Had the BBC's censors noticed the not-so-subtle sexual metaphor in the phrase "four of fish and finger pie," they would no doubt have banned "Penny Lane," as they later did "I Am the Walrus" (with far less basis for doing so). Less blatant, but still intentional, is the phallic imagery in the line "He likes to keep his fire engine clean / It's a clean machine."

"Penny Lane" / "Strawberry Fields Forever"

Despite the existence of CD singles, the concept of a "single" has virtually lost its meaning in the age of compact discs. But from the 1950s through the early 1980s, singles—and specifically hit singles—drove the music market. Usually the A-side was a hit (or a song its promoters *hoped* would be a hit), whereas B-sides ranged from absolute dogs to quirky tracks not found elsewhere—as in the case of "The Inner Light," B-side to "Lady Madonna." Every once in a while, something out of the ordinary would slip through, as when Gary Glitter's A-side "Rock and Roll (Part One)" died without a whimper in the 1970s, whereas the B-side—Part Two—became a huge hit, played regularly at football games. But generally, the pattern held: the A-side was a hit, the B-side a throwaway. Hence Blue Oyster Cult later sang of "Time everlasting / Time to play B-sides."

Then there's the phenomenon of a "double A-side" single, a term used to describe a record on which the B-side is every bit as good as the A-side. The Beatles' February 1967 release—without a doubt one of the greatest singles of all time, if not *the* greatest—was the ultimate double A-side. In fact, it literally did not have a B-side. Hence, though it is generally referred to as "Penny Lane" / "Strawberry Fields Forever" simply because the former song was more accessible and therefore more popular, it could just as easily be called "Strawberry Fields Forever" / "Penny Lane." Thus "Strawberry Fields Forever" is correctly identified as the "flip-side" (not the B-side) of "Penny Lane."

This particular single is more like a miniature album. In fact, the Beatles put far more effort into these two songs than they did their first album, *Please Please Me*. Also, the two compositions have similar themes, reexamining places from childhood.

Their Greatest Single a Failure?

For all its merits, and in spite of the fact that it followed the longest silence during the Beatles' career as a group—six months without a new record—the single did not perform as well on the British charts as its predecessors. In the U.S., "Penny Lane" hit Number One and its flip-side Number Eight, but in the U.K., where charts are based on an average of the figures for both sides of a single, it fell short of the top slot.

Prior to that time, "Love Me Do" had been the only Beatles single that did not reach first place in Britain. It had been followed by twelve straight Number Ones, from "Please Please Me" to "Yellow Submarine"; then, with the group's fourteenth single, the Beatles seemed to have stumbled.

The song that kept it out of the top slot, by the way, was "Release Me" by Engelbert Humperdinck.

Percussion

In the area of rhythm, as with melody and harmony, the Beatles introduced countless innovations or improvements on existing methods.

And as with other types of instruments, the group made use of a wide and varied palette—in all, fourteen different types of percussive instruments aside from standard rock drums. (And aside from percussive instruments played by guest musicians, such as the Indian artists on "Within You Without You.")

Percussion pieces played by members of the group include the African drum, anvil, bongos, castanets, claves, conga drum, cowbell, finger cymbals, firebell, loose-skinned Arabian bongo, maracas, packing case, tambourine, and timpani. And not nearly all of these performances were by Ringo—George, John, and particularly Paul provided the percussion on many tracks. (The packing case, incidentally, was on "Words of Love.")

Yet there are seven songs with no percussion at all, either by the Beatles or their guests: "Yesterday," "Eleanor Rigby," "She's Leaving Home," "Julia," "Good Night," "Because," and "Her Majesty."

Philippines

The people of the Philippines are among the world's friendliest, and excel as hosts. Given the graciousness of the people, and the nation's openness to Western ways—from 1898 to 1946, it was a territory of the United States—it is surprising that the Beatles encountered greater hostility in the Philippines than anywhere else on earth. (The lone exception might be the American South during the "We're More Popular Than Jesus" brouhaha, which occurred around the same time as the Philippine fiasco.)

The Beatles spent two days in the Philippines, between July 3 and 5, 1966, and these were among the most harrowing of their career. Filipino *fans,* who came out to see them at the Jose Rizal Memorial Football Stadium, loved them. But they ran afoul of higher authorities.

Just the year before, Ferdinand Marcos had been elected president, a position he would hold for the next twenty-one years, effectively making himself president-for-life when he declared martial law in 1972. Like the Maos in China, the Perons in Argentina, and later the Clintons in the U.S., the Marcoses offered a two-for-one package: First Lady Imelda Marcos, who would later become infamous for her vast shoe collection, was at least as forceful as her husband.

Imelda, who had risen from the slums to Malacañang, the presidential palace, did not get where she was by accepting *no* for an answer. Therefore when she sent one of her aides to give Brian Epstein a "suggestion" that the boys call at Malacañang before their afternoon concert, she expected to be obeyed. But the Beatles were tired, and Brian replied that while they appreciated the gracious offer, they needed to rest.

George Martin remembered the return telegram as something like this: "They must come nevertheless. The offer cannot be refused." An armed military escort arrived at the hotel to take them to the palace, but Epstein bravely ran interference for the group, asleep and oblivious in their rooms. Later, when he turned on the television, he began to realize how much trouble they were in: the commentators were talking about nothing else, and a riot atmosphere spread around the Beatles.

Between the stadium and the flight out, all kinds of nasty things happened. Their driver was pushed down the stairs, and the road managers discovered that the escalator at the airport was out of order; once they had dragged the gear up the stairs, the escalators suddenly began working again. The group was informed that special taxes would eat up their entire proceeds from the Manila concerts, and Philippine Air Lines sent their luggage to Sweden—despite the fact that they were on their way to India.

But as Ringo recalled in *The Beatles Anthology* TV special, they got the last laugh on the Marcoses, when the co-dictators were deposed in a 1986 popular revolution.

"Please Please Me"

"Please Please Me," the Beatles' second single, was their first to reach Number One in any country—on February 16, 1963, in Great Britain. (It would be eleven months before "I Want To Hold Your Hand" became their first U.S. Number One.)

Whereas "Love Me Do" would not sound all that remarkable a few decades later, the excitement of "Please Please Me" remains as clear as the day it was recorded. The song showcased melody lines and harmonies entirely new in pop music, and also introduced the trademark thundering drums that Ringo would soon contribute to "She Loves You."

It is important, therefore, to remember that when they recorded this song, the Beatles' grasp on success was *extremely* tenuous. They had enjoyed a minor hit with "Love Me Do," and on the basis of that, EMI/Parlophone invited them to have another go at it in the studio. On the day they recorded "Please Please Me," Lennon and McCartney showed George Martin a new song they'd been working on, "Tip of My Tongue," but Martin didn't like it, so the Beatles never released it. It did come out in July 1963 in a recording by another of Brian Epstein's artists, Tommy Quickly, and appeared on the 1979 album *The Songs Lennon and McCartney Gave Away*.

After they recorded "Please Please Me," George Martin said to them through the intercom from the control room: "Gentlemen, you've just made your first Number-One record."

Martin liked the recording the group made on the first take, even though Paul forgot the words in the first chorus and John forgot them in the finale. They put this version, in stereo, on the album of which it became the title track. The mono version, used for the single, sounds almost identical even though it is a different recording.

John said that he came up with the song's title—the first-ever example of Beatles wordplay—based on a Bing Crosby line that he liked: "Please, listen to my pleas." Aspects of the tune bore a very faint resemblance to another favorite, Roy Orbison's "Only the Lonely." (Later in 1963, the Beatles went on tour with Orbison, one of their heroes.)

Please Please Me

Please Please Me, released in England on March 22, 1963, was the Beatles' first album anywhere in the world.

The group recorded the entire album of fourteen songs in the course of less than ten hours between 10:00 a.m. and 10:45 p.m. on Monday, February 11, 1963. To top it off, John Lennon had a bad cold, and spent the whole day struggling through with the help of Zubes lozenges.

Even though it doesn't sound like it—his singing is strong throughout—Lennon was saving his energy for his vocal-cord-wrenching recording of "Twist and Shout." This was one of the few times that the last song recorded for an album became the actual last song on the album. By contrast, "Tomorrow Never Knows" and "A Day in the Life," the last songs on *Revolver* and *Sgt. Pepper* respectively, were begun first.

"Polythene Pam"

The lyrics of "Polythene Pam," one of John Lennon's three contributions to Paul McCartney's lengthy song cycle on Side Two of *Abbey Road*, are virtually unintelligible to most listeners. This is because most of it is in scouse, the Liverpool dialect. The acoustic demo, on *The Beatles Anthology 1*, is much easier to understand.

John wrote this obscene piece of hard rock about a prostitute he met in Jersey during the group's touring days. The lady dressed in polythene (clear plastic) as a "gimmick."

Popularity

Though individual albums by artists such as Michael Jackson have certainly outperformed various of the Beatles' records, they will probably always remain the all-around most successful musical act in history.

They had more Number One records (twenty) and more Number One albums (fifteen) than any other band. Not only did they have the most gold records (forty-two), but the *Guinness Book of World Records* credits the Beatles with greatest worldwide sales, estimated at 100,000,000 singles and 100,000,000 albums. "Yesterday" has received more covers than any other song—1,186 versions in the first eight years of its release—and "Can't Buy Me Love" still holds the record for greatest advance sales: 2,100,000 copies shipped in early 1964.

They have, of course, enjoyed at least as much popularity with critics as with fans. A group of leading music critics in the 1970s conducted a poll among themselves as to the all-time greatest albums, which they published in *Rock Critics' Choice: The Top 200 Albums*. The Top 20 from this includes a number of Dylan records, of course, as well as several by the Stones and even an Elvis album, although his best years predated the album era. But the Beatles held fully one-quarter of the top twenty slots, including the top one with *Sgt. Pepper's Lonely Hearts Club Band* (voted greatest album of all time), *Revolver, Abbey Road, Rubber Soul*, and *The Beatles*.

Creative Marketing
But before all that, the Beatles were an obscure bar band just trying to get by.

In December 1961, for instance, the group resorted to stuffing ballot boxes just to win a popularity contest, the "favorite Merseyside band" poll conducted by *Mersey Beat*, the Liverpool music paper. Fearing stiff competition from Gerry and the Pacemakers, Lennon and McCartney bought up dozens of copies of the magazine and filled in the entry blanks using assumed names. The Beatles won the contest.

To reinforce the idea that the boys were really popular, Brian Epstein designed a poster in early 1962 which bore the following claims about the group:

> MERSEY BEAT POLL WINNERS!
> POLYDOR RECORDING ARTISTS!
> PRIOR TO EUROPEAN TOUR!

The *"Mersey Beat* poll winners" had stuffed the ballot box. The "Polydor recording artists" had issued a minor single, "My Bonnie" / "The Saints," as Tony Sheridan's backup band while in Germany. And "European Tour" was a fanciful way of referring to the fact that the group was on its way back to Hamburg to play at the Star Club.

Two years later and a lifetime away, this was the makeup of *Billboard's* U.S. Top Five list for April 4, 1964:

1. "Can't Buy Me Love"—The Beatles
2. "Twist and Shout"—The Beatles
3. "She Loves You"—The Beatles
4. "I Want to Hold Your Hand"—The Beatles
5. "Please Please Me"—The Beatles

This had never been done before, has not been done since, and probably will never be done again. The following week, fourteen Beatles songs made it to the American Hot Hundred, meaning that the Beatles by themselves controlled one-seventh of the charts.

Billy Preston

If any performer could claim to be a "fifth Beatle," it was American keyboardist Billy Preston, who made his Beatles debut on both sides of the April 1969 single "Get Back" / "Don't Let Me Down." The German subsidiary of EMI listed the artist on that record as "The Beatles with Billy Preston."

The group knew Preston from his days in Little Richard's band, which had played at the Star Club in Hamburg at the same time as the Beatles in 1962. When he stopped by for a visit at the Apple offices on January 22, 1969, Preston was met by an eager George Harrison, who rushed the bewildered keyboardist downstairs to the studio. It must have seemed as though they were waiting for him, and in a sense they were.

Because they wanted to record their new album (then titled *Get Back*) live in the studio, the Beatles needed another player to flesh out the sound, since Paul couldn't overdub piano if he was already playing bass. In addition, the presence of an outsider caused the four, who had devolved into bickering, to shape up, and with Preston's arrival their relations in the studio improved. The group members briefly considered making Preston a fifth Beatle, but by then the group was moving more toward disintegration than expansion.

In addition to the "Get Back" / "Don't Let Me Down" single, Preston plays on "Old Brown Shoe," "I Me Mine," "Dig It," "Let It Be," and the four songs from the January 30, 1969, "rooftop concert" that appear on *Let It Be:* "Dig a Pony," "I've Got a Feeling," "One After 909," and "Get Back." He later went on to record solo albums released by Apple, and to work with several former Beatles, most notably on Harrison's *Concert for Bangladesh* in 1971.

The Quarry Men

The roots of the Beatles went back more than five years before the recording of "Love Me Do," to a time before even Paul or George were in the picture.

In 1956, Liverpool was abuzz with a form of music called "skiffle." Skiffle, whose leading star was Lonnie Donegan, had a slow, shuffling beat that made it easy to play, and it was an economical art form: most skiffle instruments, such as a washboard and tea-chest bass, could easily be constructed from stolen or borrowed parts.

A Liverpool teenager named John Lennon had become infatuated with rock 'n' roll after hearing Elvis Presley's "Heartbreak Hotel" in May 1956, but when he formed a group in March 1957, it was a skiffle band. This was the Quarry Men (sometimes rendered "Quarrymen"), named after the Quarry Bank High School for Boys, which the group's two members— Lennon and Pete Shotton—attended. Lennon first wanted to call them the Black Jacks, but decided instead on the name suggested in the Quarry Bank school song: "Quarry Men, strong before our birth."

Shotton, never a very enthusiastic Quarry Man, had a brief stint as washboard player. In addition to Lennon on guitar and vocals, the group included at one time or another Eric Griffiths on guitar; Rod Davis on banjo; Bill Smith, Len Garry, Ivan Vaughan, and Nigel Whalley successively on tea-chest bass; John Lowe (nicknamed "Duff") on piano; and Colin Hanton on drums.

Then of course there were the two other most famous Quarry Men: Griffiths would introduce Lennon to his schoolmate Paul McCartney (see **Lennon–McCartney Partnership**) on July 6, 1957, and within a few months McCartney in turn brought in his young friend George Harrison.

Verbal Cuts, Cuts in the Lineup, and Other Cuts

The Quarry Men had a somewhat elastic lineup, changing from month to month, performance to performance. This was due in part to the ordinary disorganization that accompanies any high school band, but it also had something to do with the group's leader. Lennon, with his sharp tongue and cruel, taunting manner, drove away all but the bravest.

The history of the group was one of disappointments and obstructions. They were often beaten out in skiffle competitions by a band that featured a midget named Nicky Cuff, who could stand on his tea-chest bass while playing it. Finding a place to practice was also a problem. When she was alive, they had often played at the apartment of John's mother Julia, who saw nothing strange in their habit of practicing in the bathtub in order to achieve more echo. Later Mrs. Harrison allowed them to practice at her home.

Even skiffle itself eventually let them down, as the craze began to flicker and die in the late 1950s. The mid-1960s would see a short-lived "skiffle revival," from which emerged perhaps the most famous skiffle song of all time, "In the Summertime" by Mungo Jerry. But for the Quarry Men skiffle was over, and they began adding more rock 'n' roll to their act.

The public, however, was not always receptive to the new trends. At one club, the group was happily thumping away at a rock tune when the management handed them a note that said "Cut out the bloody rock."

In early 1960, the Quarry Men changed their name and thus ceased to exist. (See **Birth of the Beatles.**)

"Revolution"

John Lennon had three songs called "Revolution" or some variation thereof, the first of which he released in August 1968 on the first Apple single, as the B-side to "Hey Jude."

John wanted a hard, dirty sound for this recording, so he and George distorted the sounds of their guitars by overloading the pre-amps, and Ringo thumped out an electronically compressed drumbeat. When fans first purchased the single, many thought that their copies were defective because of the gritty guitars.

But the words caused even more surprise than the music. Instead of embracing the violence of New Left groups, the song calls for reason, moderation, thoughtful discussion—none of which were very fashionable in 1968. Lennon places himself at odds with those who "go carrying pictures of Chairman Mao" or have "minds that hate," and calls on them to "free your mind instead." It was one of the few rock songs ever to take a stance squarely against the chic leftism typically embraced by artists such as, say, the later John Lennon.

After the song came out, the backlash against Lennon in the rock music press was swift and decisive. One magazine described "Revolution" as a plank from the platform of the "Democratic Death Party" at the Chicago Convention. With the release of the White Album in November, however, the mavens of radical chic had a version of the song more to their liking—"Revolution 1," actually recorded first.

"Revolution 1"

John Lennon's acoustic version of "Revolution," from Side Four of *The Beatles*, sounds like a takeoff on the earlier song. In fact, this was actually the first recording; as with *Abbey Road* and *Let It Be* later, they were released out of sequence.

Besides being much softer than the version on the single, this one included a changed word: on "Revolution" he had said, regarding any type of violence, "don't you know that you can count me out"; now he substituted the word "in." He said later that he put in the contradictory statement because everyone has an underlying violent streak; whatever the case, a lot of people—Charles Manson included—liked the changed line.

There are several misunderstandings regarding this song and "Revolution." Lennon did not record "Revolution 1" to appease the counterculture he'd offended with the other song; that would have been hard to do, since he recorded "Revolution 1" nearly six weeks before "Revolution." At that point, "Revolution 1" *was* "Revolution": Lennon had intended all along for the track to have a subdued sound, as it did on the White Album. But Paul and George both felt that it didn't sound strong enough to be a single, so a few weeks later, the group recorded the more hard-driving version that they released along with "Hey Jude." The White Album track received the title "Revolution 1" to distinguish it.

Also, it was on "Revolution 1," and not on "Revolution," that Lennon sang lying on the floor in order to alter his voice quality.

"Revolution 9"

At eight minutes, fifteen seconds, "Revolution 9" is the longest Beatles composition—not *song*, though, since it contains no music except for assorted snippets, particularly the piano piece toward the beginning. This lengthy mishmash of voices and other noises near the end of the White Album might be called an "instrumental," though that doesn't quite describe it either. Many fans would have quite another word for it: in a 1971 magazine poll, they voted it the worst Beatles song of all time.

Paul McCartney fought to keep it off the White Album, but John, then reasserting himself as leader of the group, insisted that it stay on. Lennon later said that he spent more time assembling the tape loops for his third "Revolution" than he spent on half the songs he'd ever written. Ironically, Paul ended up providing some of the only non-prerecorded musical instrumentation for "Revolution 9," the piano piece at the beginning.

Most ironic of all was the fact that Paul himself may have provided the precedent for "Revolution 9": On January 5, 1967, he recorded thirteen minutes, forty-eight seconds of various noises for a psychedelic event called the "Carnival of Light Rave," to begin in London later that month. The recording consisted of sounds such as a church organ, a person gargling, and John and Paul screaming non sequiturs such as "Are you alright?" and "Barcelona!"

The Mad Scientist at Work

The name "Revolution 9" is not as arbitrary as it sounds. It was not the ninth of anything, perhaps, but nine was Lennon's favorite number. And "Revolution 9" did grow out of "Revolution 1."

The first song taped for the White Album, on May 30, 1968, was "Revolution 1," which at that time was simply "Revolution." With the eighteenth take, the group had the basic track down, but the recording went on for a total of ten minutes, seventeen seconds. The last six minutes were made up of a jam that disintegrated into formlessness, and on this outtake Lennon began to build "Revolution 9."

It is significant that the May 31 session, when John began adding feedback, screaming, and other overdubs to the basic track, marked the first of many, many appearances by Yoko Ono at the Abbey Road studios. Equally telling was the fact that when John started to put the composition together on June 10, both George and Ringo were out of the country. And perhaps most pertinent of all was the confluence of events on June 20 and 21. On the first day (night, actually, since that was when the Beatles did their recording once they became superstars), McCartney went into one studio to record "Blackbird" while Lennon worked on "Revolution 9" in another. Never before had the Beatles worked separately like this.

Then on June 21, when Paul left town, Lennon took over the Abbey Road/EMI studios. Like a mad scientist, he put people to work in all three studios, helping him run together some thirty tapes while he, Yoko, and George added numerous voice-overs.

The Landscape of "Revolution 9"

"Revolution 9" starts with a snippet of conversation, which sounds like it could be from a radio or TV program. A man's voice says "Will you forgive me?" and another answers "Yes." In fact these were the voices of Apple office manager Alistair Taylor and George Martin, who presumably didn't know they were being taped. They were in the studio control room at Abbey Road, and Taylor was asking Martin to forgive him for not bringing him a bottle of claret (a red wine) that Martin had presumably requested.

Paul's piano begins, along with a disembodied voice chanting "Number nine, number nine." This, the most famous element of "Revolution 9," came from an old Royal Academy of Music examination tape stored in the Abbey Road archives.

From there the program segues into a series of various pieces of music played backwards, and John says "Everybody knew that as time went by they'd get a little bit older and a little bit slower." More backwards music, some hideous female laughter, "Number nine," and the sound of a baby crying.

George asks "Who is to know?" More "Number nine," the sound of a symphony, and John shouting "Riot! Riot! Riot!" followed by another series of "Number nine's." Car horns honk, children are heard laughing and playing, George says, "The situation . . ." and someone comments, "They are standing still." George: ". . . upon a telegraph." A weird-sounding voice moans, followed by a referee's whistle and a crowd cheering. John says, "I couldn't tell what he was saying, his voice was low, and his eyes . . . his eyes . . ."

Just as he had done in "Revolution" and "Revolution 1," John can be heard half-singing, half-shouting the word "Alright!" This time, however, it becomes "All riiiot!" A crowd cheers, the ubiquitous "Number nine" says his piece, and an extremely disturbing voice comes in. It sounds at best half-human, and makes grunts and snapping noises like a beast ripping flesh. More backwards music, and John (presumably) describes his first acid experience: "We went to see a bloody dentist, which wasn't really a dentist. . . ."

A crowd at a football game shouts "Block that kick!" and Ringo (?) says, "My broken chair, my wings are broken and so is my hair. I'm not in the mood for [wearing clothes?]." A voice speaking in a foreign language (or perhaps English recorded backwards) shouts something against what sounds like a crackling fire, and then moans as though in agony. There are more sounds of gunfire, followed by George saying ". . . to find the night watchman." Ringo says "A new suit," to which George replies ". . . of his presence." John, like a BBC commentator, says, "Industrial allowance, financial imbalance, the watusi, the twist."

"El Dorado" and "Take this, brother—may it serve you well" are followed by various sounds, including Yoko's voice saying, "Maybe it's not that, maybe even then you expose . . ." A man's baritone voice sings "Again and again," backed by whistling. Yoko says, ". . . like being naked . . . if . . . you become naked." Finally, out of opposite channels on the stereo, come responsive chants from a football crowd: "Hold that line!" turns into "Block that kick!"

These are a few of the sounds in "Revolution 9"; repeated listenings—particularly on CD—would undoubtedly reveal many more.

Revolver

Some fans and critics consider *Revolver*, released in August 1966, the Beatles' finest album. Whereas on *Sgt. Pepper* the parts remain dependent on the whole, each song on *Revolver* is a separate piece that can stand on its own.

After the innovations of *Rubber Soul*, *Revolver* proved to anyone who still doubted it that the Beatles had begun taking new directions both with music and lyrics. This was the first of several albums to span a wide musical spectrum, from "classical" to acid rock to ballads.

Remarkable Songs

Not long before his death in 1980, John Lennon said that two of his favorite Beatles songs were McCartney's "Here, There and Everywhere" and "For No One." At other times he had praised another McCartney composition from this album, "Got to Get You into My Life."

On *Revolver*, George Harrison had more songs than on any Beatles record except the White Album: three, including "Taxman," "I Want to Tell You," and his first composition using only Indian instruments, "Love You To."

None of the Beatles plays on the latter recording, or on "Eleanor Rigby." "For No One" utilizes only the talents of Paul and Ringo, and "Good Day Sunshine" employs only two instruments: George Martin's piano and Ringo's double-tracked drums.

"Got to Get You into My Life" set some sort of record when it became a U.S. Top Ten hit in the summer of 1976, ten years after its release. The end of that song, bridging into the next, is one of those powerful transitions often found on Beatles albums, the most notable example being the clucking chicken at the end of "Good Morning Good Morning" that becomes the electric guitar of "Sgt. Pepper's Lonely Hearts Club Band (Reprise)." In this case, the final horn blast of "Got to Get You into My Life" turns into the droning sitar of *Revolver*'s final track, "Tomorrow Never Knows." The latter, with its promise of things to come, could *only* be at the end of the album.

The Cover and the Name

The album cover itself was the third in a series of innovative Beatles record jackets, beginning with *Rubber Soul* and continuing though the banned "Butcher Sleeve" of America's *"Yesterday"*. . . *and Today*. Designed by Klaus Voorman, the group's friend from Hamburg, the cover features two photos previously used on the *Rubber Soul* back cover. Voorman himself makes a Hitchcock-like appearance in his own production, sticking his head out of George's hair.

The name *Revolver* describes a record spinning on a turntable—not a pistol, as some fans thought at the time. At one point the group had considered calling it *Abracadabra!*

The songs on *Revolver* are all relatively short: only two even reach the rock 'n' roll "standard" of three minutes. (But the average track was still much longer than on *Revolver*'s predecessor—see the song list under **Rubber Soul.**)

* * * * *

Revolver Song List

Title	Composer	Time
Side One		
Taxman	Harrison	2:36
Eleanor Rigby	McCartney	2:11
I'm Only Sleeping*	Lennon	2:58
Love You To	Harrison	3:00
Here, There, and Everywhere	McCartney	2:29
Yellow Submarine	McCartney	2:40
She Said She Said	Lennon	2:39
Side Two		
Good Day Sunshine	McCartney	2:08
And Your Bird Can Sing*	Lennon	2:02
For No One	McCartney	2:03
Dr. Robert*	Lennon	2:14
I Want to Tell You	Harrison	2:30
Got to Get You Into My Life	McCartney	2:31
Tomorrow Never Knows	Lennon	3:00

*British version only.

The Rolling Stones

The Rolling Stones' group lineup differed greatly from that of the Beatles—for one thing, there were five of them, and no single Beatle was as much a star of the show as Mick Jagger—but there were similarities too. For instance, they had their own songwriting partnership, Mick Jagger and Keith Richards. The function of George Harrison, as the third man and the quiet one, fell to Brian Jones and Bill Wyman together, and the Stones had their own shy and much-loved drummer, Charlie Watts.

Just as the Beatles had once been the Silver Beatles, so the Stones were at one time—in 1962—the Silver Rolling Stones. The Stones' second single in December 1963 became their first Top Fifteen British hit: "I Wanna Be Your Man," written by Lennon and McCartney.

In 1967, the Stones would take on a manager who in 1969 became the Beatles' manager as well. Neither group would end up on good terms with the hard-nosed Allen Klein.

The Beatles' Shadow

The Stones benefited by contrasting with the Beatles, maintaining a grittier, dirtier sound and image. They failed when they tried to emulate the Beatles, and such was the case with their own *Sgt. Pepper* imitation, *Their Satanic Majesties Request*.

Not only did the Stones' title have the same number of syllables as the Beatles'; it also made use of the missing apostrophe motif in the word "Majesties," which the Beatles had used in "Hearts." The cover was another kaleidoscopic picture, with two Beatles' faces hidden among its various trappings in response to the Rolling Stones doll on the cover of *Sgt. Pepper*. Side Two of the album, in fact, begins with the voice of a carnival barker who mentions the Beatles.

Their Satanic Majesties Request has its own theme song, "Sing This All Together," and like "Sgt. Pepper's Lonely Hearts Club Band," this one has a reprise—which begins with a flute portion almost identical to the opening of "Strawberry Fields Forever." There is an Eastern-sounding piece, "Gomper," and a "Day in the Life"-style dream-waking sequence, "In Another Land." The British version of *Sgt. Pepper* had its inner groove, a few seconds of gibberish just after "A Day in the Life," and the Stones' album has a longer piece of noise, which sounds just a bit like "Within You Without You."

Critics attacked the Stones for trying to follow the Beatles, and on *Beggar's Banquet*, the group returned to their trademark blues-influenced style with one of their best albums ever. It is interesting to note that the Stones' best work began at about the time the Beatles broke up: first came *Let It Bleed* in 1969, when the Beatles were recording their last two albums, then *Sticky Fingers* and *Exile on Main Street* in 1971 and 1972 respectively. It was as though the Beatles had to leave the stage before the Stones could excel to their fullest.

Guest Appearances

Three Beatles songs feature members of the Rolling Stones: "Yellow Submarine," with Brian Jones joining in the chorus; "All You Need Is Love," with Jagger and Richard on background vocals; and "You Know My Name (Look Up the Number)," featuring Jones on saxophone. (Jones died of a drug overdose less than a month after the recording.) Jagger was present at the taping of the orchestral portion of "A Day in the Life," and later accompanied the group to visit the Maharishi in Bangor, Wales, in August 1967.

On the other hand, rumors that Lennon and McCartney sang on the Stones' "Sing This All Together" were untrue. However, they did sing backup on "We Love You," a song dedicated to Stones fans who had supported Jagger and Richard while they were in jail on drug charges.

Rubber Soul

Rubber Soul was the first of many albums in which the Beatles made dramatic leaps ahead, and progressed so much as artists that it seemed as though years, not mere months, had passed since their earlier work.

In fact the group recorded *Rubber Soul* under enormous pressure. Previously they had always released two albums a year, and with 1965 fast drawing to a close, they needed to come up with their second after *Help!*, but they lacked enough new material to flesh the new album out. Yet somehow it came together.

Issued in Britain and America in December 1965, *Rubber Soul* was the first Beatles album with the same title and cover on both sides of the Atlantic. It was also the only album on which the American version included tracks not available on the British one—only because those two songs, "I've Just Seen a Face" and "It's Only Love" had already appeared on the British *Help!* The British album, on the other hand, included four tracks later released on the American *"Yesterday". . . and Today.* No wonder, then, that the Beatles posed as "butchers" for the cover of *"Yesterday". . .* to symbolize what Capitol Records was doing to their albums.

Rubber Faces

Fans were shocked to see the distorted faces, looking like something out of a nightmare, on the cover of *Rubber Soul.* The brownish-tinged photograph, with its curved space, was without a doubt the most innovative sleeve on the market at the time; aside from all else, nobody had ever issued an album without the name of the band somewhere on the front of the jacket.

Other bands had the justifiable fear that if buyers didn't know immediately who the artist was, they might not purchase the album. But the Beatles could have issued a record in a plain white sleeve—which they later did—and it still would have sold. Since 1965, of course, groups like Led Zeppelin have issued albums that mention the name of the group nowhere but on the record label itself; the Beatles, however, were the first to try this surprisingly effective form of soft sell.

Like the title of *Revolver* after it, *Rubber Soul*'s made use of a simple, almost ludicrous pun. This did not come from the Beatles' chief punster, John Lennon, but from Paul McCartney. On take 1 of "I'm Down," from *The Beatles Anthology 2*, McCartney can be heard using an early version of the phrase: "plastic soul, man, plastic soul."

As for *Rubber Soul*, the name suggests the expanding and contracting human soul; then again, maybe it's just rubber-soled shoes and soul music.

* * * * *

Rubber Soul Song List

Title	Composer	Time
Side One		
Drive My Car*	McCartney	2:25
I've Just Seen a Face**	McCartney	2:04
Norwegian Wood (This Bird Has Flown)	Lennon	2:00
You Won't See Me	McCartney	3:19
Nowhere Man*	Lennon	2:40
Think for Yourself	Harrison	2:16
The Word	Lennon	2:42
Michelle	McCartney	2:42
Side Two		
What Goes On?*	Lennon–McCartney–Starkey	2:44
It's Only Love**	Lennon	1:53
Girl	Lennon	2:26
I'm Looking Through You	McCartney	2:20
In My Life	Lennon	2:23
Wait	Lennon	2:13
If I Needed Someone*	Harrison	2:19
Run for Your Life	Lennon	2:21

*British version only.

**American version only.

"Run for Your Life"

George Harrison considered "Run for Your Life," the fierce track that closes out *Rubber Soul*, one of John Lennon's best songs. Lennon himself, however, dismissed it as a "throwaway." He took the opening line, "I'd rather see you dead, little girl, than to be with another man" from Elvis Presley's 1955 song "Let's Play House" by Arthur Gunter.

"Savoy Truffle"

George Harrison wrote "Savoy Truffle," from Side Four of *The Beatles*, about his sweet-toothed friend Eric Clapton, who had to undergo major dental work.

George was at Clapton's house one day when his host happened to have a box of Mackintosh's Good News Chocolates. Harrison—never one to shy away from moralizing—decided to write a cautionary song about Clapton's addiction to sweets. Besides referring to "Good News" by name in the song, Harrison also mentions some of the flavors included in the box: creme tangerine, montelimar, ginger sling, coffee dessert, and savoy truffle.

"Sexy Sadie"

John Lennon wrote "Sexy Sadie," from Side Three of the White Album, in India. Disillusioned by his discovery that the Maharishi had nonspiritual designs on Mia Farrow, he originally titled the song "Maharishi, What Have You Done, You Made a Fool of Everyone," but he decided to make it a bit less blatant.

"Sgt. Pepper Inner Groove"

The "Sgt. Pepper Inner Groove" is, at two seconds, the Beatles' shortest recording. Rumored to be a snippet of conversation from a party held after the final taping of "A Day in the Life," it is actually all four Beatles chanting nonsense and making strange sounds.

After the group made the two recordings that went into the "Inner Groove," engineer Geoff Emerick more or less applied the methodology

John and the Maharishi at Rishi Kesh at the foot of the Himalayas, March 8, 1968.
Archive Photos

used for "Mr. Kite": he cut up the tapes and reassembled them in a haphazard fashion, then ran them backwards. In its final form, the "Inner Groove"—which, not surprisingly, was John Lennon's idea—sounds like a very short burst of laughter, noise, and what some have translated as a voice saying "Fuck me like a superman."

This minuscule piece, tacked on to the end of "A Day in the Life," constituted the only *audible* difference between the British *Sgt. Pepper* and its American counterpart. (Though no humans could hear it, the British version also featured a 20,000-Hz tone audible only to dogs.) The "Inner Groove" came not at the end of "A Day in the Life," but all the way on the inner label on the record, so that if the listener's tone-arm did not pick up automatically, it would play over and over and over.

The "Sgt. Pepper Inner Groove" did not become available to American listeners until 1980, with the release of the *Rarities* album.

Sgt. Pepper's Lonely Hearts Club Band

Sgt. Pepper's Lonely Hearts Club Band, released on June 1, 1967, has long since transcended the realm of music, becoming a part of modern mythology. This disc set the standard for sound recording, and *Sgt. Pepper* is a synonym for greatness; hence people commonly refer to an artist's finest achievement as his or her *Sgt. Pepper*.

Even though the Beatles themselves disavowed the assertion, *Sgt. Pepper* was really the first "concept" album—that is, an LP that unites all or most of its songs under a common theme. Unlike the sometimes too-earnest efforts of other groups that would follow the Beatles, the theme in *Sgt. Pepper* is more a matter of style than of "message." Whether the Beatles fully intended it or not, the listener's consciousness fills in the idea of a complete and unified work, a sort of psychedelic vaudeville show. Little touches throughout—the audience sounds that recur after "Within You Without You," the "Sgt. Pepper" theme reprise—reinforce this sense.

When the Beatles recorded their first album, *Please Please Me*, a scant four years before, the entire recording took place in one thirteen-hour session and cost only £400 (about $1,000). *Sgt. Pepper's Lonely Hearts Club Band*, their eighth album, took four months to record and cost £50,000, or $120,000. Engineer Geoff Emerick, who after the Beatles and George Martin deserved the most credit for the finished product, calculated that the group devoted 700 hours to the making of the album.

The Long Silence

In August 1966, the Beatles had issued *Revolver* and played their last concert. For the next three months they rested, and all except for Ringo tried new experiences.

John Lennon appeared in Richard Lester's *How I Won the War*—the first movie to feature one Beatle without the other three—as well as the Dudley Moore British comedy show, *Not Only—But Also*.

Paul McCartney composed the music for *The Family Way* soundtrack, the first Beatles solo album, and went on a Kenyan safari with Jane Asher. He attended "classical" concerts, plays, and art exhibits with Jane, and told a newsman, "I'm trying to cram everything in, all the things I've missed. People are saying things and painting things and writing things and composing things that are great, and I must know. . . ."

George Harrison went to India to study sitar under Ravi Shankar. There he learned the rudiments of the instrument and of Hinduism, both of which would soon become popular among Western youth largely due to his influence.

In December 1966, the four vacationers reassembled at Abbey Road Studios and began work on a follow-up to *Revolver*, but after a month they had worked on only three tracks: "Strawberry Fields Forever," "Penny Lane," and "When I'm Sixty-Four." They broke for Christmas, and this would be the first holiday season in four years that did not see the release of a new Beatles album, since their records had traditionally hit the stores right at gift-buying time.

On January 19, 1967, they returned to the studios, and soon afterward decided to release a single using the two best songs from the previous sessions. So in February, the group issued "Penny Lane" / "Strawberry Fields Forever." The public had waited six months between *Revolver* and the single—the longest they had ever, or would ever, wait for new Beatles material between October 1962 and May 1970.

The "Concept" Emerges

The previous year, Paul had written an insignificant song about a fictitious Victorian bandleader. Neither he nor the other Beatles set out to create a "concept" for the album; it just evolved, and eventually the idea emerged that they should use this track as the album's theme song.

At that time, Victoriana was the rage in London, though as with most revival movements, those styles were reinterpreted in keeping with the times. Hence the quasi-Victorian idea of Sgt. Pepper and his lonely hearts club band fit squarely with the zeitgeist, as did the outlandish name. As Paul recalled three decades later, in 1967 there were a number of West Coast groups with long, colorful-sounding names, the most famous probably being Janis Joplin's original band, Big Brother and the Holding Company.

So the title song created the idea of a fictitious group, a sort of Beatles alter ego, and the already completed "When I'm Sixty-Four," with its 1920s-style melody, fit with the old-fashioned motif. The next song the group began recording was "A Day in the Life," to which they continued adding touches throughout the making of *Sgt. Pepper*. Eventually it became apparent that the real theme of the album was not the shadow marching band or the Victorian concept, but experimentation—with drugs least of all, but rather with ideas, with technology, with music itself.

John drew upon ordinary fixtures of everyday experience—a child's painting, a circus poster, a corn flakes commercial, and a series of random newspaper clippings—to create some of the most remarkable songs he ever wrote: "Lucy in the Sky with Diamonds," "Being for the Benefit of Mr. Kite!" "Good Morning Good Morning," and "A Day in the Life." George interpreted the Hindu scriptures, and used the Eastern music he had studied while in India for "Within You Without You." Besides playing his most

The Beatles display a photograph of themselves in their Sgt. Pepper *costumes.* Archive Photos/Express Newspapers

accomplished performance as the lovable buffoon in "With a Little Help from My Friends," Ringo provided a solid, strong drum backing on all tracks except "She's Leaving Home" and "Within You Without You." (The former used no percussion, and the latter featured the talents of an Indian musician on tabla.)

Other Voices, Other Sounds

One of the most remarkable aspects of *Sgt. Pepper*, a feature that greatly served to enhance the idea that the whole record was a performance by a band other than the Beatles, was the inclusion of extraneous voices and sounds throughout the album.

A number of the audience sounds came from the Abbey Road sound archives. One of the tapes used most was "Volume 28: Audience Applause And Atmosphere, Royal Albert Hall and Queen Elizabeth Hall." The name of the tape sounded like something from *Sgt. Pepper*, and it was even recorded partially at a place mentioned in "A Day in the Life." More effects came from "Volume 6: Applause and Laughter," made in 1961 at a London show called *Beyond the Fringe*.

As for the sound of an orchestra warming up at the very beginning of the album, that came from recordings of the musicians who performed in "A Day in the Life"—when they actually were warming up. Hence this was not just a "canned" effect, imported from elsewhere and made to fit into the context of the album.

Nor was the applause that Martin and Emerick used to cover the transition from the intro song to "With a Little Help from My Friends." This came from the then-unreleased recordings of the Beatles live at the Hollywood Bowl, not issued until almost exactly ten years later, in May 1977.

Faces in the Crowd

The Beatles completed most of *Sgt. Pepper's Lonely Hearts Club Band* before April 3, 1967, since Paul was flying to the U.S. that day. By then they had long before decided that to complement a work of such color and originality, they needed an appropriate cover, and they commissioned designer Peter Blake to stage the project.

Having decided that the jacket would show a collage "crowd scene" standing behind the band members, each of the Beatles selected various contemporary and historical characters to include. Naturally, the executives at EMI were not excited by such a controversial idea, but the Beatles usually got their way. So it was that Brian Epstein's assistant Wendy Hanson wrote to each person—or, in the case of the deceased, to their estates—requesting permission to include them on the cover of the Beatles' latest album.

Someone—probably George—had wanted Gandhi on the cover, but EMI drew the line, saying that this might seem offensive in India, and would therefore hurt sales. They also nixed an idea from (who else?) John that Hitler appear in the already-motley crowd.

Those pictured on the cover of *Sgt. Pepper* are, from left to right, back row: Sri Yukteswar Giri, an Indian guru; Aleister Crowley, black magician and self-styled "Beast 666"; Mae West; comedian Lenny Bruce; Karlheinz Stockhausen, a German composer; W. C. Fields; C. G. Jung, psychologist and author of *Synchronicity*; Edgar Allan Poe; Fred Astaire; Richard Merkin, an American artist; woman [some sources list her as "the Vargas Girl," though she may be Clara Bow, silent film starlet]; Huntz Hall, bowery boy actor; Simon Rodia, folk artist who created the Watts Towers in Los Angeles; and Bob Dylan.

[Second row from back]: Stuart Sutcliffe, the fifth Beatle, who died in 1961; [above him] Aubrey Beardsley, Victorian illustrator; [woman in green hat unidentified, though one source lists her as "wax hairdresser's dummy"];

Sir Robert Peel, pioneer in police investigative work (in whose honor British policemen are nicknamed "bobbies"); Aldous Huxley, author of *Brave New World*; Dylan Thomas, Welsh poet; Terry Southern, author of *Candy* and *The Magic Christian* (Ringo would later star in the film versions of both books); Dion, of Dion and the Belmonts; Tony Curtis; Wallace Berman, California artist and actor; Tommy Handley, wartime comedian; [looking up] missionary and explorer Dr. David Livingstone, in wax; Marilyn Monroe; author William S. Burroughs; Sri Mahavatara Babaji, a guru; Stan Laurel of Laurel and Hardy; Richard Lindner, New York artist; Oliver Hardy of Laurel and Hardy; Karl Marx; H. G. Wells; Sri Paramahansa Yogananda, a guru; a cardboard cutout of T. E. Lawrence, or Lawrence of Arabia; [unidentified woman in yellow-and-red striped hat above Lawrence—may be hairdresser's dummy].

[Second row from front]: unidentified woman [may be hairdresser's dummy]; Max Miller, comedian; another unidentified woman [some sources list her as "The Petty Girl"]; Marlon Brando; Tom Mix, cowboy star of silent films; Oscar Wilde, Irish playwright; actor Tyrone Power; Larry Bell, painter; Johnny Weismuller, star of several *Tarzan* films; [waving] Izzy Bonn, comedian; [behind him] Stephen Crane, author of *The Red Badge of Courage*; playwright George Bernard Shaw, in wax; Albert Stubbins, Liverpool football star; Sri Lahiri Mahasaya, guru; Albert Einstein; Lewis Carroll.

[Front row]: boxer Sonny Liston, in wax; the Beatles' Madame Tussaud wax figures, depicting them as they appeared in 1964; the Beatles in the flesh, as they appeared in 1967, John holding a French horn, Ringo a trumpet, Paul a *cor anglais,* and George a piccolo (uniforms by Douglas Hayward); Bobby Breen, child singer; actress Marlene Dietrich, in a cardboard cutout; unidentified man in fez; [in front of him] Shirley Temple; and Diana Dors, actress, in wax.

(Though most people on the *Sgt. Pepper* cover are readily identifiable, there is some disagreement about the more obscure figures. An excellent online source of information, which provides profiles of each person depicted—and which differs with the above in some particulars—is "Sgt. Pepper's Lonely Hearts Club Members" by Rebecca Proctor and Alea Schroeder at http://students.cedarcrest.edu:81/users/rlprocto/web/index2.html.)

Sgt. Pepper's Lonely Hearts Club Band and their illustrious guests had apparently gathered for a funeral—to mourn the passing of the old Beatles. The four dark-clothed wax figures to the left stare down at a grave whose flowers form the word "BEATLES," as well as the shape of a star and a guitar.

Various dolls, selected from the group members' own homes, surround the grave. They range from the prim sky-blue Victorian on the left to the four-armed, red-robed Hindu goddess in the very front of the group. Off to the far right sits a doll wearing a sweater that says "WELCOME THE ROLLING STONES" and, on the sleeve, "GOOD GUYS."

Though its "men in suits" spent hours haggling over the cover, EMI missed one little detail. Lining the Beatles' grave—in one of the most clever "hidden messages" ever used by the group—is a row of marijuana plants. (Peter Blake, however, insisted that these were ordinary houseplants.)

Innovative Packaging

The cover was by far the most detailed piece of artwork ever used on an album, but it was far from the only innovation in the packaging of *Sgt. Pepper*.

At the time, the idea of a double album was almost unheard of, except for Dylan's *Blonde on Blonde* a year before, and—in the following year—the Beatles' own White Album. At least as unusual was the notion of a single album that opened up in the middle just like a double one, which this one did. (According to one unlikely account, this was because the group had originally considered making a double album, but decided against it when they realized they didn't have enough material.)

Inside, the fans found a brightly colored picture of Sgt. Pepper's Band. Early versions of the album also included several cardboard cutouts, much like prizes inside a cereal box.

But the greatest innovation of all, or at the least the most ultimately significant one, lay on the back cover. There, superimposed over yet another view of the band, were the lyrics to the songs. The idea of a lyrics sheet, followed to its logical conclusion, promoted the concept that rock 'n' roll was an art form. And that was exactly what the Beatles were saying by clearly displaying the lyrics on the back cover.

Eventually lyrics sheets and elaborate album covers would become de rigueur, but the Beatles were the first.

Praise and Aspersions

Unlike most music at the frontiers of experimentation, *Sgt. Pepper* was eminently listenable, and hence it swept that bastion of safety and commercialism, the Grammy Awards. Not only did it take Album of the Year for 1967, it also earned the title of Best Contemporary Rock 'n' Roll Recording. Geoff Emerick took the Best Engineered Recording award for his work on *Sgt. Pepper*. As for Best Album Cover, the album was a shoo-in.

But the praise was not universal. Dr. Joseph Crow, lauded by certain groups as "America's number-one expert on musical subversion," wrote that

> For them [Lennon and McCartney] to have written some of their songs is like someone who had not had physics or math inventing the A-Bomb. . . . Because of its technical excellence it is possible that this music is put together by behavioral scientists in a 'think tank.'. . . I have no idea whether the Beatles know what they are doing or

whether they are being used by some enormously sophisticated people. . . .

And then there were the drug references. A few years after its release, Vice President Spiro Agnew tried to have "With a Little Help from My Friends" banned for the line "I get high with a little help from my friends." On another drug charge, for Paul's smoke-induced "dream" and John's "I'd love to turn you on," the BBC took "A Day in the Life" off the air.

A few barbs directed at the album came from much closer to home. There was, first of all, the rumor that Bob Dylan had snapped "turn that off!" when he heard the album. More certain—and closer still—was Brian Epstein's dislike of the cover. Ever conscious of the group's image and the need not to offend, a sensitivity he had no doubt developed growing up gay in postwar England, Epstein thought the cover was simply too much. Before he boarded a plane in early 1967, prior to the album's release, he scrawled out a last wish in case the plane crashed: "Brown paper bags for *Sgt. Pepper*."

* * * * *

Sgt. Pepper's Lonely Hearts Club Band Song List

Title	Composer	Time
Side One		
Sgt. Pepper's Lonely Hearts Club Band	McCartney	1:59
With a Little Help from My Friends	Lennon–McCartney	2:46
Lucy in the Sky with Diamonds	Lennon	3:25
Getting Better	McCartney	2:47
Fixing a Hole	McCartney	2:33
She's Leaving Home	McCartney	3:24
Being for the Benefit of Mr. Kite!	Lennon	2:36
Side Two		
Within You Without You	Harrison	5:03
When I'm Sixty-Four	McCartney	2:38
Lovely Rita	McCartney	2:43
Good Morning, Good Morning	Lennon	2:35
Sgt. Pepper's Lonely Hearts Club Band (Reprise)	McCartney	1:20
A Day in the Life	Lennon–McCartney	5:03
20,000-Hz tone*		0:08
Sgt. Pepper Inner Groove*		0:02

*British version only.

"Sgt. Pepper's Lonely Hearts Club Band (Reprise)"

The reprise of the "Sgt. Pepper" theme, a thundering piece of rock 'n' roll that announces the final coup-de-grace of *Sgt. Pepper*, occurred to Paul McCartney almost as an afterthought. On April 1, 1967, the last day that he participated in the recording of *Sgt. Pepper*, he decided to do the reprise in order to further the concept that the whole album was a single show by Sgt. Pepper's band.

The song shares certain characteristics with "The End" on *Abbey Road* two years later. Both George Harrison and John Lennon play lead guitar (no rhythm guitar), and all three sing lead vocal, without any backing.

At the beginning of the song, Paul counts the intro: "One, two, three, four." Just between the two and the three, John's voice says "'Bye."

"She Loves You"

"She Loves You," the Beatles' fourth single, became the group's first gold record. From the time of its release in 1963 until late 1977 it was the biggest-selling single of all time in Great Britain. The song that replaced it was Paul McCartney's "Mull of Kintyre."

Years later, John Lennon would recall that even though he and Paul often wrote their songs separately, this one was truly a Lennon–McCartney composition. They wrote it sitting on twin beds at a hotel in Newcastle, and recorded it five days later.

Several things about the song are unusual. First of all, instead of what was then the usual first-person framework for love songs—"I love you"—this one used second person: "*She* loves *you*." Thus it had something both for the girls, the group's principal fans at that point, and for the boys—who would presumably be flattered by the message. Musically the song is remarkable because it begins with the chorus, rather than the first verse. And of course it introduced the phrase "Yeah yeah yeah." This would become the Beatles' trademark line in that early period of their popularity, even though very few of their songs other than this one used the phrase.

"She Said She Said"

John Lennon later described the events that led to the writing of "She Said She Said," the last song on Side One of *Revolver*.

He and Ringo were in California in early 1966, doing acid at a house they had rented somewhere in the hills. It was a sunny day, and everybody with them was having a great time—except for one of the guests, who kept going around saying "I know what it's like to be dead." This was Peter Fonda, four years before he made *Easy Rider*—and many, many years before a later generation would know him as Bridget Fonda's dad.

John and Ringo kept telling him to shut up, but he wouldn't. Lennon later reversed Fonda's sex and wrote "She Said She Said."

Tony Sheridan

On the Beatles' second trip to Hamburg in 1961, Polydor Records executive Bert Kaempfert arranged what would become the group's first commercial recording, as backup to popular nightclub singer Tony Sheridan.

The recordings, at Friedrich Ebert Halle in Hamburg on June 22, featured the Beatles backing Sheridan on five songs and performing two of their own. The two most famous Sheridan–Beatles recordings are "My Bonnie" and "The Saints," released as a single that later sparked the interest of Liverpool businessman Brian Epstein. In Germany, however, the single listed the backup band as the Beat Brothers because the marketing people at Polydor were afraid Germans would mistake "Beatles" for the slang "peedles," which means *penis*.

The two recordings made solely by the Beatles during this session were "Ain't She Sweet," a cover of the 1920s song, for which John sings lead; and "Cry for a Shadow." The title of the latter refers to the Shadows, a popular British group who had backed singer Cliff Richard, but originally it had a less imaginative name: "The Beatle Bop." This is the only Lennon–Harrison songwriting collaboration known to exist, and was also the group's first instrumental, the second not appearing until six years later with "Flying" from *Magical Mystery Tour*.

All of the above-named songs, except for "The Saints," appear on *The Beatles Anthology 1*. (See also **The Beat Brothers**.)

"She's Leaving Home"

"She's Leaving Home," written by Paul McCartney, is the only *Sgt. Pepper* track on which none of the Beatles plays a single instrument. Both

McCartney and John Lennon sing, but the backing comes entirely from guest musicians on harp and strings.

It is also the only song in the group's history, of the ones which involved "classical" instruments, that George Martin did not score. Since neither John or Paul could read music, they normally had to describe to Martin what they wanted, and then he would write down the notation for the instruments. But on this song, Mike Leander did the scoring.

Though this is Paul's song, John apparently came up with the counterpoint lines he sings, from the parents' point of view: "What did we do that was wrong?" etc.

Sitar

George Harrison first discovered the sitar on the set of *Help!*, where it was being used as an exotic prop. On the Beatles' final tour, Harrison, McCartney, and Lennon purchased sitars from a music store in India, and though the other two never developed much interest in the instrument—which is considerably harder to master than the guitar—Harrison stayed with it. Eventually he popularized the sitar in the Western world, and became the world's most famous sitar player. (After all, he was the one who made his friend, sitar master Ravi Shankar, famous in the West.)

Yet Harrison actually played the instrument on only six Beatles songs: "Norwegian Wood (This Bird Has Flown)," "Girl," "Tomorrow Never Knows," "Lucy in the Sky with Diamonds," "Within You Without You," and "Across the Universe." Two other Harrison compositions feature only Indian musicians playing the sitar and other traditional instruments such as the tabla: "Love You To" and "The Inner Light."

"Something"

"Something," one of George Harrison's two *Abbey Road* compositions, proved that he could write songs every bit as good as those of Lennon and McCartney.

The single "Something" / "Come Together," released in October 1969, was Harrison's first and only A-side as a Beatle. It sold more copies than any of the group's songs except "Hey Jude" and "I Want to Hold Your Hand." Frank Sinatra called it "the greatest love song of the past fifty years" (though

George learns to play the sitar from Ravi Shankar, August 7, 1967. Archive Photos/Popperfoto

he routinely attributed it to Lennon and McCartney), and John Lennon said it was his favorite *Abbey Road* track. Outside of "Yesterday," it has been covered more times than any Beatles song.

Yet the single was the first since "Penny Lane" / "Strawberry Fields Forever" not to reach Number One in Britain. This was probably because the album of its origin came out *before* the single, the first time this ever happened in the Beatles' career, and hence a lot of fans already owned copies of *Abbey Road*.

George wrote the song for his wife, Patti. He lifted the opening line, "Something in the way she moves," from the title of an early hit by Apple recording artist James Taylor. (Then again, Taylor used the phrase "I feel fine" in his own song.)

Songs

The Beatles released 118 songs from 1962 to 1966, and 97 songs from 1967 to 1970, making a total of 215 compositions. Of these 215, the largest number—161—are listed as Lennon–McCartney compositions. (Of course the vast majority of those 161 were composed by either Lennon *or* McCartney, but not both.)

Cover Versions

The next most numerous category of songs are those composed by others. Before the Lennon–McCartney songwriting partnership matured, the group supplemented their own songs with those of other, more established writers. These included many of the artists they had admired during the Liverpool and Hamburg days, such as Chuck Berry, Charles Hardin Holly (a.k.a. Buddy Holly), Richard Penniman (a.k.a. Little Richard), and Carl Perkins.

The twenty-four Beatles cover versions are as follows, in order of their release:

"Anna (Got to Him)"—Arthur Alexander
"Chains"—Gerry Goffin / Carole King
"Boys"—Luther Dixon / Wes Farrell
"Baby It's You"—Hal David / Burt Bacharach / Barney Williams
"A Taste of Honey"—Ric Marlow / Bobby Scott
"Twist and Shout"—Phil Medley / Burt Russell
"Till There Was You"—Meredith Willson
"Please Mr. Postman"—Brian Holland / Robert Bateman / Berry Gordy
"Roll Over Beethoven"—Chuck Berry
"You Really Got a Hold on Me"—William "Smokey" Robinson
"Devil in Her Heart"—Richard B. Drapkin
"Money"—Janie Bradford / Berry Gordy
"Long Tall Sally"—Enotris Johnson / Richard Penniman / Robert "Bumps" Blackwell
"Matchbox"—Carl Perkins

"Slow Down"—Larry Williams
"Rock and Roll Music"—Chuck Berry
"Mr. Moonlight"—Roy Lee Johnson
"Kansas City"—Jerry Lieber / Mike Stoller; "Hey-Hey-Hey-Hey!"—
  Richard Penniman
"Words Of Love"—Charles Hardin "Buddy" Holly
"Honey Don't"—Carl Perkins
"Everybody's Tryin' to Be My Baby"—Carl Perkins
"Dizzy Miss Lizzie"—Larry Williams
"Bad Boy"—Larry Williams
"Act Naturally"—Vonie Morrison / Johnny Russell

George's Songs

Next most numerous are George Harrison's compositions, which number twenty-two. They are, along with the years of their release:

1963:	"Don't Bother Me"
1965:	"I Need You"
	"You Like Me Too Much"
	"Think for Yourself"
	"If I Needed Someone"
1966:	"Taxman"
	"Love You To"
	"I Want to Tell You"
1967:	"Within You Without You"
	"Blue Jay Way"
1968:	"The Inner Light"
	"While My Guitar Gently Weeps"
	"Piggies"
	"Long Long Long"
	"Savoy Truffle"
1969:	"Only a Northern Song"
	"It's All Too Much"
	"Old Brown Shoe"
	"Something"
	"Here Comes the Sun"
1970:	"I Me Mine"
	"For You Blue"

Ringo's Songs and the Rest

Ringo Starr wrote two Beatles songs, "Don't Pass Me By" from the White Album, and "Octopus's Garden" on *Abbey Road*.

There are two songs composed by all four Beatles: "Flying" from *Magical Mystery Tour*, and "Dig It," a snippet of which appears on *Let It Be*.

On two more songs, Lennon and McCartney share composing credits with three translators. These were the versions of "I Want to Hold Your Hand" and "She Loves You" recorded in German: "Komm, Gib Mir Deine Hand" (whose translators' last names are listed as Nicholas and Hellmer) and "Sie Liebt Dich" (Nicholas and Montague).

The only three-way composition in the Beatles catalogue is the 1965 Lennon–McCartney–Starkey song "What Goes On?"

Finally, the Beatles' short recording of "Maggie Mae," a Liverpudlian song of unknown authorship, is listed on *Let It Be* as "traditional, arranged by Harrison–Lennon–McCartney–Starkey."

Longest, Shortest, and Worst

The Beatles' shortest "song" is the "Sgt. Pepper Inner Groove." Their shortest *actual song* is "Her Majesty" from *Abbey Road*, just twenty-three seconds long. There are three other Beatles tracks, all recorded in 1968 and 1969, that are under one minute long: the uncredited "Can You Take Me Back" (0:27) from the White Album; and "Maggie Mae" (0:39) and "Dig It" (0:51) from *Let It Be*.

When "Hey Jude" came out in August 1968 it was, at seven minutes, eleven seconds, the longest single ever released by a major rock artist. The longest *song* by the Beatles is Lennon's "I Want You (She's So Heavy)," which runs for 7:49. And the Beatles' longest recording or composition, as opposed to song, is "Revolution 9," at eight minutes, fifteen seconds.

"Revolution 9" is further distinguished by the fact that, in a 1971 poll conducted by New York radio station WPLJ and the *Village Voice*, it won the title of "Worst Beatles Song of All Time." The runners up were, in order, "Mr. Moonlight," "You Know My Name (Look Up the Number)," "Helter Skelter," and "Do You Want To Know a Secret."

Songs Featuring Only Three, Two, One . . .

When Paul McCartney introduced the world to "Yesterday" in 1965, he did more than simply launch one of the most popular songs of all time. He also started a phenomenon that would help lead to the Beatles' breakup: a solo song presented as a group effort. For the first time ever, the Beatles released a song on which John, George, and Ringo played no part. From then on, there would be songs in which three, two, or even just one Beatle played or sang. In the one-man-band area, the versatile McCartney would prove most adept, but George had his Indian-only compositions, and even Ringo performed alone with an orchestra.

Listed below are songs that—as far as it is possible to tell—feature the vocals and/or instrumentation of fewer than four Beatles, though they may include outsiders (and often do):

Three: (Lennon, McCartney, Harrison)
           "Back in the U.S.S.R."
           "Because"
           (Lennon, McCartney, Starkey)
           "I Will"
Two: (Lennon, McCartney)
           "She's Leaving Home"
           "The Ballad of John and Yoko"
           (McCartney, Starkey)
           "For No One"
           "Why Don't We Do It in the Road"
One: (McCartney)
           "Yesterday"
           "Eleanor Rigby"
           "Wild Honey Pie"
           "Martha My Dear"
           "Blackbird"
           "Mother Nature's Son"
           "Can You Take Me Back"
           "Her Majesty"
           (Harrison)
           "Love You To"
           "Within You Without You"
           "The Inner Light"
           (Starkey)
           "Good Night"
           (Lennon)
           "Julia"

. . . Or None of the Beatles

The emergence of recordings that involved three, two, or only one Beatle resulted from the fact that the group was bringing in more and more guest musicians to augment the work of themselves and George Martin—another phenomenon inaugurated with "Yesterday."

Though Paul strums a guitar on "Yesterday," a string quartet provides the majority of the musical backing. The next album, *Rubber Soul*, made use of no musicians other than the group members, Martin, and road manager Mal Evans, but *Revolver* showed the work of numerous guest instrumentalists.

That album's second track, "Eleanor Rigby," heralded a further departure from conventional ideas about what a rock song should be. Paul sings a double-tracked vocal, but otherwise neither he nor any of the Beatles plays a single note, that job being given to a string octet. Likewise on "Love You To," the instrumentation was too complex to accommodate George's limited experience with the sitar, so he turned over all the instrumental work to the Indian musicians who play on the song. Other than George's vocals, no Beatle performs at all on that recording.

There are three other Beatles songs on which no Beatle plays an instrument: "She's Leaving Home," "The Inner Light," and "Good Night."

Where's the Title?

In the vast majority of Beatles songs, the title appears as part of the chorus: "She loves you," "I want to hold your hand," etc. Bob Dylan, by contrast, made a fashion of recording songs that do not include the title anywhere in the lyrics: "Positively Fourth Street," "Rainy Day Women #12 and #35," "Ballad of a Thin Man." There are only eight Beatles songs like this, most by John and George and all from the LSD/meditation phase or later: "Love You To," "Tomorrow Never Knows," "A Day in the Life," "Blue Jay Way," "The Inner Light," "Yer Blues," "The Ballad of John and Yoko," and "For You Blue." (See also the discussion of the "title line" recording under **"I Will."**)

Songs About the Beatles

As seen from the proliferation of Beatles merchandise in 1964 and 1965, entrepreneurs could make money from almost anything having to do with the Beatles—including songs about them. These are not to be confused with cover versions of Beatles songs; these are actual songs *about* the Beatles, the majority of which appeared in the mid-1960s.

Some of the offerings from the early days include "We Want the Beatles" by the Vernon Girls; "Beatle Crazy" by Bill Clifton; "The Boy with the Beatle Hair" by the Swans; and "A Beatle I Want to Be" by Sonny Curtis, best remembered for his hit "I Fought the Law."

Ringo was apparently the most popular musical inspiration, as the titles "Ringo for President" and "You Can't Go Far Without a Guitar Unless You're Ringo Starr" (the latter by Neil Sheppard) reveal. When Ringo married Maureen Cox on February 11, 1965, a group of resolute female admirers called Angie and the Chiclettes recorded "Treat Him Tender Maureen." Of special interest was "I Love Ringo," a 1964 recording produced by Phil

Spector and sung by Bonnie Jo Mason. Within half a decade Miss Mason would create her own phenomenon under a new name—Cher.

In July 1964, England's *New Musical Express* reported that a group called "The Bumblers" were recording a Beatles parody. The Bumblers, a rare example of a group in which the sum of the parts was actually *greater* than the whole, consisted of Frank Sinatra, Sammy Davis, Jr., Bing Crosby, and Dean Martin. Several months after the Bumblers recording, Sinatra and Martin, like many other people half their age, tried and failed to get tickets to the Beatles' Hollywood Bowl concert.

Probably the most inspired Beatles takeoff—one that has often been attributed to the Beatles themselves—was "L.S. Bumble Bee" / "Bee Side," released in early 1967 on Decca, a label that had rejected the Beatles five years before. Peter Cooke sang background vocals, and on lead vocal was the distinctly Lennonesque voice of Dudley Moore. At that time, Moore was well known in Britain, but it would be another twelve years before he gained a U.S. audience with the success of *10* in 1979.

Another comedian released a Beatles parody, this one in 1966, a single of "A Hard Day's Night" backed with "Help!" Long before he met the Beatles, George Martin had produced early comedy records by this artist—Peter Sellers—who went on to star in films ranging from *Dr. Strangelove* to *Being There* (and who appeared with Ringo in *The Magic Christian* in 1969).

In the wake of the "Paul Is Dead" hoax of the late 1960s, another wave of Beatles-related recordings appeared. These consisted mainly of tributes to the "late" Paul McCartney, such as "St. Paul" by Terry Knight, who would later create Grand Funk Railroad; and "The Ballad of Paul (Follow the Bouncing Ball)" by The Mystery Tour.

In 1975, the English group Barclay James Harvest scored a minor hit with "Titles," composed of Beatles song titles strung together: thus the line "Lady Madonna, let it be."

Richard Starkey, a.k.a. Ringo Starr, Drummer for the Beatles

Born: July 7, 1940, at 9 Madryn St., Dingle, Liverpool.

Family: Father, Richard Starkey; Mother, Elsie Starkey. Only child.

Schools: St. Silas Primary, Dingle Vale Secondary.

Married: Maureen Cox, hairdresser, on February 11, 1965. Divorced 1975 (Maureen died 1994). Married Barbara Bach, actress, on April 27, 1981.

Children: Three, all by Maureen: two sons, Zak and Jason; one daughter, Leigh.

In the early days of Beatlemania, Ringo was the favorite of the girls, even though he was the least conventionally handsome. The majority of songs written about the Beatles in 1964 and 1965 were for Ringo, and many assumed he was the leader of the group, because his unique name and size (he was 5'8", whereas the other three all stood 5'11") made him stand out.

From the beginning, Ringo played the role of the sad buffoon, and he had a guaranteed vocal spot on virtually every album. He was like a latter-day Charlie Chaplin, and his mournful voice gave just the right touch to songs such as "Honey Don't" and "Act Naturally." As the group evolved, he provided a much-needed counterpoint to the sometimes exaggerated self-importance of the other three.

Ringo Starr and wife Maureen leave a London maternity hospital, September 22, 1965. A nurse holds their newborn son, Zak. Archive Photos/Popperfoto

Ringo the Renaissance Man

John Lennon himself expressed distaste for the idea that he was the Beatle with the highest I.Q., and Ringo the one with the lowest. *A Hard Day's Night*, he said, annoyed him with its portrayal of "me witty, Ringo dumb and cute."

Ringo's report card at age twelve described him as "quiet, thoughtful, a slow worker—but doing his best." In later life, however—perhaps because he lagged behind the others musically—he would establish himself as the most versatile of the four band members.

There was his music, of course; aside from his own solo albums, he played backup for his former bandmates, their onetime idol Lonnie Donegan, Peter Frampton, and many others. He appeared on *The Concert for Bangladesh*, and played on the superstar ensemble for the Band's ostensible 1976 farewell, *The Last Waltz*.

But music was only part of it. There was acting, too, which he pursued with far more vigor than did the other three Beatles. Besides his Beatles roles, he was in numerous other movies, including *Candy* (1968); *The Magic Christian* (1969), *200 Motels* as Frank Zappa (1969); *Blindman* (1971); *Born to Boogie*, a documentary about the musician Marc Bolan/T. Rex which Ringo directed (1972); *That'll Be the Day* (1973); *Son of Dracula* (1974); *Lisztomania* (1975); *Stardust* (1976); and *Caveman* (1981).

He also took the photographs of the Beatles at home featured in Hunter Davies's *Authorized Biography*, and began designing furniture for his own company, Ringo or Robin, Ltd., in 1975. He even had a brief foray as a restaurateur in Atlanta during the 1980s.

How Ringo Got His Sad Look

Whereas George enjoyed a relatively happy and normal childhood and Paul would have if his mother hadn't died, the two older Beatles had a harder time of it. John's younger years were far from idyllic, and Ringo's were downright dismal.

The eldest of the four Beatles came from one of Liverpool's poorest sections, the Dingle. His parents divorced when he was three, and his mother remarried when he was eleven. The boy suffered a series of illnesses, and had to spend long periods in the hospital for pleurisy (and also once for appendicitis).

In 1955 he left his hospital bed for the last time, having missed so much school that he could hardly even read and write. The headmasters at Dingle Vale Secondary did even not remember who he was, and he finally gave up on trying to complete his education. (Interestingly, however, once the Beatles became popular, the Dingle Vale administrators miraculously found the desk where Ringo had once sat, and charged visitors admission to view it.)

Ringo had first discovered the drums while in the hospital, and received a drum kit for Christmas in 1959, when he was nineteen years old. He joined the Eddie Clayton skiffle group soon afterward, and later left to play for Rory Storme and the Hurricanes.

Around this time, Richard Starkey became Ringo Starr. He had first been called "Rings" Starkey because of the many rings he wore on his fingers, but he changed this to "Rings" *Starr*, so that his drum performance could be called "Starr Time." He eventually changed this to the cowboyish pseudonym of Ringo Starr.

As with John, who almost moved to New Zealand in his childhood and thus probably wouldn't have met Paul, the world very nearly missed Ringo. In 1961, he applied to the Houston Chamber of Commerce, hoping to come to America to be a cowboy. Ringo had always been fascinated with the cowboy mystique, and when he saw on a record jacket that bluesman Lightnin' Hopkins came from Houston, he decided to move to that city. But he changed his mind when, in his own words, ". . . the really big [immigration] forms arrived, all about was your grandfather's great dane a commie."

Ringo's Fans

After joining the Beatles in 1962, Ringo began playing with them at Liverpool's Cavern Club, where he met his future wife, Maureen Cox. Maureen, a hairdresser, later recalled that jealous female fans would come to her to get their hair done and threaten her while they were under the hair dryer.

Ringo took his driver's test twice, and failed both times. On the third try, however, he passed, having driven without a license for two years. And in March 1964, Ringo Starr, who had the equivalent of a grammar school education, became the honorary Vice President of Leeds University in England.

But the sickliness that had shadowed him as a child, keeping him in the hospital and out of school, continued to dog him in adulthood. Between June 4 and June 15, 1964, Ringo was ill with throat trouble, and Jimmy Nicol sat in as the group's drummer while they continued to tour. In November of that year, Ringo had his tonsils removed. While American fans stood constant vigil, radio stations kept them posted on the latest details of the operation and recovery. People offered him fantastic sums of money for the tonsils once they were removed, but he requested that they be destroyed.

And yet Ringo collected a little fan memorabilia of his own. Just as Paul McCartney got his hero Buddy Holly's cufflinks, Ringo received a cowboy holster from Elvis Presley. He hung it behind the bar of his home in Weybridge, Surrey.

Even Ringo Had His Detractors

A reporter for the *Jewish Chronicle* once contacted Ringo, assuming that because of his nose, he must be Jewish. Less friendly people sometimes made the same assumption, hurling anti-Semitic epithets at him.

Ringo usually distinguished himself by how well he got along with people—but not always. In early 1963, when the Beatles toured Britain as backup band for child star Helen Shapiro, he got himself ejected from a ball at the Carlisle Hotel. The reason for his expulsion was "excessive scruffiness."

At another function, a masked ball held by the British Ambassador in Washington during the Beatles' first visit to the U.S. in 1964, Ringo cursed at the wife of an American diplomat who had lunged at him with a pair of scissors, intent on cutting off a lock of the famous Beatle hair.

Bringing Others Together

Although he wrote only two songs for the Beatles, "Don't Pass Me By" and "Octopus's Garden," Ringo composed several others that the group didn't record—presumably for legal reasons. In Ringo's words, "I'd write tunes that were already written and just change the lyrics, and the other three would have hysterics tellin' me what I'd rewritten."

Later, Ringo brought the four ex-Beatles closer to a reunion than they would ever again come. His 1973 album *Ringo*, critically acclaimed as one of the best post-Beatles albums by any of the four, featured the songwriting talents of John Lennon on "I'm the Greatest"; Paul McCartney on "Six O'Clock"; and George Harrison on "Sunshine Life for Me" and "You and Me (Babe)." Harrison wrote the melody, and Ringo the words, for what would become the hit song "Photograph." All four Beatles perform on the album, though they did not record together.

George and Paul, with their wives, attended Ringo's second wedding in 1981, when he became the only Beatle to marry someone already famous in her own right. This was actress Barbara Bach, who he met while filming *Caveman*. They were married at Marlyebone Register Office in Liverpool, the same place where Paul and Linda McCartney had said their vows twelve years before.

In December 1994, Ringo's former wife Maureen died after a bone-marrow transplant she had received for a pre-leukemic disease. She had married Isaac Tigrett, co-founder of the Hard Rock Cafe, with whom she had a seven-year-old daughter. Ringo, along with his and Maureen's three children, was with her when she died.

"Strawberry Fields Forever"

John Lennon's song "Strawberry Fields Forever" appeared with Paul McCartney's "Penny Lane" on a February 1967 single that ushered in a new era for the Beatles.

Just as Paul romanticized his Liverpool childhood in "Penny Lane," John in this song took his own journey through childhood. As a boy, his aunt Mimi had taken him to the Strawberry Field Salvation Army Home for an annual garden party. It was a happy memory for him, but it must have been tinged with something else, because Strawberry Field was an orphanage, and John eventually lost both of his parents—one to desertion and one to death. Hence it seemed an appropriate setting for his ode to uncertainty.

Long after he left the Beatles, Lennon still referred to "Strawberry Fields," along with "Help!" and "In My Life," as one of his best songs because of its honesty concerning who he was and what he was thinking. He also explained the cryptic verse that begins with the line "No one I think is in my tree." When he was a child, Lennon said, he had noticed he wasn't quite like anyone else—that no one was "in his tree." He had wondered whether he were a genius or a fool—hence the line ". . . it must be high or low."

A Feat of Artistry and Engineering

The recording of "Strawberry Fields Forever" is actually two different versions woven together, and it became one of the Beatles' most complex productions.

Lennon had originally wanted a rock song, so he and the rest of the group recorded an upbeat version with electric guitars and drums. But upon listening to the playback, he decided that this one sounded too raucous for what he had intended as an introspective piece. Therefore he and George Martin assembled a group of musicians, including cellists and trumpeters, and did a more subdued version. However, this didn't please him either.

Then, after listening to the playbacks of both versions, Martin discovered that the slower one could be speeded up 5 percent, so that it corresponded both to the tempo and key of the other. This was far from an obvious solution, but Martin pulled it off, combining the two tapes at a point sixty seconds into the song.

The Surprise Ending

"Strawberry Fields" introduced an innovation that, like other Beatles experiments, has been imitated numerous times since then: the surprise ending, or more accurately, the surprise return or non-ending.

In the few seconds of the surprise return at the end of "Strawberry Fields Forever," John says something that "Paul Is Dead" scholars concluded was "I buried Paul." But Lennon claimed he said "Cranberry sauce," which is clear if one listens to the song. Just *why* he would want to say "Cranberry sauce," on the other hand, is not clear.

Another misconception is that the title of "Strawberry Fields" has something to do with the needle tracks on a junkie's arm. Inasmuch as junkies in the 1960s used the term to describe the telltale marks of their habit, the expression came *after* the song, not vice versa.

"Sun King"

The idea for John Lennon's "Sun King," from Side Two of *Abbey Road*, supposedly came from a dream.

The song certainly makes use of a dream language, which is not really a language at all. The chanting in the middle sounds like it could be Spanish, French, or Italian, and though it borrows from all three, it's really just Lennon nonsense.

As for the enchanting harmonies on the recording, Lennon performs all those himself, double-tracking and multi-tracking his voice in places.

The Sun King, in history at least, was Louis XIV of France, who ruled from 1642 to 1714—seventy-two years, the longest reign of any European monarch. They called it the "golden age" of French history; while his people lived under poverty and oppression, he built the magnificent Palace of Versailles and condemned to death anyone who joked about the fact that he was completely bald under his wig.

Stuart Sutcliffe

During his brief stay in art college in the late 1950s, John Lennon became friends with a moody young man named Stuart Fergusson Victor Sutcliffe. Though Lennon was often exceedingly cruel to the younger boy, they remained close, and together they came up with the name "Beatles."

Stuart was born to be a visual artist, not a musician, and he proved his talent when the noted artist John Moores purchased one of his paintings. This was a great honor, and the £65 Moores paid for the canvas was a huge sum of money then. Such was Lennon's sway that he persuaded Stuart to invest it all in a Hofner President bass guitar, much to the chagrin of Stuart's parents.

Stuart Sutcliffe, an original member of the Beatles, died in 1962.
Archive Photos/Popperfoto

As a bass player, Stuart was never more than a curiosity. He fumbled with the notes, and to compensate for his shyness on stage, usually turned sideways. Yet when promoters and booking agents tried to encourage the others to dump him, they always closed ranks and defended Stuart.

Though Lennon constantly taunted the quiet Sutcliffe, he nonetheless admired him for his artistic sensibilities and his brooding James Dean image. In fact it was Stuart—and his girlfriend Astrid Kirchherr—who introduced the others to the idea of cultivating an *image*, a factor that would become extremely important to their later success.

Stuart played with the Beatles on their first Hamburg trip, but quit before the second; having fallen in love with Astrid, he had decided to get married. When the Beatles returned for their third visit, they were met by a tearful Astrid, who told them that Stuart had died of a brain hemorrhage. On Friday the 13th of April, 1962, the day the group played their first show at the Star Club, Stuart's mother arrived to make funeral arrangements. Some biographers have suggested that his hemorrhage was the result of an injury sustained in a scuffle after an early Beatles show.

Years later, the Beatles paid tribute to their friend by putting his picture on the cover of *Sgt. Pepper*. (See also **Birth of the Beatles; Hamburg.**)

"Taxman"

"Taxman" belongs to a minority of pre-1967 Beatles songs—i.e., the ones that appear on exactly the same album in both the U.S. and Britain. In its case, it was the opening track of *Revolver* on both sides of the Atlantic.

It is also remarkable as one of the very, very few rock songs that express a political viewpoint *other* than the standard left-wing line. Opposing rampant taxation has never been a big cause with the Left, after all, and George Harrison's "Taxman" is the anthem of all those who believe that they, and not others, have a right to the fruits of their labor. Some of the only political rock songs that express a conservative (i.e., anti-revolutionary/totalitarian) viewpoint are "I'd Love to Change the World" by Ten Years After, "Won't Get Fooled Again" by the Who—and "Revolution" by the Beatles. "Taxman" is virtually unique, however, in its stance, more libertarian than strictly conservative.

This may seem like over-analysis of the political content in a rock song, but clearly Harrison intended it to be overtly political, a fact signified by the song's mention of two British leaders in the dubbed-in line "Uh-uh Mister Wilson / uh-uh Mr. Heath." Harold Wilson of the Labour Party was British Prime Minister at the time the song was recorded, while the Conservative

Party's Edmund Heath was chief opposition leader. (Heath would become prime minister in 1974.) Clearly Harrison blamed both sides for the ultra-high taxation necessary to fund the British welfare state, taxation which ultimately led the Beatles to take measures to guard their income from the taxman. Apple may have been a "counterculture corporation," but it was also a tax shelter, and John Lennon may have later professed a type of fuzzy socialism, but when it came to the realities of his own life, he wanted to protect what he had earned.

The term "taxman," incidentally, is a British expression that long predates this song.

"Ticket to Ride"

"Ticket To Ride" first came out as a single from the soundtrack of an upcoming film. At the last minute, the film was renamed *Help!*, but in the U.S., a few singles released in April 1965 bore the announcement: "From the United Artists Release, *Eight Arms to Hold You*." Copies of this single are extremely valuable.

"Tomorrow Never Knows"

Out of the speakers comes a single note that builds in intensity until it explodes into shards of a melody that spill forward and downward endlessly, speeded along by the beat of a pagan drum that strikes the listener in the marrow of the soul. Presiding over this, like a guide on a journey to the center of Time, is a voice that sounds a million years old and a million miles high. "Turn off your mind, relax and float downstream," the unearthly voice counsels, "It is not dying." The music seems in a constant state of climax, and thunders forward relentlessly until it deposits the listener in a new and undiscovered land. . . .

Then the tone-arm picked up, returning control of their record players to millions of listeners who wondered what they had just heard. This was "Tomorrow Never Knows," last song on *Revolver*.

John Lennon based the song, originally titled "The Void," on a book called *The Psychedelic Experience*, a reading of the Tibetan Book of the Dead under the influence of LSD. Its authors were two Ph.D.s—Timothy Leary and Richard Alpert, later Baba Ram Dass—who had been removed from the Harvard faculty three years before for their experiments with the then-legal drug.

Lennon dropped his ponderous title after hearing Ringo say offhand-edly, "Tomorrow never knows"—i.e., let's just focus on today's worries. John appropriated the expression for the title, thus giving the song a much-needed light touch.

A Thousand Chanting Monks

For the recording of "Tomorrow Never Knows"—which during the record-ing phase bore the prosaic working title "Mark I"—Lennon had wanted to have a thousand Tibetan monks chanting in the background. Instead, he and the others concocted a series of tape loops run backwards.

Lennon sang through a megaphone, the sound of which he and George Martin ran through the Leslie speaker of a Hammond organ. This produced one of his (or anybody else's) most unusual vocal performances.

"Tomorrow Never Knows" used neither rhymes nor chords, and its structure and message showed fans—whether they liked it or not—the vast gulf that separated "Yesterday" and "Tomorrow." The last lines of the song are ". . . the end / Of the beginning," and that is exactly what it was.

It is interesting to note that the group started work on "Tomorrow Never Knows" at the *beginning* of the *Revolver* project. Thus while Lennon was making the song, the Beatles hadn't even stopped touring yet; as *The Beatles Anthology 2* illustrates, they were still having to perform songs from the Fab Four era.

"Twist and Shout"

The Isley Brothers had a Number Seventeen hit with "Twist and Shout" in 1962, and John Lennon sang the Beatles' famous cover in 1963. Though this song did not appear in the U.S. on an album until *The Early Beatles* in March 1965, the Beatles had recorded it more than two years before, in the sessions for the first Beatles album, *Please Please Me*.

Supposedly, at the end of the grueling thirteen-hour day in which they recorded that album in its entirety, George Martin discovered that they had space left on the record for one more song. Lennon selected one of his favorite current hits, and in one take (his voice probably couldn't have stood another) belted out one of the most throat-ripping vocals in history.

More likely, though, he knew all along he was going to sing "Twist and Shout." On the day of the recording, John had a bad cold, which he alter-nately soothed with lozenges and exacerbated with cigarettes. It must have been all he could do to sing as he did, even on a good day, and he surely would have been conserving his vocal strength to do the song.

In July 1976, Parlophone Records released a Beatles reissue single, "Back in the U.S.S.R." / "Twist and Shout." This was the first time a song not written by the Beatles had appeared on a British Parlophone single from the group.

Union of Soviet Socialist Republics

The U.S.S.R. is one of only two nations mentioned in the title of a Beatles song, the other being the adjective in "Norwegian Wood."

"Back in the U.S.S.R.," from the White Album, served to convince some extreme conservatives in America that the Beatles were agents of Soviet subversion. In actuality, the only "endorsement" the Beatles ever received from Communists had occurred five years before, in late 1963, and it didn't come from any Eastern Bloc or Bamboo Curtain countries, but from right back home in the U.K. Nor did the Reds mention the Beatles specifically, instead lumping them under an all-inclusive heading that included Gerry and the Pacemakers, Billy J. Kramer and the Dakotas, and others. A late 1963 editorial in *The Daily Worker*, the paper of the British Communist Party, said that "The Mersey Sound is the voice of 80,000 crumbling houses and 30,000 people on the dole."

The Reverend David Noebel observed in *Communism, Hypnotism, and the Beatles*: "Beatle music [is being used] to hypnotize American youth and prepare them for future submission to subversive control." How odd, then, that the Rev. Noebel's words should mirror observations made in the Soviet paper *Pravda* regarding the four long-haired proletarians with the electrified balalaikas: "The Beatles are a plot by the . . . ruling classes to distract . . . youngsters from politics."

Recognized by Moscow

Concert promoter Vic Lewis, in July 1968, attempted to arrange a Beatles concert back in the U.S.S.R. Not surprisingly, the Soviets nixed the idea.

The Moscow government did not officially recognize the Beatles' existence until 1972. The sale of Beatles music was forbidden on the open market, although albums by the group brought as much as $200 on the black market.

The first official release in the U.S.S.R. was *Let It Be*, issued on the Melodia label. In typical Soviet fashion, they brought out the worst available product—and no doubt people stood in line to buy it nonetheless.

United States of America

For eleven weeks leading up to February 7, 1964, when the Beatles touched down at New York City's Kennedy Airport, America was in the grip of shock that followed the Kennedy assassination. Then the Beatles landed, breaking through the gloom.

Late in 1963, a few discerning journalists had begun to notice the phenomenon surrounding a new singing group from Britain. Here and there, a more progressive radio station would play a single, issued on one low-budget label or another. (Capitol Records, which owned the rights to the Beatles' music in America, had no interest in groups with guitars at the time. One of those "low-budget" singles, "Please Please Me" on V-J Records, was worth $200 in the 1980s.)

Radio station WMCA in New York claims the first "important" broadcast of a Beatles single in America, at 12:50 p.m. on December 29, 1963, when it played "I Want to Hold Your Hand." Later on, WWDC disputed this claim, saying it was the first.

A film clip of the group singing "She Loves You" aired on the *Jack Paar Show* on January 3, 1964, but few in the press saw anything spectacular in this. One writer for the *New York Times* referred to the song as "a number apparently entitled 'With a Love Like That, You Know You Should Be Bad'," and went on to say that he did not think the Beatles would have a great deal of success in America, since the era of screaming teenage girls had ended in 1959. The implication was that Americans were far too sophisticated to fall for a British craze.

The Beatles Are Coming

But teenagers had a different reaction to the Beatles, and suddenly sales of "I Want to Hold Your Hand" began to climb. That was when Capitol Records decided to put $50,000—a laughably small budget now, but an unheard-of sum in those days—into publicity. Middle-aged company executives donned Beatles wigs, and the company printed millions of Beatles buttons and newsletters. Stickers reading "The Beatles Are Coming" appeared everywhere in the United States.

(For a copy of the original December 23, 1963, Capitol Records memo outlining the promo campaign, see *The Beatles Are Coming Promotion* [http://www.rarebeatles.com/photopg2/comstk.htm] on the World Wide Web; also see this author's entry on "The Beatles Are Coming" in *Encyclopedia of Major Marketing Campaigns,* Detroit: Gale, 1999.)

The Beatles arrive at Kennedy Airport in New York, February 7, 1964.
Archive Photos/Popperfoto

On Their Way to America

January 19, 1964, began the last week in history that no recording by a British artist appeared on the American Hot Hundred.

Still, things did not seem too promising to the Beatles as they flew across the Atlantic with a Liverpool journalist (whose name happened to be George Harrison) and American producer Phil Spector, who would complete production on their *Let It Be* album six eventful years hence. John Lennon later admitted that he had low expectations: "We were only coming over to buy LPs." To further disquiet the nervous quartet, they had received H-2 work classifications for the period of their stay in the United States. The permits allowed them to play for a two-week period "so long as unemployed American citizens capable of performing this work cannot be found." But their fears disappeared when they saw thousands of girls waiting for them at the recently renamed Kennedy Airport.

Reporters at the airport found themselves immediately impressed by the Beatles' calm, casual presence, and their irrepressible wit. But it still didn't seem like a big story. On the NBC News broadcast for February 7, 1964, Chet Huntley stated that the network had sent three cameramen to the airport earlier that day "Like a good little news organization. . . . However, after surveying the film our men returned with, and the subject of that film, I feel there is absolutely no need to show any of that film."

Two days later the group that wasn't big enough for the evening news would make television history.

The Greatest

When Elvis Presley appeared on the *Ed Sullivan Show* in 1958, an incredible 7,000 people had made requests for tickets to the 800-seat television studio. For the Beatles' performance on February 9, 1964, 60,000 people requested tickets.

The largest audience for a television entertainment program at that time—70,000,000 people, or 60 percent of all television viewers in America—watched the Beatles that night. During the broadcast, the nation's crime rate dropped to its lowest point in the previous fifty years. In all five boroughs of New York City, no one reported a single hubcap stolen.

On February 12, the group played at New York's prestigious Carnegie Hall, a performance attended by the state's First Lady, "Happy" Rockefeller, and her two children. The administrators of Carnegie Hall had previously rejected booking requests from Elvis Presley and Carl Perkins, and never would have knowingly booked a rock act this time. But Sid Bernstein—who would organize the Beatles' famous Shea Stadium concert a year later—told the Carnegie Hall representative that the Beatles were a phenomenon. The woman was from Eastern Europe, not a native English-speaker, and she assumed that a phenomenon must be some sort of string quartet. So she went ahead and booked them, urged on by Bernstein's beguiling suggestion that allowing a British group to perform at the Hall would "promote international understanding."

After playing Carnegie, the group flew to Miami. Much to their dismay, they found that someone had cancelled their first-class reservations and booked them in tourist class as a "practical joke." While in Miami, they appeared again on the *Ed Sullivan Show*. In the audience that night were two boxers, Joe Louis and Sonny Liston (who later appeared on the cover of *Sgt. Pepper*).

The group visited another boxer in the same city. His name at the time was Cassius Clay, and he was about to battle Liston for the heavyweight title—a match in which he would emerge the victor. Thirteen years later, after having written a song for Ringo called "I'm The Greatest," Lennon would again meet Muhammad Ali, at President Carter's 1977 Inauguration Ball.

Unwashed Sheets and Pillowcases

The Beatles' second trip to the United States was their first actual tour of the country, in the summer of 1964. On that trip, they traveled 22,441 miles, or 600 miles a day.

Among the places the group played was Kansas City—where they played the song "Kansas City," though they had yet to record their version of the Lieber–Stoller composition. The sheets they slept on at the Muehlback Hotel there, as well as the ones from the Whittier in Detroit, were sold (unwashed) for $1,150. These were then divided into one-inch-square pieces totaling about 150,000, which sold for $1 apiece. The unwashed pillowcases were placed in a bank vault.

The Summer 1965 North American Tour, the Beatles' third trip to America, included the Shea Stadium concert on August 15, 1965. At the time, this was the largest concert ever held: 55,600 people. Amidst the screaming, the Beatles struggled to hear what they were playing. Precisely because nobody was listening, the Beatles had begun to shorten the length of their performances; Shea Stadium lasted only thirty minutes, during which time the band earned approximately $100 a second.

Not everybody was cheering for them, either. One of New York's finest, keeping the peace at Shea, said to a journalist, "Dey stink. Dey de woist."

The Last Trip West

The Beatles' fourth trip to America would be their last. Not only was their current music impossible to reproduce on stage, but touring had become a chore and a danger.

A famous psychic who had supposedly predicted President Kennedy's assassination announced that three of the Beatles would die during their Summer 1966 Tour. Many other performers refused to travel with them. In addition, the entire group was under censure for their controversial "Butcher Cover" of *"Yesterday"... and Today,* and Lennon had gotten himself singled out for particular disapprobation because of his nonchalant comment to a British journalist that the Beatles were "more popular than Jesus."

In New York, two girls threatened to jump from a twenty-story ledge if someone didn't let them in to see the Beatles. Police coaxed them down from the ledge and had them committed to a local hospital. In the same city a young man appeared holding a sign that read "John Is a Lesbian."

The Beatles played their last concert anywhere in the world at San Francisco's Candlestick Park on August 29, 1966. Though Harrison would return to that city a year later and Lennon and McCartney would go to New York to announce the formation of Apple a year after that, the Beatles as a group would never again return to America.

Web Sites

When the Beatles flourished, back in the technological dark ages, the Internet already existed, but it was far from the user-friendly realm that it is today. There are scores—perhaps hundreds—of Beatles Web sites and pages, many of them appealing to the most obscure interests. What follows is a survey of a few useful or interesting sites, presented with the caveat that (a) this list is far from exhaustive; and (b) the Internet being the fluid creature it is, any of these may cease to exist at any point.

Perhaps the best jumping-off point is *Beatles Fans at the Mining Co.* (http://beatles.miningco.com/mbody.htm), a site with a vast array of links in categories such as Bootlegs; Controversy; December 8, 1980; and Paul Is Dead. (More about that later.) Among its offerings are a message board called the Bird and Bee; a series of links concerning Lennon "assassination" conspiracy theories; various sites related to the *Anthology* CDs and film; Rutles pages; and a Beatles chat every Thursday from 8:00 to 10:00 p.m. Eastern Standard Time.

The Net is rife with discography pages, but one of the very best is *The Beatles Revolution* (http://www.ozemail.com.au/~revolution/beatles/

index.htm), operated by a genial Australian with an extensive knowledge of the group's music. It includes information on each song, and Real Audio sound files for many tracks.

Other useful sites (with plenty of links) include *WAITE'S WEB WORLD—The Beatles Collection* (http://pages.prodigy.com/waite/ waite17.htm); *The Beatles* (http://www.columbia.edu/~brennan/beatles/), which includes links to a number of interesting essays; *Past Masters: A Beatles Tribute* (http://members.aol.com/hahahahno/private/beatles.htm); and *The Complete Beatles Discography* (http://www.thadonline.cbd/left.html), which also has several articles about Ringo, Charles Manson, and other topics.

Among specialty sites are *"What Goes On": The Beatles Anomalies List,* a collection of "mistakes" (http://www.pootle.demon.co.uk/wgo.htm); *Beatle Books,* an annotated bibliography (http://mccoy.lib.siu.edu/snackeru/beatles/beatbook.html); *All About the Beatles Butcher Cover* (http://www.eskimo.com/~bpentium/butcher.html); and *Troni's Beatles Archive: Anthology related material* (http://nobile.wirtschaft.tu-ilmenau.de/~weigmann/antho.html), which is partly in German. (See also **Christmas Records** and *Sgt. Pepper's Lonely Hearts Club Band.*)

In the world of Usenet, the leading newsgroup is rec.music.beatles. Good luck trying to keep up with the daily postings; it's a full-time job. Two offshoots are rec.music.beatles.info, which concerns the latest news about the group, and rec.music.beatles.moderated, for analytical and investigative articles. Another general newsgroup is fido7.ru.beatle.club; specialized newsgroups include alt.binaries.sounds.midi.beatles, as well as es.rec.musica.grupos.beatles, the latter for Spanish-speaking fans.

"Paul Is Dead" Pages

Then, to get back to the Web, there are the "Paul Is Dead" pages. There seem to be dozens of them, including *The Paul is DEAD Page* (http://www.psci.net/~jmarsh/pauldead.html) and *PAUL IS DEAD* (http://rrq.simplenet.com/music/Beatles/Dead.html), which has quite a few links to other "Paul Is Dead" sites.

Particularly entertaining is *Everyone BUT Paul is dead!* (http://tor-pw1.netcom.ca/~mccabe/everyonebutpaul.html). There we learn, for instance, that George is the only Beatle with his back to the camera on the cover of *A Hard Day's Night,* and the only one holding a cigarette; therefore he must have died.

On the more serious side is *Paul is dead?!?* (http://www.geocities.com/Hollywood/Lot/3722/mccartneybio.html), which presents a highly informative essay on the origins of the rumor.

The "We're More Popular Than Jesus" Scandal

John Lennon, throughout his career, had a habit of speaking his mind with almost no consideration of consequences. Such was the case on March 4, 1966, when he told journalist Maureen Cleave of the London *Evening Standard* that

> Christianity will go. It will vanish and shrink. I needn't argue about that, I'm right and will be proved right. We're more popular than Jesus Christ now. I don't know which will go first, rock 'n' roll or Christianity. Jesus was all right, but his disciples were thick and ordinary. It's them twisting it that ruins it for me.

It was one of many things he said in a lengthy interview, and the British public—who were used to his offhand remarks—didn't pay much attention to the statement.

Not so in America. In July of that year, Lennon's words reached the U.S. fan magazine *Datebook*, and suddenly a furor erupted. The focal point of the outrage lay in the rural South and Midwest, where churches, radio stations, and various conservative groups sponsored the destruction of anything having to do with the Beatles. People gathered to burn, shred, or grind to bits records, magazines, and photographs of the group.

One anti-Beatles radio station, KLUE of Longview, Texas, was struck by lightning and put off the air for the night. The station had held a Beatles bonfire earlier that day, and the program director was knocked unconscious by the bolt. However, KLUE resumed programming the following morning.

The world soon began to react. Spain and the Vatican denounced Lennon, but the press in Hong Kong—a predominantly Buddhist city—questioned what all the fuss was about. South Africa banned Beatles music from its airwaves. Years later, after the group broke up, the apartheid regime allowed the music of McCartney, Starkey, and Harrison on the radio, but John Lennon's songs remained under ban.

"I Was Not Saying We Are Greater"

By the time Lennon had an opportunity to clarify his statement, stock in Northern Songs, the Beatles' publishing company, had dropped from $1.64 to $1.26 a share.

In Chicago on August 11, 1966, Lennon held perhaps the most difficult press conference of his career. Appearing quite shaken by the outrage he had inadvertently caused, he told reporters

John, accompanied by George and Ringo, apologizes at a Chicago news conference on August 12, 1966, for his remark that the Beatles "are more popular than Jesus."
AP/Wide World Photos

I suppose if I had said television was more popular than Jesus, I would have gotten away with it. I'm sorry I opened my mouth. I'm not anti-God, anti-Christ, or anti-religion. I was not knocking it. I was not saying we are greater or better.

People generally accepted his apology, although the Ku Klux Klan tried unsuccessfully to keep the group from playing a show in Memphis.

A few months later, in October 1966, the Archbishop of Boston agreed that the Beatles were more popular than Jesus Christ, modern times being what they were.

It is interesting to observe that one reason why nobody cared about Lennon's comment in Britain was that they assumed it was just one man's opinion. In America, on the other hand, much of the furor had its wellspring in the fact that the Beatles enjoyed a status larger than mere mortals, and their opinions were not just opinions. Hence the very reaction to his comment helped to prove John's point.

"What Goes On"

Like "Drive My Car," "What Goes On" belonged to *Rubber Soul,* but in the U.S. it appeared as part of *"Yesterday"*. . . *and Today,* an album patched together from pieces of several other albums.

As early as March 1963, the Beatles had intended to record "What Goes On," a Lennon and McCartney tune written much earlier. They finally made the recording in November 1965, with Ringo on vocal. He made some adaptations: hence the "Lennon–McCartney–Starkey" credit, the only song in the Beatles *oeuvre* thus designated.

The group, which especially in its later years would often go through dozens of takes before they were satisfied enough with a song to lay down a master track, recorded "What Goes On" in one take.

"When I'm Sixty-Four"

Though it ended up on *Sgt. Pepper,* where its style fit perfectly, "When I'm Sixty-Four" was actually recorded during the sessions that stretched from November 1966 to January 1967 and yielded perhaps the greatest single of all time, "Penny Lane" / "Strawberry Fields Forever." The recording of "When I'm Sixty-Four" took place in December, while "Strawberry Fields" was still in the works, and "Penny Lane" was just getting started.

The group had been playing this song since its Cavern Club days. When he included it on *Sgt. Pepper,* Paul McCartney intended to honor his father, Jim, who turned sixty-four that year.

"While My Guitar Gently Weeps"

The title of "While My Guitar Gently Weeps" came about by accident. George Harrison had been reading the Chinese *I Ching,* or Book of Changes, and he resolved to put into practice the book's teaching that everything is related to everything else in one way or another. Deciding that he would write a song using the first phrase he saw, he opened a book to the words "Gently weeps."

The recording, from Side One of the White Album, features the guitar work of George's friend Eric Clapton.

"Wild Honey Pie"

Paul McCartney's "Wild Honey Pie," from the White Album, runs for just sixty-two seconds and consists simply of the words "honey pie" sung over and over, with "I love you" tacked on at the end. McCartney seems to have been fond of the phrase, since it also appears in the title of a much more polished recording on Side Four.

Paul multi-tracked his vocals, along with guitars and a bass drum, during an August 20, 1968, session while the other three Beatles were elsewhere. That night he also recorded a demo of a song he named "Etcetera," the single tape of which was lost immediately thereafter.

"With a Little Help from My Friends"

"With a Little Help from My Friends," the first song after the intro theme on *Sgt. Pepper*, originally had the title "Badfinger Boogie." Later the Iveys, a band signed on by Apple Records, shortened this to "Badfinger" and adopted it as their group name.

Vice President Spiro Agnew conducted an unsuccessful crusade in 1970 to have "With a Little Help from My Friends" banned from U.S. radio, charging that the line "I get high with a little help from my friends" was a drug reference. He did, however, admit that it was a nice song.

With the Beatles

The Beatles' second British album, *With the Beatles*, came out on the day of President John F. Kennedy's assassination, November 22, 1963. The first album by any artist to sell a million copies in the United Kingdom, it later came out in the U.S.—with several of its songs removed and farmed out to other albums—as *Meet the Beatles!*

"Within You Without You"

"Within You Without You" is, along with "A Day in the Life"—both of which last for five minutes, three seconds—the longest song on *Sgt. Pepper's Lonely Hearts Club Band.*

Indian music, as George Harrison conceded in his introduction of Ravi Shankar's performance on *The Concert for Bangladesh*, "is a lot different from our music." Though "Within You Without You" contains some exquisite melodies and instrumentation, as well as an unusual time signature (5/4) in the middle, a lot of fans consider it too ponderous and dirgelike. But George realized that the song might seem too "heavy" to some listeners, and he and George Martin attempted to eliminate some of its weight by adding in the laughter that separates it from "When I'm Sixty-Four."

"Words of Love"

Despite the fact that the name "the Beatles" was influenced by that of Buddy Holly's group, the Crickets, the group only released one Buddy Holly cover, "Words of Love," between 1962 and 1970. Volume 3 of *The Beatles Anthology,* however, contains a cover of a little-known song by Holly, "Mailman, Bring Me No More Blues," and Volume 1 includes the first-ever recording by the Quarry Men, a cover of his "That'll Be the Day."

The recording of "Words Of Love," which appeared on *Beatles for Sale* in Britain and *Beatles VI* in the United States, features Ringo beating time on a packing case.

"Yellow Submarine"

Though John Lennon was probably involved, Paul McCartney most likely composed the bulk of "Yellow Submarine." Donovan contributed two lines as well.

Most of the group's contribution to the recording of this *Revolver* track involved sound effects, since the music itself consisted of little more than simple guitar strums and the thump of a bass drum. They sloshed water around in a bucket to produce the sound of waves lapping the side of the craft just after the line "So we sailed unto the sun." John blew bubbles into a bucket, and they clinked glasses together to complement the line "And our friends are all aboard." A real military brass band played for five seconds on Ringo's cue of "And the band begins to play."

John is the one shouting "Full speed ahead, Mister Captain!" and other appropriately nautical-sounding commands. There was another spoken part, however, that didn't make the final cut, a thirty-one-second soliloquy by all four Beatles backed by the sound of coal rattling around in a cardboard box to replicate the sound of marching feet. Intended for the beginning of the song, it was: "And we will march to free the day to see them gathered there, from Land O'Groats to John O'Green, from Stepney to Utrecht, to see a yellow submarine." These words would be at least marginally comprehensible to a Briton, since Land's End lies at the far southwest corner of England and John O'Groats at the northeast end of Scotland.

Everyone joined in the final chorus: not only the four Beatles, but George Martin; the Rolling Stones' Brian Jones; Mick Jagger's sometime companion Marianne Faithfull; sound engineer Geoff Emerick; road managers Mal Evans and Neil Aspinall; and Patti Harrison. Evans led the others around the studio, beating on a bass drum as they followed him, single file, singing.

Yellow Submarine (Film)

The Beatles' fourth film, in 1968, was a cartoon, and it came together almost without any involvement on the Beatles' part.

John Lennon may have introduced the idea for the film with a phone call to producer Al Brodax one night at 3:00 a.m. "Wouldn't it be great if Ringo was followed down the street by a yellow submarine?" he asked the sleepy film producer. But John—no doubt tripping when he made that call—forgot the idea and moved on.

This did not stop *Yellow Submarine* from becoming, next to *A Hard Days' Night*, the Beatles' most critically acclaimed motion picture. It introduced a whole new era in animation—an alternative cinema best described as a combination of Walt Disney and Andy Warhol. The animation itself—colorful and combining a variety of styles—represented the finest in pop art, and each of its five million sketches was later sold separately. The engaging if flimsy script was cowritten by Erich Segal, who later became famous as the author of *Love Story*.

Aside from a soundtrack consisting of four throwaways along with previously released classics, the Beatles' only contribution to the film was an anticlimactic appearance at the end. The film's premiere, on July 17, 1968, was the last time the group would ever be mobbed by crowds.

A collection of pin-back buttons displays images from the Beatles' 1968 film Yellow Submarine. Archive Photos/Blank Archives

Yellow Submarine (LP)

Of the four songs that the Beatles introduced on the soundtrack of *Yellow Submarine*, the question is not which is best, but which is worst?

Certainly this title would not go to the two previously released songs: "Yellow Submarine" from *Revolver*, and (one of *Yellow Submarine*'s few selling points) a stereo version of "All You Need Is Love," unlike the one found on *Magical Mystery Tour*. John Lennon's "Hey Bulldog" has its good qualities, as does George Harrison's "It's All Too Much," though it's all too long. But Paul McCartney's "All Together Now" is enough to give anybody sugar shock, and George's "Only a Northern Song" is beneath contempt. The songs are exactly what their authors called them— "throwaways."

Giving It Their Worst

The late Brian Epstein had signed a contract for the group, stating that they would supply at least three new songs for the soundtrack of the film *Yellow Submarine*. Displeased to be encumbered by this obligation, the three song-writers determined that they would give it their worst.

Originally they had planned "Baby You're a Rich Man," another below-standard Beatles track, for inclusion on the album, but they released it instead as the B-side of "All You Need Is Love," and later on *Magical Mystery Tour*. (The song would have carried its weight better amongst the refuse on *Yellow Submarine* than it did on the *Mystery Tour* album, where it creates a weak spot between "Penny Lane" and "All You Need Is Love.") But the Beatles did manage to dig up some pretty hideous dogs—a fact that Lennon, with characteristically brutal honesty, seems to admit in the title of his contribution.

The album's failings lie not only in the fact that Side One consists of rereleases and throwaways; Side Two, like the American versions of *A Hard Day's Night* and *Help!*, is made up of incidental film music by the George Martin Orchestra. This is especially unfortunate since several previously released Beatles songs appeared in the film and could have been used here to at least make this a true Beatles album: "Nowhere Man," "Think for Yourself," "Love You To," "Eleanor Rigby," "Sgt. Pepper's Lonely Hearts Club Band," "With a Little Help from My Friends," "Lucy in the Sky with Diamonds," "Within You Without You," "When I'm Sixty-Four," "A Day in the Life," and "Baby You're a Rich Man."

An even better idea would have been to combine several recent singles on Side Two, as they had done on *Magical Mystery Tour*. They could have used "Lady Madonna," "The Inner Light," "Hey Jude," and "Revolution." All of these, except for "The Inner Light," ended up instead on the American *Hey Jude* album in February 1970.

* * * * *

Yellow Submarine Song List

Title	Composer	Time
Side One		
Yellow Submarine	McCartney	2:40
Only a Northern Song	Harrison	3:23
All Together Now	McCartney	2:08

Hey Bulldog	Lennon	3:09
It's All Too Much	Harrison	6:27
All You Need Is Love	Lennon	3:47

Side Two
[Incidental film music by the George Martin Orchestra]

"Yesterday"

"Yesterday" has a listing in the *Guinness Book of World Records* as the world's most-recorded song, with 1,186 cover versions between 1965 and 1973.

Originally titled "Scrambled Eggs," "Yesterday" could be considered the first song of Paul McCartney's solo career. The recording, from *Help!* in Great Britain and *"Yesterday". . . and Today* in the U.S., features Paul without the other three, his solo vocal and acoustic guitar backed by a string quartet.

"Yesterday". . . and Today

Released in the U.S. in June 1966, the album *"Yesterday". . . and Today* contained some fine Beatles songs, including the title track, "We Can Work It Out," "Day Tripper," and "Nowhere Man."

But the album, which consisted of songs sliced out of the British *Help!*, *Rubber Soul*, and *Revolver*, is equally famous for its original—extremely gory—cover. Robert Whitaker took the photograph, which showed the four lovable moptops with evil grins, dressed in butcher smocks and clutching pieces of raw meat and mangled dolls.

Capitol Records immediately issued an apology for what soon gained the nickname of "The Butcher Cover," and set about to change the sleeve using the less remarkable picture of the group that later adorned the album. The offensive jacket had to be replaced on 750,000 records, an undertaking that cost Capitol Records upwards of $200,000. Consequently, though it hit Number One like every other Beatles album, this one proved much less profitable for the record company.

There's an irony in that.

Butchered Albums

Parlophone Records in Britain, Capitol's sister company under the EMI umbrella, issued eight Beatles albums prior to *Sgt. Pepper*—seven containing new material, and one compilation, *A Collection of Beatle Oldies*. Each of these records had a running time between thirty and forty minutes. Capitol, on the other hand, managed to turn these eight albums into eleven—not including the excessively padded *Beatles' Story* two-record interview album—and none of these was over thirty minutes long.

First Capitol stretched the British *With the Beatles*, along with several singles, to create both *Meet the Beatles!* and *The Beatles' Second Album*. *A Hard Days' Night* came out under the label of United Artists, the company that released the film, and Capitol took five songs from the UA version, plus several cuts from the British soundtrack and assorted singles, to create an album whose title seemed like a deliberate slap in the face: *Something New*.

From the fans' perspective, Capitol was profiteering; from the Beatles' point of view, the company was cutting up their creations willy-nilly, mixing up pieces as though they were making sausage instead of music. And the butchering had just started.

Beatles for Sale in Britain turned into two U.S. albums, *Beatles '65* and *Beatles VI*. Aside from *The Early Beatles* (Capitol's version of the British *Please Please Me*, minus three songs), the company served up an abbreviated *Help!*, a distorted *Rubber Soul*, and a truncated *Revolver*.

But when Capitol managed to squeeze a fourth album, *"Yesterday,"* from the three just mentioned, the Beatles decided that they had seen their albums get cut up just one time too many. Hence the significance of the "Butcher Cover"—even though the impetus for the picture came not from the Beatles, but from Whitaker, who had no axe to grind with Capitol. He was interested only in creating an interesting-looking, avant-garde cover; later, however, it would seem that the whole thing had been an intentional act on the Beatles' part.

Covering Up

Capitol's recall of the "Butcher" cover did not prove entirely effective. In many cases, record company employees simply pasted the new cover over the old one, and a few lucky buyers ended up with the "Butcher Cover" in disguise. It is now worth hundreds of dollars.

Of course many others, mistakenly thinking they had the "Butcher Cover" underneath the later cover, ended up marring their albums trying to get to the "real" cover. Later the cover appeared, in all its gore, on the inside sleeve of the American *Rarities* album.

After *"Yesterday"... and Today*, Capitol straightened up its act. It never again butchered any albums, and even brought out two compilations not available in Britain for many years: *Magical Mystery Tour* and *Hey Jude*.

"You Know My Name (Look Up the Number)"

"You Know My Name (Look Up the Number)" came out as the B-side of "Let It Be" in March 1970 and later on the American and British *Rarities* albums.

Even though the Beatles themselves professed to love it, from a fan's perspective this was definitely not one of the group's classic compositions. Outside of certain ad-libs and spoken portions, its lyrics consist of the title sung over and over, and in style it closely resembles the group's absurd Christmas records issued each year to Fan Club members.

John was waiting for Paul at the latter's house one day when he saw a phone book propped up on the piano. Across the front of the directory were the words "You know my name—look up the number." The group recorded the instrumental tracks during jam sessions following the completion of *Sgt. Pepper,* with Brian Jones, guitarist for the Rolling Stones, playing saxophone. Lennon and McCartney, without the other two Beatles, added vocals in April 1969.

Zapple Records

Zapple was Apple Records' only subsidiary label. When they established it in early 1969, the group intended it as a "paperback records concept." The label would release spoken-word recordings of writers such as Ken Kesey, Richard Brautigan, and Allen Ginsberg reading from their own material and holding forth on subjects of their choosing. The "paperback records" idea meant that these recordings would be low-priced affairs that people could listen to a few times and then give—or throw—away.

But in those last days of the Beatles, such ideas disappeared as rapidly as they appeared, and by the time Zapple came anywhere close to realization, they had all moved on. The label was destined to have only two releases, neither of them "paperback records," but rather quasi-musical recordings by John Lennon and George Harrison.

Zapple's *Oeuvre*

The album designated as Zapple 01 was John Lennon and Yoko Ono's *Life with the Lions*, their follow-up to *Two Virgins*. The people who bought this record—and there weren't many—discovered that it was more of the same. Even *Rolling Stone*, a publication usually sympathetic of John's Onoistic shenanigans, had uncharitable things to say. Describing Yoko's twenty-six minutes of screaming, backed by feedback from John's guitar, a reviewer wrote that she sounded "like a severely retarded child being tortured." The album also included twelve minutes of radio static and two minutes of silence.

Zapple 02 was George Harrison's *Electronic Sounds*. Though Harrison would later put the synthesizer to good use on *Abbey Road*, *Electronic Sounds* seemingly served no other purpose than to let fans hear what he sounded like while he was learning to play the instrument. There has even been some question whether or not one side of the album was merely a synthesizer demonstration given to Harrison by Bernard Krause, a pioneer in the use of electronic music.

Both Zapple releases belied the original promise of being low-priced: the price was the same as for Beatles albums, even if the quality wasn't. At least they did fulfill the other half of Zapple Records' stated purpose—these two albums were certainly meant to be listened to once and then tossed.

Life with the Lions spent eight weeks on the U.S. Top Two Hundred Album Chart, during which time it peaked at Number 174. *Electronic Sounds* did not enjoy such popularity; in its two weeks on the charts, it reached Number 191 before being enveloped by oblivion.

There is a paradox here: because the albums were so unpopular, they went out of print. And because they went out of print, both are now extremely valuable collectors' items.

"If It's Good, We'll Charge"

After those two releases in May 1969, Zapple went dormant; then New York businessman Allen Klein became the Beatles' third and last manager in February 1970.

Klein immediately began turning Apple Records into something it had never been: a real business, with number-crunchers and men in suits. As for the hangers-on around the offices, he tossed them out. He dismissed all unneeded employees, of which there were quite a few, and for the first time in months, Apple started making money.

In the midst of his housecleaning project, Klein discovered the existence of Zapple Records. With five words, he simultaneously disavowed Zapple's hippie mission statement and dismantled the label: "If it's good, we'll charge."

Appendix 1

From "Across the Universe" to "You've Got to Hide Your Love Away": The Beatles' Songs Alphabetized

For those who care, there are two ways to alphabetize: by letter or by word. The list below is by word, meaning that all the songs beginning with the *word* "I" are in order, then "If," "I'll," etc. One could just as easily have done it by letter, so that the "If I Fell," for instance, would come just after "I Feel Fine," and "I Me Mine" would follow "I'm Down." Somehow, though, this seemed rather confusing, so for the list that follows, the word method was applied.

Also, this list contains only the 215 canonical songs. To be part of the canon, a song had to be:

- Recorded after Ringo joined the group and they began working with George Martin in the EMI Studios—that is, during or after the late summer and early fall of 1962.
- Recorded by the Beatles with the express intention of releasing it later as a single or part of an EP or LP—no live recordings, bootlegs, or outtakes of the kind included later in the *Beatles Anthology* CDs.

Two of the "songs" named below—"Sgt. Pepper Inner Groove" on *Sgt. Pepper* and "Can You Take Me Back" on *The Beatles*—are fragments unlisted on the covers of their respective albums. Nonetheless, they seem to have an existence separate from the pieces that precede and (in the case of the latter) follow them, so they made the list.

An asterisk (*) accompanies the titles of all songs which have a separate entry in this book.

*Across the Universe
*Act Naturally

All I've Got to Do
*All My Loving
*All Together Now
*All You Need Is Love
*And I Love Her
And Your Bird Can Sing
Anna (Go to Him)
Another Girl
Anytime at All
Ask Me Why
Baby It's You
*Baby You're a Rich Man
*Baby's in Black
*Back in the U.S.S.R.
Bad Boy
*The Ballad of John and Yoko
*Because
*Being for the Benefit of Mr. Kite!
*Birthday
*Blackbird
*Blue Jay Way
*Boys
*Can You Take Me Back
*Can't Buy Me Love
*Carry That Weight
Chains
*Come Together
*The Continuing Story of Bungalow Bill
*Cry Baby Cry
*A Day in the Life
Day Tripper
*Dear Prudence
Devil in Her Heart
*Dig a Pony
*Dig It
Dizzy Miss Lizzie
*Do You Want to Know a Secret
*Doctor Robert
*Don't Bother Me
*Don't Let Me Down
*Don't Pass Me By

*Drive My Car
*Eight Days a Week
*Eleanor Rigby
*The End
Every Little Thing
*Everybody's Got Something to Hide Except Me and My Monkey
Everybody's Trying to Be My Baby
*Fixing a Hole
*Flying
*The Fool on the Hill
For No One
For You Blue
*From Me to You
*Get Back
*Getting Better
*Girl
*Glass Onion
*Golden Slumbers
*Good Day Sunshine
*Good Morning Good Morning
*Good Night
*Got to Get You into My Life
*Happiness Is a Warm Gun
*A Hard Day's Night
*Hello Goodbye
*Help!
*Helter Skelter
*Her Majesty
*Here Comes the Sun
Here, There and Everywhere
*Hey Bulldog
*Hey Jude
Hold Me Tight
*Honey Don't
Honey Pie
*I Am the Walrus
I Call Your Name
I Don't Want to Spoil the Party
*I Feel Fine
*I Me Mine
I Need You

*I Saw Her Standing There
I Should Have Known Better
*I Wanna Be Your Man
*I Want to Hold Your Hand
*I Want to Tell You
*I Want You (She's So Heavy)
*I Will
If I Fell
If I Needed Someone
I'll Be Back
I'll Cry Instead
I'll Follow the Sun
I'll Get You
I'm a Loser
*I'm Down
I'm Happy Just to Dance with You
*I'm Looking Through You
I'm Only Sleeping
*I'm So Tired
*In My Life
*The Inner Light
It Won't Be Long
It's All Too Much
*It's Only Love
I've Got a Feeling
*I've Just Seen a Face
*Julia
*Kansas City/Hey-Hey-Hey-Hey!
*Komm, Gib Mir Deine Hand
*Lady Madonna
*Let It Be
Little Child
The Long and Winding Road
*Long Long Long
Long Tall Sally
*Love Me Do
*Love You To
Lovely Rita
*Lucy in the Sky with Diamonds
*Maggie Mae
Magical Mystery Tour

Martha My Dear
Matchbox
*Maxwell's Silver Hammer
*Mean Mr. Mustard
*Michelle
Misery
Money (That's What I Want)
*Mother Nature's Son
Mr. Moonlight
The Night Before
No Reply
*Norwegian Wood (This Bird Has Flown)
Not a Second Time
Nowhere Man
*Ob-La-Di, Ob-La-Da
Octopus's Garden
*Oh! Darling
Old Brown Shoe
*One After 909
*Only a Northern Song
Paperback Writer
*Penny Lane
Piggies
Please Mr. Postman
*Please Please Me
*Polythene Pam
P.S. I Love You
Rain
*Revolution
*Revolution 1
*Revolution 9
Rock and Roll Music
Rocky Raccoon
Roll Over Beethoven
*Run for Your Life
*Savoy Truffle
*Sexy Sadie
*Sgt. Pepper Inner Groove
Sgt. Pepper's Lonely Hearts Club Band
*Sgt. Pepper's Lonely Hearts Club Band (Reprise)
She Came in Through the Bathroom Window

*She Loves You
*She Said She Said
She's a Woman
*She's Leaving Home
*Sie Liebt Dich
Slow Down
*Something
*Strawberry Fields Forever
*Sun King
A Taste of Honey
*Taxman
Tell Me What You See
Tell Me Why
Thank You Girl
There's a Place
Things We Said Today
Think for Yourself
This Boy
*Ticket to Ride
Till There Was You
*Tomorrow Never Knows
*Twist and Shout
Two of Us
Wait
We Can Work It Out
*What Goes On
What You're Doing
When I Get Home
*When I'm Sixty-Four
*While My Guitar Gently Weeps
Why Don't We Do It in the Road
*Wild Honey Pie
*With a Little Help from My Friends
*Within You Without You
The Word
*Words of Love
*Yellow Submarine
Yer Blues
Yes It Is
*Yesterday
You Can't Do That

*You Know My Name (Look Up the Number)
You Like Me Too Much
You Never Give Me Your Money
You Really Got a Hold on Me
You Won't See Me
Your Mother Should Know
You're Gonna Lose That Girl
You've Got to Hide Your Love Away

Appendix 2

From "Love Me Do" to *Let It Be*: The Beatles' Songs in Order of Appearance

The following is a chronological listing of the Beatles' songs, from the first single in October 1962 to the last album in May 1970. Dates given are for the *first* release of that song anywhere in the world, which in almost all cases occurred in Britain. (Exceptions are noted.) All British releases prior to March 1968 were on the Parlophone Label, and American records except *A Hard Day's Night* were on Capitol; beginning in March 1968, all releases were on the Apple label. All 215 of the group's songs are listed, along with significant alternate versions of five songs (see respective entries for explanation of the differences): "Love Me Do," "All You Need Is Love," "Across the Universe," "Get Back," and "Let It Be."

It should be pointed out that, whereas the Beatles in their early days simply recorded songs and put them out—whether on 45s, albums, or EPs—things became more complicated in the group's latter years, and there came to be a marked difference between the order of recording and the order of release. The most notable instance of this, of course, was the case of *Abbey Road*, actually the group's last recording, and *Let It Be*, which came out eight months later. But this was not the only situation in which recording and release dates got mixed up; the songs on *Yellow Submarine*, for instance, date back to the end of the *Sgt. Pepper* sessions, and both versions of "Across the Universe" came out long after the song's recording.

An asterisk (*) accompanies the titles of all songs which have a separate entry in this book.

*Love Me Do [Version 1: Ringo on drums]   single, October 1962
P.S. I Love You

•••

*Please Please Me   single, January 1963
Ask Me Why

. . . .

*I Saw Her Standing There   *Please Please Me*, March 1963
Misery
Anna (Go to Him)
Chains
*Boys
*Love Me Do [Version 2: Andy White on drums, Ringo on tambourine]
Baby It's You
*Do You Want to Know a Secret
A Taste of Honey
There's A Place
*Twist and Shout

. . . .

*From Me to You   single, April 1963
Thank You Girl

. . . .

*She Loves You   single, August 1963
I'll Get You

. . . .

*I Want to Hold Your Hand   single, November 1963
This Boy

. . . .

It Won't Be Long   *With the Beatles*, November 1963
All I've Got to Do
*All My Loving
*Don't Bother Me
Little Child
Till There Was You
Please Mr. Postman
Roll Over Beethoven
Hold Me Tight
You Really Got a Hold on Me
*I Wanna Be Your Man
Devil in Her Heart
Not a Second Time
Money (That's What I Want)

. . . .

*Komm, Gib Mir Deine Hand   single, January 1964
*Sie Liebt Dich   [EMI Records, Germany]

. . . .

*Can't Buy Me Love   single, March 1964
You Can't Do That

Long Tall Sally   *Long Tall Sally* EP, June 1964
I Call Your Name
Slow Down
Matchbox

*A Hard Day's Night   *A Hard Day's Night*, June 1964
Tell Me Why   [United Artists Records, U.S.]
I'll Cry Instead
I'm Happy Just to Dance with You
I Should Have Known Better
If I Fell
*And I Love Her

Things We Said Today   single, July 1964
            [B-side of "A Hard Day's Night," released in Great Britain]

Anytime At All   *A Hard Day's Night*, July 1964
When I Get Home   [British version]
I'll Be Back

*I Feel Fine   single, November 1964
She's a Woman

No Reply   *Beatles for Sale*, December 1964
I'm a Loser
*Baby's in Black
Rock and Roll Music
I'll Follow the Sun
Mr. Moonlight
*Kansas City/Hey-Hey-Hey-Hey!
*Eight Days a Week
*Words of Love
*Honey Don't
Every Little Thing
I Don't Want to Spoil the Party
What You're Doing
Everybody's Trying to Be My Baby

*Ticket To Ride   single, April 1965
Yes It Is

....

You Like Me Too Much   *Beatles VI*, June 1965
Bad Boy   [Capitol Records, U.S.]
Dizzy Miss Lizzie
Tell Me What You See

....

*Help!   single, July 1965
*I'm Down

....

The Night Before   *Help!*, August 1965
You've Got to Hide Your Love Away
I Need You
Another Girl
You're Gonna Lose That Girl
*Act Naturally
*It's Only Love
*I've Just Seen a Face
*Yesterday

....

We Can Work It Out   single, December 1965
Day Tripper

....

*Drive My Car   *Rubber Soul*, December 1965
*Norwegian Wood (This Bird Has Flown)
You Won't See Me
Nowhere Man
Think for Yourself
The Word
*Michelle
*What Goes On
*Girl
*I'm Looking Through You
*In My Life
Wait
If I Needed Someone
*Run for Your Life

....

Paperback Writer   single, May 1966
Rain

....

I'm Only Sleeping   *"Yesterday". . . and Today*, June 1966
*Doctor Robert   [Capitol Records, U.S.]

And Your Bird Can Sing
••
*Yellow Submarine   single, August 1966
*Eleanor Rigby
••
*Taxman   *Revolver,* August 1966
*Love You To
Here, There and Everywhere
*She Said She Said
*Good Day Sunshine
For No One
*I Want to Tell You
*Got to Get You into My Life
*Tomorrow Never Knows
••
*Penny Lane   single, February 1967
*Strawberry Fields Forever
••
                        Sgt. Pepper's Lonely Hearts Club Band, June 1967
Sgt. Pepper's Lonely Hearts Club Band
*With a Little Help from My Friends
*Lucy in the Sky with Diamonds
*Getting Better
*Fixing a Hole
*She's Leaving Home
*Being for the Benefit of Mr. Kite!
*Within You Without You
*When I'm Sixty-Four
Lovely Rita
*Good Morning Good Morning
*Sgt. Pepper's Lonely Hearts Club Band (Reprise)
*A Day in the Life
*Sgt. Pepper Inner Groove
••
                                                     single, July 1967
*All You Need Is Love [Version 1, from the *Our World* television broadcast]
*Baby You're a Rich Man
••
*Hello Goodbye   single, November 1967
*I Am the Walrus

Magical Mystery Tour   *Magical Mystery Tour,* November 1967
*The Fool on the Hill   [Capitol Records, U.S.]
*Flying
*Blue Jay Way
Your Mother Should Know

*Lady Madonna   single, March 1968
*The Inner Light

*Hey Jude   single, August 1968
*Revolution

*Back in the U.S.S.R.   *The Beatles,* November 1968
*Dear Prudence
*Glass Onion
*Ob-La-Di, Ob-La-Da
*Wild Honey Pie
*The Continuing Story of Bungalow Bill
*While My Guitar Gently Weeps
*Happiness Is a Warm Gun
Martha My Dear
*I'm So Tired
*Blackbird
Piggies
Rocky Raccoon
*Don't Pass Me By
Why Don't We Do It in the Road
*I Will
*Julia
*Birthday
Yer Blues
*Mother Nature's Son
*Everybody's Got Something to Hide Except Me and My Monkey
*Sexy Sadie
*Helter Skelter
*Long Long Long
*Revolution 1
Honey Pie
*Savoy Truffle
*Cry Baby Cry
*Can You Take Me Back

*Revolution 9
*Good Night

••
*Only a Northern Song   *Yellow Submarine,* January 1969
*All Together Now
*Hey Bulldog
It's All Too Much
*All You Need Is Love [Version 2, recorded a few hours prior to the *Our World* television broadcast]

••
*Get Back [Version 1—studio recording]   single, April 1969
*Don't Let Me Down

••
*The Ballad of John and Yoko   single, May 1969
Old Brown Shoe

••
*Come Together   *Abbey Road,* September 1969
*Something
*Maxwell's Silver Hammer
*Oh! Darling
Octopus's Garden
*I Want You (She's So Heavy)
*Here Comes the Sun
*Because
You Never Give Me Your Money
*Sun King
*Mean Mr. Mustard
*Polythene Pam
She Came in Through the Bathroom Window
*Golden Slumbers
*Carry That Weight
*The End
*Her Majesty

••
*Across the Universe [Version 1, without choir]   December 1969
        [from *No One's Gonna Change Our World,* Regal Starline]

••
*Let It Be [Version 1: shorter than Version 2]   single, March 1970
*You Know My Name (Look Up the Number)

••
Two of Us   *Let It Be,* May 1970
*Dig a Pony

*Across The Universe [Version 2, with choir]
*I Me Mine
*Dig It
*Let It Be [Version 2]
*Maggie Mae
I've Got a Feeling
*One After 909
The Long and Winding Road
For You Blue
*Get Back [Version 2, from the "Rooftop Concert"]

Appendix 3

A Cross-Reference of British and American Releases Prior to *Sgt. Pepper*

As stated elsewhere (See *"Yesterday"... and Today*), British and American Beatles albums prior to 1967 bore little relation to each other: only four (*A Hard Day's Night, Help!, Rubber Soul,* and *Revolver*) had the same title, and even then the contents were not the same.

The following is an alphabetical listing of all 118 Beatles songs released between October 1962 and August 1966. On the left below the song title is the name and date of its first British album release, and on the right is the name and date of its first American album release. All British albums were issued on the Parlophone label, and all American releases were by Capitol Records, with three exceptions: *A Hard Day's Night* (United Artists), and *Hey Jude* and *The Beatles 1962–1966*, both issued by Apple.

Act Naturally
Help! (August 1965)   *"Yesterday"... and Today* (June 1966)

All I've Got to Do
With the Beatles (November 1963)   *Meet the Beatles!* (January 1964)

All My Loving
With the Beatles (November 1963)   *The Beatles 1962–1966* (April 1973)

And I Love Her
A Hard Day's Night (July 1964)   *A Hard Day's Night* (June 1964)

And Your Bird Can Sing
Revolver (August 1966)   *"Yesterday"... and Today* (June 1966)

Anna (Go to Him)
Please Please Me (March 1963)   *The Early Beatles* (March 1965)

Another Girl
Help! (August 1965)   *Help!* (August 1965)

Anytime at All
A Hard Day's Night (July 1964)   *Something New* (July 1964)

Ask Me Why
Please Please Me (March 1963)   *The Early Beatles* (March 1965)

Baby It's You
Please Please Me (March 1963)   *The Early Beatles* (March 1965)

Baby's in Black
Beatles for Sale (December 1964)   *Beatles '65* (December 1964)

Bad Boy
A Collection of Beatles Oldies   *Beatles VI* (June 1965)
(December 1966)

Boys
Please Please Me (March 1963)   *The Early Beatles* (March 1965)

Can't Buy Me Love
A Hard Day's Night (July 1964)   *A Hard Day's Night* (June 1964)

Chains
Please Please Me (March 1963)   *The Early Beatles* (March 1965)

Day Tripper
A Collection of Beatles Oldies   *"Yesterday"*. . . *and Today* (June 1966)
(December 1966)

Devil in Her Heart
With the Beatles (November 1963)   *The Beatles' Second Album* (April 1964)

Dizzy Miss Lizzie
Help! (August 1965)   *Beatles VI* (June 1965)

Do You Want to Know a Secret
Please Please Me (March 1963)   *The Early Beatles* (March 1965)

Doctor Robert
Revolver (August 1966)   *"Yesterday". . . and Today* (June 1966)

Don't Bother Me
With the Beatles (November 1963)   *Meet the Beatles!* (January 1964)

Drive My Car
Rubber Soul (December 1965)   *"Yesterday". . . and Today* (June 1966)

Eight Days a Week
Beatles for Sale (December 1964)   *Beatles VI* (June 1965)

Eleanor Rigby
Revolver (August 1966)   *Revolver* (August 1966)

Everybody's Trying to Be My Baby
Beatles for Sale (December 1964)   *Beatles '65* (December 1964)

Every Little Thing
Beatles for Sale (December 1964)   *Beatles VI* (June 1965)

For No One
Revolver (August 1966)   *Revolver* (August 1966)

From Me to You
A Collection of Beatles Oldies   *The Beatles 1962–1966* (April 1973)
(December 1966)

Girl
Rubber Soul (December 1965)   *Rubber Soul* (December 1965)

Good Day Sunshine
Revolver (August 1966)   *Revolver* (August 1966)

Got to Get You into My Life
Revolver (August 1966)   *Revolver* (August 1966)

A Hard Day's Night
A Hard Day's Night (July 1964)   *A Hard Day's Night* (June 1964)

Help!
Help! (August 1965)   *Help!* (August 1965)

Here, There and Everywhere
Revolver (August 1966)   *Revolver* (August 1966)

Hold Me Tight
With the Beatles (November 1963)   *Meet the Beatles!* (January 1964)

Honey Don't
Beatles for Sale (December 1964)   *Beatles '65* (December 1964)

I Call Your Name
Rock 'n' Roll Music (June 1976)   *The Beatles' Second Album* (April 1964)

I Don't Want to Spoil the Party
Beatles for Sale (December 1964)   *Beatles VI* (June 1965)

I Feel Fine
A Collection of Beatles Oldies
(December 1966)   *Beatles '65* (December 1964)

I Need You
Help! (August 1965)   *Help!* (August 1965)

I Saw Her Standing There
Please Please Me (March 1963)   *Meet the Beatles!* (January 1964)

I Should Have Known Better
A Hard Day's Night (July 1964)   *A Hard Day's Night* (June 1964)

I Wanna Be Your Man
With the Beatles (November 1963)   *Meet the Beatles!* (January 1964)

I Want to Hold Your Hand
A Collection of Beatles Oldies
(December 1966)   *Meet the Beatles!* (January 1964)

I Want to Tell You
Revolver (August 1966)   *Revolver* (August 1966)

If I Fell
A Hard Day's Night (July 1964)   *A Hard Day's Night* (June 1964)

If I Needed Someone
Rubber Soul (December 1965)   *"Yesterday"*. . . *and Today* (June 1966)

I'll Be Back
A Hard Day's Night (July 1964)   *Beatles '65* (December 1964)

I'll Cry Instead
A Hard Day's Night (July 1964)   *A Hard Day's Night* (June 1964)

I'll Follow the Sun
Beatles for Sale (December 1964)   *Beatles '65* (December 1964)

I'll Get You
Rarities (October 1979)   *The Beatles' Second Album* (April 1964)

I'm a Loser
Beatles for Sale (December 1964)   *Beatles '65* (December 1964)

I'm Down
Rock 'n' Roll Music (June 1976)   *Rock 'n' Roll Music* (June 1976)

I'm Happy Just to Dance with You
A Hard Day's Night (July 1964)   *A Hard Day's Night* (June 1964)

I'm Looking Through You
Rubber Soul (December 1965)   *Rubber Soul* (December 1965)

I'm Only Sleeping
Revolver (August 1966)   *"Yesterday"*. . . *and Today* (June 1966)

In My Life
Rubber Soul (December 1965)   *Rubber Soul* (December 1965)

It Won't Be Long
With the Beatles (November 1963)   *Meet the Beatles!* (January 1964)

It's Only Love
Help! (August 1965)   *Rubber Soul* (December 1965)

I've Just Seen a Face
Help! (August 1965)

Rubber Soul (December 1965)

Kansas City/Hey-Hey-Hey-Hey!
Beatles for Sale (December 1964)

Beatles VI (June 1965)

Komm, Gib Mir Deine Hand
Rarities (October 1979)

Something New (July 1964)

Little Child
With the Beatles (November 1963)

Meet the Beatles! (January 1964)

Long Tall Sally
Rock 'n' Roll Music (June 1976)

The Beatles' Second Album (April 1964)

Love Me Do
Please Please Me (March 1963)

The Early Beatles (March 1965)

Love You To
Revolver (August 1966)

Revolver (August 1966)

Matchbox
Rock 'n' Roll Music (June 1976)

Something New (July 1964)

Michelle
Rubber Soul (December 1965)

Rubber Soul (December 1965)

Misery
Please Please Me (March 1963)

Rarities (March 1980)

Money (That's What I Want)
With the Beatles (November 1963)

The Beatles' Second Album (April 1964)

Mr. Moonlight
Beatles for Sale (December 1964)

Beatles '65 (December 1964)

The Night Before
Help! (August 1965)

Help! (August 1965)

No Reply
Beatles for Sale (December 1964)

Beatles '65 (December 1964)

Norwegian Wood (This Bird Has Flown)
Rubber Soul (December 1965) *Rubber Soul* (December 1965)

Not a Second Time
With the Beatles (November 1963) *Meet the Beatles!* (January 1964)

Nowhere Man
Rubber Soul (December 1965) *"Yesterday". . . and Today* (June 1966)

Paperback Writer
A Collection of Beatles Oldies
(December 1966) *Hey Jude* (February 1970)

Please Mr. Postman
With the Beatles (November 1963) *The Beatles' Second Album* (April 1964)

Please Please Me
Please Please Me (March 1963) *The Early Beatles* (March 1965)

P.S. I Love You
Please Please Me (March 1963) *The Early Beatles* (March 1965)

Rain
Rarities (October 1979) *Hey Jude* (February 1970)

Rock and Roll Music
Beatles for Sale (December 1964) *Beatles '65* (December 1964)

Roll Over Beethoven
With the Beatles (November 1963) *The Beatles' Second Album* (April 1964)

Run for Your Life
Rubber Soul (December 1965) *Rubber Soul* (December 1965)

She Loves You
A Collection of Beatles Oldies *The Beatles' Second Album* (April 1964)
(Dec. 1966)

She Said She Said
Revolver (August 1966) *Revolver* (August 1966)

She's a Woman
Rarities (October 1979)

Beatles '65 (December 1964)

Sie Liebt Dich
Rarities (October 1979)

Rarities (March 1980)

Slow Down
Rarities (October 1979)

Something New (July 1964)

A Taste of Honey
Please Please Me (March 1963)

The Early Beatles (March 1965)

Taxman
Revolver (August 1966)

Revolver (August 1966)

Tell Me What You See
Help! (August 1965)

Beatles VI (June 1965)

Tell Me Why
A Hard Day's Night (July 1964)

A Hard Day's Night (June 1964)

Thank You Girl
Rarities (October 1979)

The Beatles' Second Album (April 1964)

There's a Place
Please Please Me (March 1963)

Rarities (March 1980)

Things We Said Today
A Hard Day's Night (July 1964)

Something New (July 1964)

Think for Yourself
Rubber Soul (December 1965)

Rubber Soul (December 1965)

This Boy
Love Songs (November 1977)

Meet the Beatles! (January 1964)

Ticket to Ride
Help! (August 1965)

Help! (August 1965)

Till There Was You
With the Beatles (November 1963)

Meet the Beatles! (January 1964)

Tomorrow Never Knows
Revolver (August 1966)

Revolver (August 1966)

Twist and Shout
Please Please Me (March 1963)

The Early Beatles (March 1965)

Wait
Rubber Soul (December 1965)

Rubber Soul (December 1965)

We Can Work It Out
A Collection of Beatles Oldies
(Dec. 1966)

"Yesterday". . . and Today (June 1966)

What Goes On
Rubber Soul (December 1965)

"Yesterday". . . and Today (June 1966)

What You're Doing
Beatles for Sale (December 1964)

Beatles VI (June 1965)

When I Get Home
A Hard Day's Night (July 1964)

Something New (July 1964)

The Word
Rubber Soul (December 1965)

Rubber Soul (December 1965)

Words of Love
Beatles for Sale (December 1964)

Beatles VI (June 1965)

Yellow Submarine
Revolver (August 1966)

Revolver (August 1966)

Yes It Is
Rarities (October 1979)

Beatles VI (June 1965)

Yesterday
Help! (August 1965)

"Yesterday". . . and Today (June 1966)

You Can't Do That
A Hard Day's Night (July 1964)

The Beatles' Second Album (April 1964)

You Like Me Too Much
Help! (August 1965)

Beatles VI (June 1965)

You Really Got a Hold on Me
With the Beatles (November 1963)   *The Beatles' Second Album* (April 1964)

You Won't See Me
Rubber Soul (December 1965)   *Rubber Soul* (December 1965)

You're Gonna Lose That Girl
Help! (August 1965)   *Help!* (August 1965)

You've Got To Hide Your Love Away
Help! (August 1965)   *Help!* (August 1965)

Bibliography

Brown, Peter and Steven Gaines. *The Love You Make: An Insider's Story of The Beatles.* New York: McGraw-Hill, 1983.

Carr, Roy and Tony Tyler. *The Beatles: An Illustrated Record.* New York: Harmony Books, 1978.

Castleman, Barry and Walter J. Podrazik. *All Together Now: The First Complete Beatles Discography, 1961-1975.* Ann Arbor, MI: Pierian Press, 1975.

Davies, Hunter. *The Beatles: The Authorized Biography.* New York: McGraw-Hill, 1968.

_____. *The Beatles.* New York: McGraw-Hill, 1985.

Doggett, Peter. *Let It Be/Abbey Road: The Beatles.* New York: Schirmer, 1998.

Fast, Julius. *The Beatles: The Real Story.* New York: Putnam, 1968.

Golson, David, editor. *The Playboy Interviews with John Lennon and Yoko Ono,* conducted by David Sheff. New York: Playboy Press, 1981.

Harrison, George. *I, Me, Mine.* New York: Simon and Schuster, 1980.

Hertsgaard, Mark. *A Day in the Life: The Music and Artistry of the Beatles.* New York: Delacorte, 1995.

Lewisohn, Mark. *The Complete Beatles Chronicle.* New York: Barnes & Noble, 1996.

Martin, George with Jeremy Hornsby. *All You Need Is Ears.* New York: St. Martin's, 1982.

_____ with William Pearson. *With a Little Help from My Friends: The Making of Sgt. Pepper.* Boston: Little, Brown, 1994.

McKeen, William. *The Beatles: A Bio-Bibliography.* Westport, CT: Greenwood, 1989.

Mellers, Wilfrid. *Twilight of the Gods: The Beatles in Retrospect.* New York: Viking, 1974.

Norman, Philip. *Shout!: The Beatles in Their Generation.* New York: Warner, 1982.

Pritchard, David and Alan Lysaght. *The Beatles: An Oral History.* New York: Hyperion, 1998.

Russell, J. P. *The Beatles on Record.* New York: Scribner, 1982.

Schaffner, Nicholas. *The Beatles Forever.* New York: McGraw-Hill, 1978.

_____. *The Boys from Liverpool: John, Paul, George, Ringo.* New York: Methuen, 1980.

Schultheiss, Thomas, compiler and editor. *A Day in the Life: The Beatles Day-by-Day, 1960–1970.* Ann Arbor, MI: Pierian Press, 1980.

Thomson, Elizabeth and David Gutman, editors. *The Lennon Companion: Twenty-Five Years of Comment.* New York: Schirmer Books, 1987.

Wenner, Jann. *Lennon Remembers: The Rolling Stone Interviews.* Harmondsworth, England: Penguin, 1973.

Wiener, Allen J. *The Beatles: The Ultimate Recording Guide.* New York: Facts on File, 1992.

About the Author

Judson Knight has been a fan of the Beatles ever since his older brother brought home a copy of *Sgt. Pepper's Lonely Hearts Club Band*. Knight was three years old at the time, and the impression the Beatles made on him then stayed with him his entire life.

Knight is a freelance writer who has penned numerous books, including *Don't Fence Me In: An Anecdotal Biography of Lewis Grizzard by Those Who Knew Him Best*. He wrote the three-volume *Ancient Civilizations* series, volume 5 of *African American Biography*, and has researched and written for the *Contemporary Musicians* and *Contemporary Authors* series.

A magna cum laude of Georgia State University, Knight resides in Atlanta with his wife, Deidre, and daughter, Tyler.